Critical
Issues
in
History

The Early Modern Era, 1648-1770

Critical
Issues
in History

UNDER THE EDITORIAL DIRECTION OF *RICHARD E. SULLIVAN*

SIX-VOLUME EDITION

TWO-VOLUME EDITION

Critical Issues in History

The Early Modern Era

1648-1770

EDITED WITH INTRODUCTIONS BY

JOHN C. RULE

Ohio State University

D. C. HEATH *and Company, Boston*

ILLUSTRATION CREDITS

Cover: Section, Facade of Louvre; *page 367;* elevation, Louvre
facing S. Germain L'Auxerrois; Jacques-François Blondel, *Architecture
Française* Paris, 1861.

Library of Congress Catalog Card Number: 67-13486
Copyright © 1967 by D. C. Heath and Company
No part of the material covered by this copyright
may be reproduced in any form without written permission
of the publisher.
Printed in the United States of America.

Printed December 1966

Boston
Englewood
Indianapolis
Dallas
San Francisco
Atlanta

PREFACE

This volume, one of a six-volume set, is intended to engage students in *problem-resolving situations* as a technique for enriching their study of European history. The editors who collaborated in preparing these six volumes are convinced that this approach has great value in stimulating interest, encouraging critical thinking, and enhancing historical-mindedness, especially when it is used to supplement the more conventional techniques employed in teaching the general introductory course in European history.

The volume opens with an interpretive essay aimed at placing the five "problems" which follow in the perspective of the period. While all of the problems follow the same structure, the topics they treat are highly diverse: in one, a single man's role in history is debated, while the next examines an ideological issue; in one problem causes are sought, while the next weighs effects.

Each of the five problems is introduced by a short statement defining the issue and directing the student to the crucial questions involved. For the most part selections have been taken from the works of modern historians, with occasional use of the observations of contemporary witnesses. In choosing the selections, the editor has tried to avoid generating conflict for conflict's sake. Rather, he has sought to show how honest divergencies emerge among historians as a result of the complexities of history, varying initial assumptions, different approaches to evidence, and all the other factors that enter into interpretation of the past. The student's efforts to understand how differing interpretations arise and to resolve these differences should increase his ability to manipulate historical data and concepts and deepen his understanding of the historian's craft.

CONTENTS

INTRODUCTION

The post-Reformation era, extending in time from the end of the Thirty Years' War (1648) to the beginnings of the active stage of the French Revolution (1788) is known in Western history as the Early Modern Era; in political-social history as the *Ancien Régime*; and in the history of ideas as the Enlightenment. The era was ushered in by violent political and intellectual storms that mark the "General Crisis of the Seventeenth Century" (*circa* 1640–1660) and departed among the equally violent storms of the Atlantic Revolutions and the rise of Romanticism, 1770–1799.

The two most important upheavals of the "General Crisis of the Seventeenth Century" were the Great English Revolution or Civil War (1640–1660) and the French parlementary and princely Frondes (1648–1652). The English Revolution, beginning in 1640 as a protest against Charles I's alleged tyrannies, was transformed by its parliamentary managers into a full-fledged revolt against the prerogatives of the crown. Oliver Cromwell, a representative of the country gentry and an ardent supporter of Puritan Independency, emerged by 1646 as the military leader of the revolution. The controversies that have raged around his character and policies form the first problem in this section. In France the Frondes constitute at once the last major uprising of the French nobility before the French Revolution and the training ground on which Louis XIV learned his first lessons of statecraft.

The troubled decades of the 1640's and 1650's also witnessed revolutionary rage engulf Naples, Catalonia, Andalusia, and Portugal—all provinces of Spain. These revolts against the government of Philip IV (1621–1665) harbingered Spain's rapid decline as a Great Power and, even more, prophesied the shift of political hegemony from the Mediterranean world of the Italian states, Spain (with Portugal), and the Ottoman Empire to the Northern European powers of England, France, the Austrian Empire, Brandenburg-Prussia, and Russia, known collectively in the eighteenth century as the Great Powers.

The rise of the Great Powers of Northern Europe denotes one of the great crises of the post-Reformation era; it marks the shift of power away from the city state and universal empire of the late medieval world to the dynastic *cum* nation state of the modern world. This shift of power was accompanied by other severe crises in the fields of economics and government; military science and international law; and the arts and ideas generally.

But before we discuss these other crises, a word about the Great Powers themselves.

The demographic and military shock of the Thirty Years' War (1618–1648) and the diplomatic and political realignments attendant on the decline of the Mediterranean world (as mirrored in the Peace of Westphalia, 1648, and the Peace of the Pyrenees, 1659) profoundly affected the history of the Holy Roman Empire. It caused the numerous independent German princely states to look inward to their own defense rather than outward to aid from the emperor; conversely, it caused the emperors to remember that they were Habsburgs and to attach more importance to the destinies of their crown lands in Hungary, Austria, Bohemia, and Italy than to the fate of "the Germanies." By the eighteenth century Austria had indeed become a Danubian Empire. Thus the treaties of Westphalia and the Pyrenees mark the emergence of the Austrian and the decline of the Holy Roman Empire.

The Habsburgs in the years following the Peace of Westphalia were fortunate in their rulers: Leopold I (1658–1705), Joseph I (1705–1710) and Charles VI (1711–1740) were pious, patient, plodding men, whose very mediocrity masked the fact that Austria was being metamorphosed into a Great Power. Their legacy was at first guarded and then somewhat dissipated by their more brillant successors, Maria Theresa (1740–1780) and Joseph II (1780–1790). Joseph, who served with his mother, Maria Theresa, as co-ruler of Austria from 1765, pursued his "enlightened" reforms with a recklessness that neither his nobles, the Church, nor the peasants could accept (see Problem 4). Only the death of Joseph and the shock of the French Revolution saved Austria from civil war.

Under the frenetic leadership of Tsar Peter I, the Great (1694–1725)—a towering man both figuratively and literally—Russia inflicted decisive defeats on the Swedish armies of Charles XII (particularly at Poltava, 1709), tilting the balance of power in the Baltic in Russia's favor as was clearly shown in peace settlement of Nystadt (1721) when the provinces of Livonia, Estonia, and Karelia were awarded to Russia, creating a "window on the West." By 1721 Russia had emerged as a Great Power. During the same period Peter and his advisers imposed domestic reforms on Russia: industry was encouraged; a new administrative capital, St. Petersburg, founded; fiscal innovations were introduced; and, through the Table of Ranks (1722), nobility was awarded on the basis of merit as well as birth. Thus did Peter's reformation begin Russia's painful translation from the middle ages to the modern era. After a chaotic interim from 1725 to 1762, Catherine II, the Great (d. 1796), took up the task of modernization left her by Peter. She has been called one of the greatest Enlightened Despots of the eighteenth century (see Problem 4). Ostensibly she was. Her *Nakaz* (Instructions) of 1767 was certainly influenced by the writers of the Enlightenment. Indeed 250 of the 526 articles in this remarkable document were drawn word for word from the writings of Montesquieu. Yet the *Nakaz* was never published in Russia. Like many of Catherine's reforms it perished still-born. Her true genius lay in the field of foreign rather than domestic policy, where, like Peter, she added windows on the West, these in Poland and on the Black Sea.

In Northern Europe, Brandenburg-Prussia began its precarious rise to the status of a Great Power under the leadership of Frederick William of Hohenzollern, the Great Elector (1640–1688), whose skilful diplomacy gained for Prussia territorial concessions along the German rim of the Baltic and in the Rhineland. His son Frederick I (1688–1713) wrested the title of King in Prussia away from the Emperor Leopold; and his son Frederick William I (1713–1740) and grandson Frederick II, the Great (1740–1786), built the Prussian army into Europe's most formidable war machine. Frederick II twice abused his position as military arbiter of Europe by gambling his troops in attacks on Austria (1740) and on France, Austria, and Russia (1756). Yet his reforms in the fields of the law, commerce, agriculture, and the bureaucracy gave him the title of Enlightened Despot (see Problem 4). Frederick's ambivalent legacy still excites heated debates among his biographers.

In Western Europe the United Provinces of the Netherlands fashioned an empire in the early seventeenth century out of the flotsum and jetsum of Spanish and Portuguese colonies. It was in this period that Amsterdam became the entrepôt of Europe and its banker; at the same time the United Provinces enjoyed a Golden Age of Culture represented in the paintings of Frans Hals, Vermeer, and Rembrandt; in the poetry of Vondel, in the scientific writings of Christiaan Huygens, and the philosophic works of Spinoza. Dutch decline after 1670, due largely to an overextension of imperial commitments and to the exhaustion of war, was as precipitous as its rise and presaged England's ascendancy.

England, blessed by nature with its "glorious ditch," the English channel, survived a string of stingy, short-sighted, self-indulgent, simple-minded Stuart rulers to emerge in 1688, under the leadership of William III of Orange-Nassau (stadtholder or military leader of Holland from 1672–1702 and king of England from 1689 to 1702), as one of the Great Powers of the eighteenth century. The era of William and Queen Anne (1689–1714) saw a remarkable burst of intellectual energy with appearance of John Locke's great treatises on religious toleration (1689 in Latin; 1694 in English); on government (1690); on human understanding (1690); of Robert Boyle's *Sceptical Chymist* (1690); of Isaac Newton's *Opticks* (1704); and of works by Swift, Pope, Addison and Steele. It also witnessed the ascendancy in the field of military science and diplomacy of John Churchill, first Duke of Marlborough and in the field of politics of Sidney Godolphin, Robert Harley, Henry St. John (Viscount Bolingbroke), and Robert Walpole, later chief minister to George I and George II.

Of all the Great Powers, France was the most favored by nature: in geographical position, richness of land, mildness of climate, and size of population (over 20 millions by the end of the seventeenth century, the largest in Europe). Louis XIV (1643–1715), with the aid of his able ministerial families, the Colberts, the Le Telliers, and the Phélypeaux, directed the vast energies of France toward the achievement of her traditional diplomatic goals: a bridgehead over the Rhine, buffer areas along the border of the Southern Netherlands, and a line of fortresses guarding the passes into Italy and Spain. To achieve these goals Louis XIV's government adopted a strategy of harassment: rapid invasion, long sieges, march and counter-march, all executed in an effort to exhaust the enemy so that France might annex yet another slice of territory (usually from Spanish possessions or from the Rhenish states of the Empire). Where Louis XIV's exaggerated sense of *gloire* (reputation) overrode counsels of prudence, as in the Dutch War (1672–78) and again in the decade of the reunions in the 1680's, coalitions of European states arose to contain French power. Coalitions soon became a conditioned reflex among European states. Even at the beginning of the War of the Spanish Succession (which lasted from 1702 to 1714), at a time when France's claims to the Spanish inheritance were legally sound, William III and the Emperor Leopold were able to form the Grand Alliance against France. In curbing French ambitions, Europe forged a new balance of power, a balance that France herself helped maintain during the long reign of Louis XV (1715–1774).

As the Great Powers emerged in the late seventeenth century Europe witnessed a sudden expansion of its military establishment: armies grew in size from 40,000 or 50,000 at the time of the Thirty Years' War to well over 300,000 in the Wars of Spanish and Austrian Successions (the latter lasted from 1740–1748). Under the guidance of such great military leaders as Cromwell and Turenne; the marquis de

Louvois (Louis XIV's war minister) and Vauban (Louis' great military engineer); and Eugene of Savoy and Marlborough, these vast new armies underwent a logistical revolution: they were better provisioned, more highly trained, better clothed and fed and cared for than their predecessors in the Reformation Era. At the same time strategy was reduced to a science of move and counter-move and the rules of war were standardized.

The standardization of the rules of war led to a reawakening of interest in the field of international law. Hugo Grotius (1583–1645) in his great work, *De Jure Belli ac Pacis* (1625), and Samuel Pufendorf (1632–94) in his treatise, *Law of Nature and Nations* (1672), helped codify the concepts of freedom of the seas, of neutrality and neutral powers, of exchange of prisoners, of territorial waters, of siege warfare, and of international congresses. The seventeenth and eighteenth centuries became the golden age of diplomats and diplomacy. Great peace congresses met in Münster (1648), in the Pyrenees (1659), Aix-le-Chapelle (1668), Nijmegen (1678–79), Ryswick (1697), Utrecht (1712–13), Aix-le-Chapelle (1748), and Paris (1763). At these congresses princes and diplomats traded counties and cities with the wordly wisdom (or cynicism) that took the name of "reason of state." In the Renaissance it was called Machiavellianism; in the nineteenth century, *Realpolitik*.

Ironically, at a time when war and famine stalked Europe, the population, overall, was expanding so rapidly that we speak of the eighteenth as the century of the first population explosion. Since the Fourth Century A.D., European population, (including Russia) had hovered at just under 100 millions. By 1700 it had risen to 120 millions and by 1800 to 190 millions. France increased in population from 20 millions in 1700 to 26 millions in 1789; Great Britain from 5 to 10 millions; Spain from 6 to 10 millions (in a startling reversal of the downward trend of the seventeenth century); Russia (including conquests) from 8 to 30 millions; and the Prussian population, which in 1740 stood at 2,500,000, numbered over 5,800,000 in 1783—and this after 500,000 men had been sacrificed on the battlefields of the Seven Years' War (1756–1763). The population explosion was due to advances in medical science; to the so-called agricultural revolution of the late seventeenth and early eighteenth centuries, and to the beginnings of the Industrial Revolution.

As the Industrial Revolution took hold of Europe in the late eighteenth century, many economists shifted their intellectual allegiance from the theory of strict state control to a belief in freedom of trade and commerce. Adam Smith, in his pioneering work on an *Inquiry into the Nature and Causes of the Wealth of Nations* (1776), berated the statesmen of the preceding century and a half for having followed the false concepts of a "mercantile system," which encouraged the hoarding of precious metals and the sterile proliferation of bureaucratic regulation of trade and industry. Nineteenth-century critics, led by Gustav Schmoller, accepted Adam Smith's concept of mercantilism as a system but tended to give it a more positive interpretation by equating mercantilism with the state-building activities of such statesmen as Cardinal Richelieu, Colbert, Peter the Great, Frederick William the Great Elector, Frederick the Great, and the Dutch merchant princes. On the other hand, some critics dealing with this century, Sir George Clark for example, deny that a "mercantile system" *qua* system actually existed. For him, as for other scholars, it represents a chimera. The great Swedish economic historian, Eli Heckscher, has countered Clark and others by redefining mercantilism as a system of power and as a new vision of society. (The arguments for and against mercantilism are presented in Problem 2.)

Linked with mercantilism is the term "absolutism." Quoting from Catherine the Great's *Nakaz* of 1767: "The Sovereign is absolute when there is no other Authority but that which centers in his single Person." Few rulers, outside of China and Turkey, did in fact possess such absolute power in the Early Modern Era. Their spokesmen might claim, as Bishop Bossuet did for Louis XIV, that the king was the fountainhead of justice and God's regent on earth; but in truth, the exigencies of geography, of religion, of provincial particularism, and of residual feudalism militated against totalitarian regimes as we know them in the twentieth century. What then is usually meant in Europe by absolutism was the attempt of the prince and his ministers to concentrate in their own hands power over justice, taxes industry, trade, and foreign policy. What success this centralization of authority in the crown did achieve was due largely to the efforts of the great ministers and secretaries of state and to their servants, the bureaucrats. These new men in politics—the bureaucrats—owed their position to merit rather than to feudal right or to the purchase of office. In many ways, then, it might be better to speak of bureaucratic absolutism rather than, simply, absolutism. (For a discussion of absolutism or enlightened absolutism and related questions see Problem 4.)

In the arts, the age of the Baroque is coeval with absolutism. By Baroque is meant that age in the history of architecture and the plastic arts that was born of the Catholic Reformation of the late sixteenth century and that is distinquished by its bold use of asymmetrical design, dramatic lighting effects, magnificent color—particularly gold ornamentation, massive cornices, bulging domes, twisting columns, and curved facades, with particular attention given to the organic integration of the whole. The tensions inherent in the Baroque are highly dramatic and gave emphasis to religious themes and later to dynastic majesty. The city of Rome was the nursery of the Baroque: home of the architects Giovanni Bernini (1598–1680) and Francesco Borromini (1599–1667) and of such great Baroque monuments as the Gesu (the mother church of the Jesuit order), the Bernini colonnade of the Piazza of St. Peter's; the baldachin or canopy over the high altar of St. Peter's; and the Church of St. Agnes on the Piazza Navona. As the Baroque spread northward and westward into the valleys of the Po, Danube, and Rhine, and into Spain and Portugal, it came increasingly to be mixed with secular architecture until when it reached France it was dramatically juxtaposed with classical motifs in Louis XIV's massive palace of Versailles. (The palace was enlarged in the 1660's by Louis Le Vau, 1612–70, and in the 1680's by J. H. Mansard, 1648–1708; it was not completed until 1710.) The style of Louis XIV's palace was evoked on a smaller scale in Marlborough's Blenheim, in the Schloss Wurttemburg outside of Stuttgart, and in the Schönbruun and Belvedere palaces in Vienna. Thus did the echoes of the Baroque carry well down into the eighteenth century when they were absorbed into the Rococo style and into a reinvigorated classicism.

The greatest crisis of the Early Modern Era, was, however, not in the field of the balance of power, military planning, government, nor economics or the arts but in the arena of ideas. The crisis began in the sixteenth century with attacks on the authority of Aristotle, Ptolemy, Galen and other Ancients made by a motley crew of neo-Platonists, neo-Pythagoreans, alchemists, nominalists, medical logicians, mystics, and mathematicians. One of the leaders of these "protestants," Nicholas Copernicus (1473–1543) attacked the complexities and absurdities of the Aristotelian-Ptolemaic world picture in a thesis entitled *On the Revolution of Heavenly Bodies*, published in the year of his death, 1543. Fortunately for Copernicus's reputation, his thesis was espoused by the great Italian mathematician and experimental scientist Galileo Galilei (1564–1642), who expressed his support for Copernicus's idea that the sun was the center of the universe and that the Earth moved in its axis around it in his influential work, *Dialogue concerning the Two Chief Systems of the World* (1632). Galileo's assertions were corroborated by Johannes Kepler's laws of planetary motion which claimed that planets follow an elliptical path around the sun, accelerating as they approach the sun's warmth and slowing down as they swing away from it.

The ideas of Copernicus, Galileo, and Kepler swayed the learned world but left many laymen confused. This confusion was expressed in the early seventeenth century by the English poet John Donne, who reflected "that the new philosophy puts all in doubt":

The sun is lost and th' earth and no man's wit
Can well direct him where to look for it.

For Donne, as for many other educated men, "All coherence [was] gone from the universe." In an attempt to restore celestial coherence Sir Isaac Newton (1642–1727) promulgated his laws of motion and gravity in one of the greatest scientific treatises of all time, the *Principia Mathematica* of 1687. In a similar effort to give coherence to the field of philosophy, René Descartes (1596–1650) applied the clear, cutting edge of rationalism to the problems of human knowledge, expounding in his *Discourse on Method* (1637) his famous aphorism: *Cogito ergo sum*, which means that I exist because I am consciously aware that I exist. I am a thinking human being, able to doubt my own existence but not to refute the fact that I am doubting. Descartes used this concept of systematic doubt as a weapon to destroy the anachronisms and myths of scholasticism. Cartesian rationalism was one of the pillars upon which the era of the Enlightenment was set.

A link between Descartes and the Enlightenment was Pierre Bayle (1647–1706) whose *Historical and Critical Dictionary* (1697) served the next generation as a model of Biblical exegesis and historical criticism, and whose *Philosophical Commentary on Christ's Words "Compel Them to Come In"* (1686) served as one of the seventeenth century's most eloquent pleas for religious toleration. Daniel Mornet calls Pierre Bayle a member of the first generation of the *philosophes*, that is, one of the men of letters who whether defending or attacking Cartesianism or Newtonianism, the New Science or the New Philosophy taught men to think. The *philosophes* urged the emancipation of man's mind from the shackles of tradition and authority, from religious superstition and princely tyranny.

Directly related to Bayle intellectually were three great *philosophes* of the second generation: Fontenelle (1657–1757), Montesquieu (1689–1755), and Voltaire (1694–1778). Fontenelle, an ardent follower of Descartes, propagated Cartesianism from his position as permanent secretary of the *Académie des Sciences* and in his popular work *Conversations on the Plurality of Worlds* (1686). Baron Montesquieu, a French noble who served as first president of the Bordeaux *parlement*, expounded his views on law and government in one of the most influential and greatest works of the Enlightenment, *The Spirit of the Laws* (1748). For Montesquieu "Law is human reason . . . [and] the political and civil laws of each nation ought to be only the particular cases in which human reason is applied. They should be adapted in such a manner to the people whom they are intended . . . They should be relative to the climate of each country, to the quality of its soil . . . to the religion of the inhabitants, to their inclinations, numbers, commerce, manners, and customs." Montesquieu's belief in a balance in the powers of government (wrongly interpreted as a separation of powers), his support of the judiciary as a moderating influence within the state, and his attack on the Cartesian *esprit géométrique* through his doctrine of relativism have remained as one of the great heritages left to us by the Enlightenment. Voltaire, another of Bayle's successors, glorified the achievements of England in the fields of government, of science, and of religious toleration in his *Letters on the English* (1733), a work that has been called "the first bomb thrown at the Old Regime." His epigrammatically brilliant tale of *Candide* (1759) employed Baylean scepticism to ridicule the hypocrisy of the ruling classes and the easy optimism of such philosophers as Leibniz, Pope, and Shaftesbury. But it was Voltaire's savage attacks on the institution of the Church and his pleas for religious toleration that endeared him to the generation of the French Revolution. For them he epitomized the spirit of secularism, scepticism, and humanitarianism.

As the Enlightenment evolved it spawned its own antithesis: Jean-Jacques Rousseau (1712–1778), who, as Sir Ernest Barker notes, looked back to pre-historic age of innocence and forward to an age of sentiment and authoritarianism. Rousseau's ideas are best expressed in his work, *Émile: or on Education*, published in 1762. Here he presents both a paradigm of progressive education and a parable of man's pilgrimage to God. For Rousseau man was born free of original sin; it was Society that corrupted him. If, therefore, the individual was carefully tutored from birth by teachers who believed in Nature's goodness and guarded against the corrupting influences of the so-called civilized world then the individual's true *amour du soi*, respect for himself and for God, would cancel out the opposing *amour propre*, self-love or pride, thus liberating man from Society's tyrannies of habit, hate, and hubris. With Rousseau's writings a new age is announced. (For a discussion of his famous work on the *Social Contract* see Problem 5.)

The Early Modern Era was *par excellence* a European era: a time in which Europe held political and economic sway over vast colonial empires and reigned supreme as the world center of light and enlightenment. Europe knew no rivals, not in the Americas, nor in Africa, nor Asia. Never again would the European "Great Powers" hold the world balance. In the nineteenth century the United States and Japan and in the twentieth China and the new nations of Africa and Asia would challenge that hegemony.

1

OLIVER CROMWELL—DICTATOR OR DEFENDER OF LIBERTY?

Oliver Cromwell was born in Huntingdon, England, on April 25, 1599, and died at the palace of Whitehall in London on September 3, 1658. He was the second son of Robert Cromwell and Elizabeth Steward. His father's family were descendants of Henry VIII's great minister, Thomas Cromwell. Oliver was educated at the Huntingdon Free School and at Sidney Sussex College in Cambridge University. He left the university at the age of eighteen and married at twenty-one. Cromwell was a vigorous man who enjoyed the hunt and the rugged sports of English county life. He was also interested in national politics; and in 1628 was elected to the House of Commons representing the borough of Huntingdon. He was reelected in 1640, following the so-called Eleven Years' Tyranny of Charles I in which no Parliament sat.

Before 1642 Cromwell had had little experience as a soldier. He proved, however, in the campaigns of August and September, 1642, to be an excellent cavalry officer; and in February, 1643, he was promoted from a captain to a colonel of the horse guards. In the campaign of 1644 Cromwell established his reputation as a field commander by leading the decisive cavalry charge at the battle of Marston Moor (July 2). In the autumn of the same year he returned to his seat in the House of Commons, where he assumed the leadership of the Independent wing of the Puritan party. At the same time Cromwell was active in training troops for what was to become known as the New Model Army. In June 14, 1645, it was this army, under the nominal command of Sir Thomas Fairfax, with Cromwell in charge of the Horse Guard, that won the decisive battle of Naseby. In 1647, he assumed an even greater role in the national political life by urging the seizure of King Charles and by prompting the purge of the Presbyterian wing in Parliament.

In the second phase of the Civil War which opened in 1648 Cromwell, as Lieutenant General of the English troops, led the attack on Scotland, winning the battle of Preston in August 1648 and entering Edinburgh in triumph in October. On January 30, 1649, when King Charles was executed, Cromwell, who had had a large hand in bringing him to trial, reportedly exclaimed that his death was a "cruel necessity," yet, for the preservation of the Commonwealth, an inevitable one. In the next year, Cromwell became Captain-General and Commander in Chief of the English land forces and in 1652, following his victory over the Scots at Worcester (September 3, 1651), the virtual ruler of England. His position was formalized in December 1653 when he took the oath of office as Lord Protector of the English Commonwealth and as guardian of its first written constitution, the "Instrument of Government." He died in 1658 exhausted by his efforts to unite England under Puritan rule.

A storm of controversy has raged around the figure of Oliver Cromwell from his day to this. Contemporary critics called him an inefficient, short-sighted initiator of policies, a "bad brave man," a supreme regicide; his supporters saw him as a "man who made all the neighboring princes fear him," a champion of religious toleration, a Puritan saint. Later commentators were no less vociferously at odds over Cromwell's character than were his contemporaries. Some early nineteenth-century Romantics, for example, branded Cromwell as an ambitious hypocrite; others, notably Thomas Carlyle, who edited Cromwell's *Letters and Speeches* (1845), pictured him as the great Hero of the Protestant cause and the champion of liberty not only in England but in the Western World. It was, however, not until writings of Samuel R. Gardiner in the late nineteenth century that there appeared a well-balanced, thoroughly researched account of Cromwell and the English Revolution. Gardiner, a cautious critic, viewed Cromwell as a moderate, a "trimmer," who wished to impose his reforms in the gradual manner of a nineteenth-century liberal statesman.

If Gardiner pictured Cromwell as "a russet-coated Gladstone," some twentieth-century critics went to the opposite extreme by identifying him with the totalitarian dictators of this century. Sir Ernest Barker likened Cromwell's accomplishments (and this was in 1937) to those of Hitler; both men, he said, were unifiers of the state, both had "purged and purified" their nations. In a more negative vein Harvard professor W. C. Abbott asserted that both Hitler and Cromwell forced their reforms on a frightened people by means of naked force. Following the Second World War, a more balanced view of Cromwell appeared in the writings of such scholars as Hugh Trevor-Roper and Christopher Hill, both of whom tended to de-emphasize the "great man" theory of history by subordinating Cromwell's role to the general economic and social trends of the times. Thus the student of modern history can in the person of one man view the changing fashions of historical interpretation.

SEVENTEENTH-CENTURY PAMPHLETEER

"THE WORLD'S MISTAKE"

In the late 1660's an anonymous pamphlet was published attacking Oliver Cromwell as the originator of England's economic and social ills. The author charged that "this late Tyrant, or Protector" had mistakenly allied himself with France against Spain. In doing so he became the dupe of the subtle Cardinal Mazarin who used English power to humble Spain and at the same time to increase enormously the power and prestige of France. The author also attacked Cromwell's acts of "oppression and injustice" within England by pointing particularly to the trial of the Leveller leader, John Lilburne; to Cromwell's "falseness and ingratitude" toward the Long Parliament; and to his "Want of Honour" in dealing "every Man's Conscience." This indictment of Cromwell's regime appealed to many Englishmen of the late seventeenth century, who, along with the author of this track, believed that Cromwell was indeed the "Favorite of Ignorance" and the "Tiberius of Dissimulation."

. . . . I will cast myself upon Providence, for the Success of this Paper; and in Reference to *Cromwell's* Government, and the present Times, make some Observations relating to both, and, in Order thereunto, shew,

First, That the *Original Cause* of the low Condition that we are now (*in Relation to Trade*) reduced unto, had its Beginning in *Oliver's* Time, and the Foundations of it, laid either by his *ignorant Mistaking* the Interest of this Kingdom, or *wilfully doing* it, for the Advancement of his own *particular* Interest.

Secondly, That his Time, for the short Continuance, had as much of *Oppression,* and *Injustice,* as any former Times.

Thirdly and *Lastly,* That he never, in his latter Days, *valued* either *Honour or Honesty,* when they stood in the Way of his Ambition, and that there is nothing to be admired in him (though so much idolised) but that the Partiality of the World should make him so great a Favourite of Ignorance, and Forgetfulness, as he seems to be.

When this late *Tyrant,* or *Protector* (as some calls him) turned out the *Long-Parliament,* the Kingdom was arrived at the highest Pitch of *Trade, Wealth,* and *Honour,* that is, in any Age, ever yet knew. The *Trade* appeared, by the great Sums offered then for the Customs and Excise, *Nine-hundred Thousand Pounds a Year* being refused. The *Riches* of the Nation shewed itself, in the high Value that Land and all our Native Commodities bore, which are the certain Marks of Opulency. Our *Honour* was made known to all the World, by a conquering Navy, which had brought the proud *Hollanders* upon their Knees, to beg Peace of us, upon our own Conditions, keeping all other Nations in Awe. And besides these Advantages, the *publick Stock* was *Five-hundred Thousand Pounds* in ready Money, the Value of *Seven-hundred Thousand Pounds* in Stores, and the whole Army in Advance, some four, and none under two Months; so that, though there might be a Debt of near Five-thousand Pounds upon the Kingdom, he met with above twice the Value in Lieu of it.

The Nation being in this flourishing and formidable Posture, *Cromwell* began his Usurpation, upon the greatest Advantages imaginable, having it in his Power to have made Peace, and profitable Leagues, in what Manner he had pleased with all our Neighbours, every one courting us then, and being ambi-

From *Harleian Miscellany,* I (London, 1744–1746), pp. 280–282, 284–288.

tious of the Friendship of *England*; but as if the Lord had infatuated, and deprived him of common Sense and Reason, he neglected all our golden Opportunities, misimproved the Victory, God had given us over the *United Netherlands*, making Peace (without ever striking a Stroke) so soon as ever Things came into his Hands, upon equal Terms with them: And immediately after, contrary to our Interest, made an unjust War with *Spain*, an impolitick League with *France*, bringing the first thereby under, and making the latter too great for *Christendom*; and by that Means broke the Balance betwixt the two Crowns of *Spain*, and *France*, which his Predecessors, the *Long-Parliament*, had always wisely preserved.

In this *dishonest War* with *Spain*, he pretended, and endeavoured, to impose a Belief upon the World, that he had nothing in his Eye, but the Advancement of the *Protestant Cause*, and the *Honour* of this Nation; but his Pretences were either fraudulent, or he was ignorant in Foriegn Affairs (as I am apt to think, that he was not guilty of too much Knowledge in them). For he that had known any Thing of the Temper of the *Popish* Prelacy, and the *French*-Court-Policies, could not but see, that the Way to increase, or preserve the *Reformed* Interest in France, was by rendering the *Protestants* of necessary Use to their King, for that, longer than they were so, they could not be free from Persecution; and that the Way to render them so, was by keeping the Balance betwixt *Spain* and *France* even, as that, which would consequently make them useful to their King: But by overthrowing the Balance in his War with *Spain*, and joining with *France*, he freed the *French* King from his Fears of *Spain*, enabled him to subdue all Factions at Home, and thereby to bring himself into a Condition of not standing in Need of any of them; and from thence hath proceeded the Persecution that hath since been, and still is, in that Nation, against the *Reformed* there; so that *Oliver*, instead of advancing the *Reformed* Interest, hath, by an Error in his Politicks, been the Author of destroying it.

The *Honour* and *Advantage* he propounded to this Nation, in his pulling down of *Spain*, had as ill a Foundation: For if true, as was said, that we were to have had *Ostend* and *Newport*, as well as *Dunkirk* (when we could get them) they bore no Proportion, in any Kind, to all the rest of the King of *Spain's European* Dominions, which must necessarily have fallen to the *French* King's Share, because of their Joining and Nearness to him, and Remoteness from us, and the Increasing the Greatness of so

near a Neighbour must have increased our future Dangers. . . .

It is confessed, that *Oliver's* Peace and League with *France* was upon honourable Articles; but, as the tottering Affairs of *France* then stood, much more could not have been sooner asked, than had: For *Mazarin*, being a Man of a large and subtle Wit, apprehending the Greatness of *England* at that Time, which was then dreadful to the World, and the vast Advantages *France* would have in pulling down, by their Help, of *Spain*, granted him, not only any Thing for the Present that he demanded, but disregarded also even his Party's making their Boasts of the Awe he had him under: Considering, that when *Cromwell* had helped him to do his Work, in bringing under the House of *Austria*, and therein casting the Balance of *Christendom* on his Side, he should afterwards have Leisure to recover what then he seemed to part with: And though nothing is more ordinary, than to hear Men brag, how *Oliver* vapoured over *France*, I do esteem *Mazarin's* Complying with him, for his own Ends, to be the chief Piece of all his Ministry; for, by that Means only, and no other, is his Master become so great at this Day, that no Factions at Home can disturb his Peace, nor Powers Abroad frighten him. Which is more than any King of *France*, since *Charles the Great*, could say: And, when his neighbour Nations have, too late I fear, experienced his Greatness, they will find Cause to curse the Ignorance of *Oliver's* Politicks; and therefore, when a true Measure is taken of *Cromwell*, the Approbation, that he hath in the World, will not be found to have its Foundation in *Sense*, or *Reason*, but proceeding from *Ignorance* and *Atheism*: From *Ignorance*, in those that take all that was done by him, as a Servant, and whilst under the Direction of better Heads, than his own, to be done by him alone; and from *Atheism*, in those that think every Thing lawful that a Man doth, if it succeed to his Advancement. But they that shall take an impartial View of his Actions, whilst he was a *Single Person*[1], and at Liberty to make Use of his own Parts without Controul, will find nothing worthy Commendations, but Cause enough from thence to observe, that the Wisdom of his Masters, and not his own, must have been that by which he first moved; and to attribute his former Performances, whilst a Servant, as is truly due, to the Judgment and Subtlety of the *Long-Parliament*, under whose Conduct and Command he was. And now, from *Crom-*

---

[1] Protector.

The Early Modern Era

well's neglecting to live in Peace, as, if he had pleased, he might have done with all the World, to the great Inriching of this Nation: The Improvement of our Victory over *Holland* in his Peace with them; his being the Cause of the Loss of our *Spanish* Trade, during all his Time; of the Loss of 1500 *English* Ships in that War; besides, by it breaking the Balance of *Europe*; of the Expence of the publick Stock and Stores he found, with the contracting a Debt of Nineteen-hundred-thousand Pounds, according to his own Account (which, for aught I know, he left behind him, but am apt to think the Debt was not altogether so great, though made so to his Son *Richard's* Assembly, as a Means to get the more Money from the poorer People:) And lastly, of the dishonourable Overthrow we met with at *Hispaniola*. It may be well concluded, that he laid the Foundation of our present Want of Trade, to what we formerly enjoyed; and that the Reason, why his Miscarriages were not sooner under Observation, is, because our Stock of Wealth and Honour, at his Coming to the Government, being then unspeakably great, stifled their Appearance, until, having since had some unhappy additional Losses, they are now become discernible as first Losses, to a Merchant, who concealedly bears up under them, are afterwards discovered by the Addition of second Losses that sink him. When I contemplate these great Failings, I cannot but apprehend the sad Condition any People are in, whose Governor drives on a *distinct contrary* Interest to theirs; for, doubtless, *Cromwell's* over-weening Care to secure his *particular* Interest, against his Majesty, then Abroad, and the Long-Parliament, whom he had turned out, with a prodigious Ambition of acquiring a glorious Name in the World, carried him on to all his Mistakes and Absurdities, to the irreparable Loss and Damage of this famous Kingdom.

To prove the *Second* Assertion, That *Oliver's* Time was full of *Oppression* and *Injustice*, I shall but instance in a few of many Particulars, and begin with *John Lilburne*, not that I think him, in any Kind, one that deserved Favour or Respect, but that equal Justice is due to the worst as well as best Men, and that he comes first in Order of Time.

I. *John*, in 1646, was, by Order of the then *Parliament*, tried for his Life, with an Intent, I believe, of taking him away; but, the Jury not finding him Guilty, he was immediately, according to Law, generously set at Liberty by those, that had Quarrel enough against him. This Example in the *Parliament*

of keeping to the Laws in the Case of one, who was a professed implacable Enemy to them, ought to have been copied by *Cromwell*; but on the Contrary, to shew that there was a Difference betwixt him and his Predecessors (the *Long-Parliament's*) Principles, when the Law had again, upon a second Tryal, occasioned by *Oliver*, cleared *Lilburne*, the *Parliament's* Submitting to the Law was no Example to him: For, *contrary to Law*, he kept him in Prison, until he was so far spent in a Consumption, that he only turned him out to die.

2dly, Mr. *Coney's* Case is so notorious, that it needs little more than Naming: He was a Prisoner at *Cromwell's* Suit, and being brought to the *King's Bench* Bar, by a *Habeas Corpus*, had his Council taken from the Bar, and sent to the *Tower*, for no other Reason, than the Pleading of their Client's Cause; an Act of Violence, that, I believe, the whole Story of *England* doth not parallel.

3dly, Sir *Henry Vane*, above any one Person, was the Author of *Oliver's* Advancement, and did so long and cordially espouse his Interest, that he prejudiced himself, in the Opinion of some, by it; yet so ungrateful was this Monster of Ingratitude, that he studied to *destroy* him, both in Life and Estate; because he could not adhere to him in his *Perjury* and *Falseness*. The Occasion he took was this, He, appointing a publick Day of Humiliation, and Seeking of God for him, invited all God's People in his Declaration, to offer him their Advice in the weighty Affairs then upon his Shoulders. Sir *Henry*, taking a Rise from hence, offered his Advice by a Treatise, called *The Healing Question*: But *Cromwell*, angry at being taken at his Word, seized, imprisoned, and endeavoured to proceed further against him, for doing only what he had invited him to do; and some may think, that Sir *Henry* suffered justly, for having known him so long, and yet would trust to any Thing he said. . . .

The . . . Assertion of *Cromwell's* knowing *no Honesty*, where he thought his particular Interest was concerned, is made good; *First*, (tho' therein he mistook his Interest) in his *odious* and *unjust* War with *Spain*, without the least Provocations, meerly out of an ambitious and covetous Design of robbing that Prince of his Silver and Gold Mines; and because he judged it for his Credit to disguise his unlawful Desires, he proceeded in it, by employing his Creatures in the City, to draw the Merchants to complain of Injuries done them by

Spain, and to petition for Reparations; but, by a cross Providence, his Project had a contrary Success; for, instead of answering his Seekings, the Merchants remonstrated to him the great Prejudice that a War with *Spain* would be to *England*; and shewed, that that King had been so far from injuring us, that he had done more for Compliance, and Preventing a Breach with *England*, than ever he had done in Favour of any other Nation; but, when *Oliver* saw his Method would not take, he called the *Remonstrators*, Malignants, and begun the War of *his own Accord*, in which, he was highly ungrateful in designing the Ruin of that Prince, who all along had been most faithful to his Party.

Secondly, his *Falseness* and *Ingratitude* appeared superlatively in turning out his Masters[2], who had not only advanced him, but made themselves the more odious by their partial Affection towards him; and in his doing it, with the Breach of a positive negative Oath, taken once a Year, when made a Counsellor of State, besides the Breach of all other Engagements, voluntary Imprecations, Protestations, and Oaths, taken frequently upon all Occasions in Discourse and Declarations; and yet further (when he had turned them out) and left them void of Protection, and exposed them to the Fury of the People, in pursuing them with false reproachful Declarations, enough to have stirred up the rude Multitude to have destroyed them, wherever they had met them.

Thirdly, his *Want of Honour*, as well as Honesty, appeareth, yet further, in that having, by a long *Series* of a seeming pious Deportment, gained, by his *Dissimulation*, good Thoughts in his Masters, the *Long-Parliament*, and, by his *Spiritual Gifts*, wound himself into so good an Opinion with his Soldiers (Men, generally, of plain Breeding, that knew little besides their military Trade, and religious Exercises) that he could impose, in Matters of Business, what Belief he pleased upon them; he made use of the Credit he had with each, to abuse both, by many vile Practices, for making himself *popular*, and the Parliament and Army *odious* to one another; and, because the Artifices he used are too many to enumerate, I shall but instance in some few: As his sly complaining Insinuations against the Army to the Parliament, and against them to the Army: His being the chief Cause of the Parliament's giving Rewards to his Creatures, and then, whispering Complaints among his Officers, of their ill Husbandry: His

obstructing the House in their Business, by long drawling Speeches, and other Ways, and then complaining of them to his Soldiers, that he could not get them to do any Thing that was good: His giving fair Words to every one without keeping Promise with any, except for his own Advantage, and then excusing all with Forgetfulness: And his deserting his Major Generals, in their Decimations, crying out most against them himself, when he only had set them at Work, because questioned by his Assembly, is not to be forgotten, etc.

I would not be understood to remember any Thing here, in *Favour* of the *Long-Parliament*, for what might be wicked in him, might be just as to them: And though, if what he did had been for the Restoration of his Majesty, he might have been excused, yet, being for his own single Advancement, it is unpardonable, and leaves him a Person to be truly admired for nothing but *Apostasy* and *Ambition*, and exceeding *Tiberius* in Dissimulation. I am not ignorant that some think it Matter of Praise in him, that he kept us in Peace, *four Years* and *nine Months*; but that hath little in it, his Majesty having done the like, almost double his Time, since his Return, with one fifth Part of that Number of Soldiers which he commanded; though he hath also had the Trouble of pressing, and sometimes forcing *Uniformity* in Religion, which he found under several Forms; whereas *Oliver* kept the Nation purposely divided in Opinions, and himself of no declared Judgment, as the securest Way of engaging all several Persuasions equally to him; which Artifice, together with his leaving the Church Lands alienated as he found them, were all the true Principles of Policy that I know of, which he kept unto.

The Honesty of these Principles I refer to the Judgment of every Man's Conscience; but, if we may judge of Things by Experience and Success, they seem to have been very happy in the World: For, in comparing the Condition of the *Protestant* Countries at Present, to what they were in Times of *Popery*, we shall find them more considerable now than formerly; for, in taking a true Survey of the *Reformed* Dominions, we shall discover them to bear no Proportion at all, in Largeness, to the *Popish*; and that there is nothing that keeps the Balance betwixt the two Parties, but the Advantage that the First hath, in being free from the Bondage of the Church of *Rome*, and the Latter's being under it: For, as the Church of *Rome's* Mercies are (by their Principles) Cruelties, so, had they Power answerable to the natural Rich-

---

[2] The *Long Parliament*.

ness of the Soil of their Countries, and Extent of their Territories, they would long before this have swallowed up the *Protestant* Churches, and made Bonfires of their Members; but, as God, in his Mercy and Wisdom, hath, by his over-ruling Hand of Providence, preserved his Church; so, for the *Romish* Church's Inability to effect that which they have *Will* and *Malice* enough to carry them on to do, there are these natural Reasons:

First, There being generally, of the *Popish* Countries, above one Moiety belonging to *Churchmen, Monks, Friars,* and *Nuns,* who, like Drones, spend the Fat of the Land, without contributing any Thing to the Good of Mankind, renders them much the less considerable.

Secondly, Marriage being *forbidden* to all *these* Sorts and Orders, occasions great Want of People every where, they being uncapable of any Children but those of Darkness, except in *France,* which is an extraordinary Case, proceeding partly, by not being so subject to *Rome,* as other Countries of that Belief are; but especially from the Multitude of *Protestants,* that are among them.

Thirdly, The *blind Devotion* of these People, carrying them on to vast Expences, in the building and richly adorning of many needless and superfluous Churches, Chapels, and Crosses, etc. with the making chargeable Presents by the better, and Pilgrimages by the meaner Sort, to their Idols, keeps all Degrees under.

Fourthly, The many *Holydays,* upon which, the labouring Man is forbidden to work, adds much to their Poverty.

But, *Fifthly* and *Lastly,* The vast Number of *begging Friars,* who living idly, and purely upon the Sweat of other Men's Brows, without taking any Labour themselves, make it impossible, for the lower Sort of People, who think they are bound, in Conscience, to relieve them, ever to get above a mean Condition; now whosoever shall seriously weigh and ponder these Circumstances, under which the *Popish* Countries lie, and consider the *Reformed's* Advantage in being free from them, must confess it the less Wonder, that the *Evangelical* Princes and States, with their small Dominions, compared to the others great, are able to bear up against them; and now as the Alienation of *Church-lands,* the Turning out the *Romish* Vermin, the *Priests, Monks, Friars,* and

Nuns, who devour all Countries wherever they come, and Freedom from the *Popish* Imposition upon Conscience, hath mightily increased the Greatness of the *Protestant* Princes and States, to what they anciently were, and the not doing the same, in the *Popish* Countries, keeps those Princes under; so, even amongst the *Reformed,* where the Church-lands are most alienated, and Liberty of Conscience most given, they prosper most, as in *Holland,* and some Parts of *Germany,* with other Places. And, on the Contrary, *Denmark,* where Church-lands are least alienated of any of the *Reformed* Countries, and the City of *Lubeck,* where, of all the free Imperial Cities of *Germany,* Liberty of Conscience is least given, they thrive least in both Places. And, I think, it will also hold, that, as this famous Kingdom, in the Times of *Popery,* was, in no Measure, so formidable as now it is; so before the Restoration of our *Hierarchy* to their Lands, their Hoarding up the Money, which before went in Trade, and their Discouraging and Driving into Corners the industrious Sort of People, by imposing upon their Consciences, it flourished more, was richer, and fuller of Trade, than now it is; and I dare undertake to be a Prophet in this, That, if ever any *Protestant* Country should be so far forsaken of the Lord, as to be suffered to turn unto *Popery,* these Observations will be made good in their visible Loss of the Splendor, Riches, Power, and Greatness, that they now know.

Had *Cromwell* been a Person of an open prophane Life, his Actions had been less scandalous; but, having been a *Professor of Religion,* they are not to be pleaded for; neither can it be consistent with religion to palliate them, which have been of so much Offence, and, as may be feared, made so many Atheists in the World; and I cannot but stand amazed, when I hear him extolled by some, not ignorant of his Practices, knowing in Religion, and, as I hope, fearing God.

Now I will suppose, I may be suspected to have been injured, or disobliged by *Oliver;* but I can with Truth affirm, I never received either Good or Evil from him in all my Life, more than in Common with the whole Kingdom, which I think, may be allowed to render me the more a competent Judge in his Case; and, that I am so far from being moved unto this, out of any Quarrel to him, that, as I have here mentioned some few of many Injustices and State-errors, that he was guilty of in his short Time, if I were conscious of any Thing more, during his *Pro-*

tectorship, worthy Applause, than I have here mentioned, I should not envy it him, but freely remember it; and, if any think I have not said enough on his Behalf, and too much to his Disadvantage, I have this for my Buckler, that I wish I could have said more for him, and had known less against him; professing, that, besides what I have here hinted, I am wholly ignorant of any one Action in all his four Years and nine Months Time, done either *wisely*, *virtuously*, or for the *Interest of this Kingdom*, and, therefore, that I am none of his Admirers, I ought to be pardoned by my Readers.

Much more might be said upon this Subject, but this may suffice to shew, that, if *Mazarin*, at the Hearing of *Oliver's* Death, thought, he had then Reason for calling him a *Fortunate Fool*, if he were now living he would find more Cause for it, *Cromwell's* Lot, as to *Reputation*, having been exceedingly much greater since his Death, than whilst he was in the World: And that from Forgetfulness of his impolitick Government, from whose Entrance we may date the Commencement of our *Trade's Decay*; and, through Want of Memory, in Men's giving to him the Cause of our former Wealth and Prosperity, which truly belongeth to others. But, what Opinion soever *Mazarin* may have had of *Oliver*, he was, without all Peradventure, a Person of *more than ordinary Wit*, and no otherwise a *Fool* than as he wanted *Honesty*, no Man being *wise* but an *honest* Man.

THOMAS CARLYLE

THE HERO

Thomas Carlyle, writing in his great work on *Heroes and Hero Worship*, praised Cromwell as one of the world's great representatives of manhood and "hero-hood," a courageous, zealous, "strong daring man," who swept aside "all manner of formulas and logical superficialities" in order to get at the truth. Carlyle pictured the Protector's quarrels with his Parliaments as the struggles of an honest man with corrupt assemblies that had sunk into "idle pedantries, constitutionalities and bottomless cavillings and questionings. . . ." Cromwell was the chosen of Providence, the representative of God's Cause on earth; and yet few mortals have been more basely treated: "His dead body was hung in chains; his 'place in History' . . . has been a place of ignominy, accusation, blackness, and disgrace." Now, said Carlyle, "Let the Hero rest. . . . Peace to him."

Poor Cromwell—great Cromwell! The inarticulate Prophet; Prophet who could not *speak*. Rude, confused, struggling to utter himself, with his savage depth, with his wild sincerity; and he looked so strange, among the elegant Euphemisms, dainty little Falklands, didactic Chillingworths, diplomatic Clarendons! Consider him. An outer hull of chaotic confusion, visions of the Devil, nervous dreams, almost semi-madness; and yet such a clear determinate man's-energy working in the heart of that. A kind of chaotic man. The ray as of pure starlight and fire, working in such an element of boundless hypochondria, *un*formed black of darkness! And yet withal this hypochondria, what was it but the very greatness of the man? The depth and tenderness of his wild affections: the quantity of *sympathy* he had with things—the quantity of insight he would yet get into the heart of things, the mastery he would yet get over things: this was his hypochondria. The man's misery, as man's misery always does, came of his greatness. Samuel Johnson too is that kind of man. Sorrow-stricken, half-distracted; the wide element of

From Thomas Carlyle, *On Heroes; Hero Worship; and the Heroic in History* (Everyman's Library), pp. 285–286, 290–293, 298–311.

mournful *black* enveloping him—wide as the world. It is the character of a prophetic man; a man with his whole soul *seeing,* and struggling to see.

On this ground, too, I explain to myself Cromwell's reputed confusion of speech. To himself the internal meaning was sun-clear; but the material with which he was to clothe it in utterance was not there. He had *lived* silent; a great unnamed sea of Thought round him all his days; and in his way of life little call to attempt *naming* or uttering that. With his sharp power of vision, resolute power of action, I doubt not he could have learned to write Books withal, and speak fluently enough;—he did harder things than writing of Books. This kind of man is precisely he who is fit for doing manfully all things you will set him on doing. Intellect is not speaking and logicising; it is seeing and ascertaining. Virtue, *Vir-tus,* manhood, *hero*-hood, is not fair-spoken immaculate regularity; it is first of all, what the Germans well name it, *Tugend* (*Taugend, dow*-ing or *Dough*-tiness), Courage and the Faculty to *do.* This basis of the matter Cromwell had in him. . . .

But in fact there are two errors, widely prevalent, which pervert to the very basis our judgments formed about such men as Cromwell; about their "ambition," "falsity," and suchlike. The first is what I might call substituting the *goal* of their career for the course and starting-point of it. The vulgar Historian of a Cromwell fancies that he had determined on being Protector of England, at the time when he was ploughing the marsh lands of Cambridgeshire. His career lay all mapped-out: a program of the whole drama; which he then step by step dramatically unfolded, with all manner of cunning, deceptive dramaturgy, as he went on,—the hollow, scheming Ὑποκριτης, or Play-actor, that he was! This is a radical perversion; all but universal in such cases. And think for an instant how different the fact is! How much does one of *us* foresee of his own life? Short way ahead of us it is all dim; an *un*wound skein of possibilities, of apprehensions, attempt-abilities, vague-looming hopes. This Cromwell had *not* his life lying all in that fashion of Program, which he needed then, with that unfathomable cunning of his, only to enact dramatically, scene after scene! Not so. We see it so; but to him it was in no measure so. What absurdities would fall-away of themselves, were this one undeniable fact kept honestly in view by History! Historians indeed will tell you that they do keep it in view;—but look whether such is practically the fact! Vulgar History, as in this

Cromwell's case, omits it altogether; even the best kinds of History only remember it now and then. To remember it duly with rigorous perfection, as in the fact it *stood,* requires indeed a rare faculty; rare, nay impossible. A very Shakspeare for faculty; or more than Shakspeare; who could *enact* a brother man's biography, see with the brother man's eyes at all points of his course what things *he* saw; in short, *know* his course and him, as few "Historians" are like to do. Half or more of all the thick-plied perversions which distort our image of Cromwell, will disappear, if we honestly so much as try to represent them so; in sequence, as they *were*; not in the lump, as they are thrown-down before us.

But a second error, which I think the generality commit, refers to this same "ambition" itself. We exaggerate the ambition of Great Men; we mistake what the nature of it is. Great Men are not ambitious in that sense; he is a small poor man that is ambitious so. Examine the man who lives in misery because he does not shine above other men; who goes about producing himself, pruriently anxious about his gifts and claims; struggling to force everybody, as it were begging everybody for God's sake, to acknowledge him a great man, and set him over the heads of men! Such a creature is among the wretchedest sights seen under this sun. A *great* man? A poor morbid prurient empty man; fitter for the ward of a hospital, than for a throne among men. I advise you to keep-out of his way. He cannot walk on quiet paths; unless you will look at him, wonder at him, write paragraphs about him, he cannot live. It is the *emptiness* of the man, not his greatness. Because there is nothing in himself, he hungers and thirsts that you would find something in him. In good truth, I believe no great man, not so much as a genuine man who had health and real substance in him of whatever magnitude, was ever much tormented in this way.

Your Cromwell, what good could it do him to be "noticed" by noisy crowds of people? God his Maker already noticed him. He, Cromwell, was already there; no notice would make *him* other than he already was. Till his hair was grown grey; and Life from the downhill slope was all seen to be limited, not infinite but finite, and all a measurable matter *how* it went,—he had been content to plough the ground, and read his Bible. . . .

But with regard to Cromwell and his purposes: Hume, and a multitude following him, come upon me here with an admission that Cromwell *was* sincere at first; a sincere "Fanatic" at first, but gradually became a "Hypocrite" as things opened round him. This of the Fanatic-Hypocrite is Hume's theory of it; extensively applied since,—to Mahomet and many others. Think of it seriously, you will find something in it; not much, not all, very far from all. Sincere hero hearts do not sink in this miserable manner. The Sun flings-forth impurities, gets balefully incrusted with spots; but it does not quench itself, and become no Sun at all, but a mass of Darkness! I will venture to say that such never befell a great deep Cromwell; I think, never. Nature's own lion-hearted Son; Antaeus-like, his strength is got by *touching the Earth,* his Mother; lift him up from the Earth, lift him up into Hypocrisy, Inanity, his strength is gone. We will not assert that Cromwell was an immaculate man; that he fell into no faults, no insincerities among the rest. He was no dilettante professor of "perfections," "immaculate conducts." He was a rugged Orson, rending his rough way through actual true *work,*—doubtless with many a *fall* therein. Insincerities, faults, very many faults daily and hourly: it was too well known to him; known to God and him! The Sun was dimmed many a time; but the Sun had not himself grown a Dimness. Cromwell's last words, as he lay waiting for death, are those of a Christian heroic man. Broken prayers to God, that He would judge him and this Cause, He since man could not, in justice yet in pity. They are most touching words. He breathed-out his wild great soul, its toils and sins all ended now, into the presence of his Maker, in this manner.

I, for one, will not call the man a Hypocrite! Hypocrite, mummer, the life of him a mere theatricality; empty barren quack, hungry for the shouts of mobs? The man had made obscurity do very well for him till his head was grey; and now he was, there as he stood recognised unblamed, the virtual king of England. Cannot a man do without King's Coaches and Cloaks? Is it such a blessedness to have clerks for ever pestering you with bundles of papers in red tape? A simple Diocletian prefers planting of cabbages; a George Washington, no very immeasurable man, does the like. One would say, it is what any genuine man could do; and would do. The instant his real work were out in the matter of Kingship —away with it!

Let us remark, meanwhile, how indispensable everywhere a *King* is, in all movements of men. It is strikingly shown, in this very War, what becomes of men when they cannot find a Chief Man, and their enemies can. The Scotch Nation was all but unanimous in Puritanism; zealous and of one mind about it, as in this English end of the Island was always far from being the case. But there was no great Cromwell among them; poor tremulous, hesitating, diplomatic Argyles and suchlike; none of them had a heart true enough for the truth, or durst commit himself to the truth. They had no leader; and the scattered Cavalier party in that country had one: Montrose, the noblest of all the Cavaliers; an accomplished, gallant-hearted, splendid man; what one may call the Hero-Cavalier.[1] Well, look at it; on the one hand subjects without a King; on the other a King without subjects! The subjects without King can do nothing; the subjectless King can do something. This Montrose, with a handful of Irish or Highland savages, few of them so much as guns in their hands, dashes at the drilled Puritan armies like a wild whirlwind; sweeps them, time after time, some five times over, from the field before him. He was at one period, for a short while, master of all Scotland. One man; but he was a man: a million zealous men, but *without* the one; they against him were powerless! Perhaps of all the persons in that Puritan struggle, from first to last, the single indispensable one was verily Cromwell. To see and dare, and decide; to be a fixed pillar in the welter of uncertainty;   a King among them, whether they called him so or not.

Precisely here, however, lies the rub for Cromwell. His other proceedings have all found advocates, and stand generally justified; but this dismissal of the Rump Parliament and assumption of the Protectorship, is what no one can pardon him. He had fairly grown to be King in England; Chief Man of the victorious party in England: but it seems he could not do without the King's Cloak, and sold himself to perdition in order to get it. Let us see a little how this was.

England, Scotland, Ireland, all lying now subdued at the feet of the Puritan Parliament, the practical question arose, What was to be done with it? How will you govern these Nations, which Providence in a wondrous way has given-up to your disposal? Clearly those hundred surviving members of the Long Parliament, who sit there as supreme authority, cannot continue for ever to sit. What *is* to be done?

[1] James Graham, fifth Earl and first Marquis of Montrose (1612–1650), a Scottish noble and follower of Charles I; a famed royalist military commander. [Editor's note.]

It was a question which theoretical constitution-builders may find easy to answer; but to Cromwell, looking there into the real practical facts of it, there could be none more complicated. He asked of the Parliament, What it was they would decide upon? It was for the Parliament to say. Yet the Soldiers too, however contrary to Formula, they who had purchased this victory with their blood, it seemed to them that they also should have something to say in it! We will not "For all our fighting have nothing but a little piece of paper." We understand that the Law of God's Gospel, to which He through us has given the victory, shall establish itself, or try to establish itself, in this land!

For three years, Cromwell says, this question had been sounded in the ears of the Parliament. They could make no answer; nothing but talk, talk. Perhaps it lies in the nature of parliamentary bodies; perhaps no Parliament could in such case make any answer but even that of talk, talk! Nevertheless the question must and shall be answered. You sixty men there, becoming fast odious, even despicable, to the whole nation, whom the nation already calls Rump Parliament, you cannot continue to sit there: who or what then is to follow? "Free Parliament," right of Election, Constitutional Formulas of one sort or the other,—the thing is a hungry Fact coming on us, which we must answer or be devoured by it! And who are you that prate of Constitutional Formulas, rights of Parliament? You have had to kill your King, to make Pride's Purges,[2] to expel and banish by the law of the stronger whosoever would not let your Cause prosper: there are but fifty or three-score of you left there, debating in these days. Tell us what we shall do; not in the way of Formula, but of practicable Fact!

How they did finally answer, remains obscure to this day. The diligent Godwin himself admits that he cannot make it out. The likeliest is, that this poor Parliament still would not, and indeed could not dissolve and disperse; that when it came to the point of actually dispersing, they again, for the tenth or twentieth time, adjourned it,—and Cromwell's patience failed him. But we will take the favourablest hypothesis ever started for the Parliament; the favourablest, though I believe it is not the true one, but too favourable.

[2] In 1648 Colonel Thomas Pride and his musketeers, under Cromwell's command, purged the House of Commons of 140 of its 200 members, leaving a docile "Rump" Parliament which later ordered Charles I's trial. [Editor's note.]

According to this version: At the uttermost crisis, when Cromwell and his Officers were met on the one hand, and the fifty or sixty Rump Members on the other, it was suddenly told Cromwell that the Rump in its despair *was* answering in a very singular way; that in their splenetic envious despair, to keep-out the Army at least, these men were hurrying through the House a kind of Reform Bill,—Parliament to be chosen by the whole of England; equable electoral division into districts; free suffrage, and the rest of it! A very questionable, or indeed for *them* an unquestionable thing. Reform Bill, free suffrage of Englishmen? Why, the Royalists themselves, silenced indeed but not exterminated, perhaps out*number* us; the great numerical majority of England was always indifferent to our Cause, merely looked at it and submitted to it. It is in weight and force, not by counting of heads, that we are the majority! And now with your Formulas and Reform Bills, the whole matter, sorely won by our swords, shall again launch itself to sea; become a mere hope, and likelihood, *small* even as a likelihood? And it is not a likelihood; it is a certainty, which we have won, by God's strength and our own right hands, and do now hold *here*. Cromwell walked down to these refractory Members; interrupted them in that rapid speed of their Reform Bill;—ordered them to begone, and talk there no more.—Can we not forgive him? Can we not understand him? John Milton, who looked on it all near at hand, could applaud him. The Reality had swept the Formulas away before it. I fancy, most men who were realities in England might see into the necessity of that.

The strong daring man, therefore, has set all manner of Formulas and logical superficialities against him; has dared appeal to the genuine Fact of this England, Whether it will support him or not? It is curious to see how he struggles to govern in some constitutional way; find some Parliament to support him; but cannot. His first Parliament, the one they call Barebone's Parliament, is, so to speak, a *Convocation of the Notables*. From all quarters of England the leading Ministers and chief Puritan Officials nominate the men most distinguished by religious reputation, influence, and attachment to the true Cause: these are assembled to shape-out a plan. They sanctioned what was past; shaped as they could what was to come. They were scornfully called *Barebones's Parliament*: the man's name, it seems, was not *Barebones*, but Barbone,—a good enough man. Nor was it a jest, their work; it was a most serious reality,—a trial on the part of these Puritan Notables how far the Law of Christ could become the Law of this England. There were men of sense among them, men of some quality; men of deep piety I suppose the most of them were. They failed, it seems, and broke-down, endeavouring to reform the Court of Chancery! They dissolved themselves, as incompetent; delivered-up their power again into the hands of the Lord General Cromwell, to do with it what he liked and could.

What *will* he do with it? The Lord General Cromwell, "Commander-in-chief of all the Forces raised and to be raised"; he hereby sees himself, at this unexampled juncture, as it were the one available Authority left in England, nothing between England and utter Anarchy but him alone. Such is the undeniable Fact of his position and England's, there and then. What will he do with it? After deliberation, he decides that he will *accept* it; will formally, with public solemnity, say and vow before God and men, "Yes, the Fact is so, and I will do the best I can with it!" Protectorship, Instrument of Government,—these are the external forms of the thing; worked out and sanctioned as they could in the circumstances be, by the Judges, by the leading Official people, "Council of Officers and Persons of interest in the Nation"; and as for the thing itself, undeniably enough, at the pass matters had now come to, there *was* no alternative but Anarchy or that. Puritan England might accept it or not; but Puritan England was, in real truth, saved from suicide thereby! I believe the Puritan People did, in an inarticulate, grumbling, yet on the whole grateful and real way, accept this anomalous act of Oliver's; at least, he and they together made it good, and always better to the last. But in their Parliamentary *articulate* way, they had their difficulties, and never knew fully what to say to it!

Oliver's second Parliament, properly his *first* regular Parliament, chosen by the rule laid-down in the Instrument of Government, did assemble, and worked—but got, before long, into bottomless questions as to the Protector's *right*, as to "usurpation," and so forth; and had at the earliest legal day to be dismissed. Cromwell's concluding Speech to these men is a remarkable one. So likewise to his third Parliament, in similar rebuke for their pedantries and obstinacies. Most rude, chaotic, all these Speeches are; but most earnest-looking. You would say, it was a sincere helpless man; not used to *speak* the great inorganic thought of him, but to act it

rather! A helplessness of utterance, in such bursting fulness of meaning. He talks much about "births of Providence": All these changes, so many victories and events, were not forethoughts, and theatrical contrivances of men, of *me* or of men; it is blind blasphemers that will persist in calling them so! He insists with a heavy sulphurous wrathful emphasis on this. As he well might. As if a Cromwell in that dark huge game he had been playing, the world wholly thrown into chaos round him, had *foreseen* it all, and played it all off like a precontrived puppet-show by wood and wire! These things were foreseen by no man, he says; no man could tell what a day would bring forth: they were "births of Providence," God's finger guided us on, and we came at last to clear height of victory, God's Cause triumphant in these Nations; and you as a Parliament could assemble together, and say in what manner all this could be *organised*, reduced into rational feasibility among the affairs of men. You were to help with your wise counsel in doing that. "You have had such an opportunity as no Parliament in England ever had." Christ's Law, the Right and True, was to be in some measure made the Law of this land. In place of that, you have got into your idle pedantries, constitutionalities, bottomless cavillings and questionings about written laws for *my* coming here—and would send the whole matter in Chaos again, because I have no Notary's parchment, but only God's voice from the battle-whirlwind, for being President among you! That opportunity is gone; and we know not when it will return. You have had your constitutional Logic; and Mammon's Law, not Christ's Law, rules yet in this land. "God be judge between you and me!" These are his final words to them: Take you your constitution-formulas in your hand; and I my *in*formal struggles, purposes, realities and acts; and "God be judge between you and me!"

We said above what shapeless, involved chaotic things the printed Speeches of Cromwell are. *Wilfully* ambiguous, unintelligible, say the most: a hypocrite shrouding himself in confused Jesuitic jargon! To me they do not seem so. I will say rather, they afforded the first glimpses I could ever get into the reality of this Cromwell, nay into the possibility of him. Try to believe that he means something, search lovingly what that may be: you will find a real *speech* lying imprisoned in these broken rude tortuous utterances; a meaning in the great heart of this inarticulate man! You will, for the first time, begin to see that he was a man; not an enigmatic chimera, unintelligible to you, incredible to you.

The Histories and Biographies written of this Cromwell, written in shallow sceptical generations that could not know or conceive of a deep believing man, are far more *obscure* than Cromwell's Speeches. You look through them only into the infinite vague of Black and the Inane. "Heats and jealousies," says Lord Clarendon himself: "heats and jealousies," mere crabbed whims, theories and crotchets; these induced slow sober quiet Englishmen to lay down their ploughs and work; and fly into red fury of confused war against the best-conditioned of Kings! *Try* if you can find that true. Scepticism writing about Belief may have great gifts; but it is really *ultra vires* there. It is Blindness laying-down the Laws of Optics. —

Cromwell's third Parliament split on the same rock as his second. Ever the constitutional Formula: How came *you* there? Show us some Notary parchment! Blind pedants: "Why, surely the same power which makes you a Parliament, that, and something more, made me a Protector!" If my Protectorship is nothing, what in the name of wonder is your Parliamenteership, a reflex and creation of that?

Parliaments having failed, there remained nothing but the way of Despotism. Military Dictators, each with his district, to *coerce* the Royalist and other gainsayers, to govern them, if not by act of Parliament, then by the sword. Formula shall *not* carry it, while the Reality is here! I will go on, protecting oppressed Protestants abroad, appointing just judges, wise managers, at home, cherishing true Gospel ministers; doing the best I can to make England a Christian England, greater than old Rome, the Queen of Protestant Christianity; I, since you will not help me; I while God leaves me life! Why did he not give it up; retire into obscurity again, since the Law would not acknowledge him? cry several. That is where they mistake. For him there was no giving of it up! Prime Ministers have governed countries, Pitt, Pombal, Choiseul; and their word was a law while it held: but this Prime Minister was one that *could not get resigned.* Let him once resign, Charles Stuart and the Cavaliers waited to kill him; to kill the Cause *and* him. Once embarked, there is no retreat, no return. This Prime Minister could *retire* nowhither except into his tomb.

One is sorry for Cromwell in his old days. His complaint is incessant of the heavy burden Providence has laid on him. Heavy; which he must bear till death. Old Colonel Hutchinson, as his wife relates it, Hutchinson, his old battle-mate, coming to see him on some indispensable business, much against his will — Cromwell "follows him to the door," in a most fraternal, domestic, conciliatory style; begs that he would be reconciled to him, his old brother in arms; says how much it grieves him to be misunderstood, deserted by true fellow-soldiers, dear to him from of old: the rigorous Hutchinson, cased in his Republican formula, sullenly goes his way. And the man's head now white; his strong arm growing weary with its long work! I think always too of his poor Mother, now very old, living in that Palace of his; a right brave woman; as indeed they lived all an honest God-fearing Household there: if she heard a shot go off, she thought it was her son killed. He had to come to her at least once a day, that she might see with her own eyes that he was yet living. The poor old Mother! What had this man gained; what had he gained? He had a life of sore strife and toil, to his last day. Fame, ambition, place in History? His dead body was hung in chains; his "place in History" place in History forsooth! has been a place of ignominy, accusation, blackness and disgrace; and here, this day, who knows if it is not rash in me to be among the first that ever ventured to pronounce him not a knave and liar, but a genuinely honest man! Peace to him. Did he not, in spite of all, accomplish much for us? *We* walk smoothly over his great rough heroic life; step over his body sunk in the ditch there. We need not *spurn* it, as we step on it! Let the Hero rest. It was not to *men's* judgment that he appealed; nor have men judged him very well. . . .

SAMUEL R. GARDINER

THE LIBERAL OUT OF SEASON

Samuel Gardiner's portrait of Cromwell in his important book, *Cromwell's Place in History* (1897), is remarkably free of rancor and of hero worship. The Protector is pictured as a harassed, lonely man, far in advance of his time politically, whose work largely perished with his death but whose experiments in government "were but premature anticipations of the legislation of the nineteenth century." For Gardiner, Cromwell becomes the harbinger of nineteenth-century liberalism, "a typical Englishman of the modern world," in fact, "the most typical Englishman of all time."

What, then, did Cromwell accomplish to change the face of history? If we inquire of popular tradition we shall have but little doubt. He won battles; he cut off the King's head; he turned out Parliaments by military compulsion; he massacred the Irish at Drougheda; he made England respected by land and sea.

Is not the popular legend at least roughly in the right? All these things, it will be seen, are negative actions. Hostile armies were not allowed to be victorious; kings were not to be allowed to wield absolute power in disregard of the conditions of the time or the wishes of their subjects; Parliaments were not allowed to disregard public opinion; Irishmen were not allowed to establish a government hostile to England; foreign Powers were not allowed to disregard the force of England. All this is so plain that it needs no further consideration. Our difficulties come in when we ask what was the effect of those constructive efforts which popular tradition passes by. Is tradition right in neglecting these, as it is pre-eminently right in magnifying the destructive blows dealt with no unstinting hand?

To the student who deals with the details of Cromwell's life a picture very different from that of the popular tradition is apt to present itself. He is compelled to dwell upon the hesitations and the long postponements of action which are no less characteristic of the man than are the swift decisive hammer-strokes which have caught the popular fancy. Yet these two sides of his character have to be harmonised in any complete estimate of the man and his work.

With the man we are here concerned only so far as a knowledge of him may enable us to understand his work, and it is enough to say that there is nothing in the combination of qualities which may fairly be ascribed to Cromwell to render it improbable that he would be as successful in statesmanship as he was in war. If we regard Cromwell's character apart from the circumstances amongst which he moved we should come to the conclusion that it was admirably fitted for the work of directing a State. If large-mindedness, combined with an open eye for facts, together with a shrinking from violence till it seems absolutely necessary to employ it, cannot fit a man to be a statesman, where can we hope to find statesmanship at all? Yet even if we set his management of Scotland and Ireland, and still more his management of foreign affairs, aside, and restrict ourselves to his dealing with English politics, of which he had far greater personal knowledge it is impossible to resist the conclusion that he effected nothing in the way of building up where he had pulled down, and that there was no single act of the Protectorate that was not swept away at the Restoration without hope of revival.

It must be remembered that no lasting effects result from any policy, whether negative or positive, which are not in accordance with the permanent tendencies of that portion of the world affected by

From Samuel R. Gardiner, *Cromwell's Place in History* (London: Longmans, Green and Company, 1897), pp. 102–116.

The Early Modern Era

them. Providence, it is said, is on the side of big battalions. Big battalions, indeed, may do much as far as the immediate future is concerned; but they can do nothing for the distant future. Evesham did not make Edward, when his time came to reign, an absolute sovereign, nor did Falkirk[1] enable him to hand down the undisputed lordship of Scotland to his son. The effect of Naseby, on the other hand, and of the King's execution never were undone. Charles II, indeed, re-ascended the throne, but he sat on it under conditions very different from those of his father, and when James II reverted to his father's conception the Stuart monarchy fell, past recall. So, too, with Cromwell's dealings with the Long Parliament. Never again did England tolerate a Parliament which, being itself but a fragment of its original numbers, set the constituencies at defiance as well as the King.

That Cromwell's success as a destructive force must have stood in the way of his success as a constructive statesman is too obvious to need much labouring, and the proposition is indeed now accepted by all who handle the subject. No man was more aware of the danger than Cromwell himself. He was, at all events, personally disinclined to rattle the sabre to the terror of civilians. It has often been noticed that when Napoleon, before setting out for Waterloo, took the oath to observe the *Acte additionnel*, he appeared in military uniform, and the circumstance has been used to enforce the belief that in heart he was a soldier first and a civilian a long way afterwards. When Cromwell took the oath of the Protectorate, he was clothed in a civilian garb. All his constitutional efforts—efforts for which he had less intellectual aptitude than for any other of the problems he assailed—were directed to the transformation of the Military State into the Civil State. If his attempts were all frustrated, it was because of the impracticability of the task. He was in one sense, as the three Colonels declared, the master of 30,000 men; in another sense, he was their servant. He could not cast them off, as the restored Charles cast them off, because he had no such weight of public sentiment in his favour to support him, to say nothing of the ties by which he was bound to them by common memories and common aspirations. Every day the popular feeling was ex-

cited not so much against Cromwell's policy and action, as against his government by military support. How strong was the antagonism aroused appears by the length of time during which fear of military intervention in politics was prolonged. At the Restoration Charles II. could only venture to keep up a very small force. In the reign of William III., when the long war came to an end by the Peace of Ryswick,[2] Parliament cut down the army first to 10,000 and then to 7,000 men. Even in the time of the younger Pitt an excellent scheme for building barracks was rejected by the House of Commons lest its adoption should, by segregating the soldiers from civilian life, lend itself to their employment against the liberties of civilians.

Revulsion against authority maintained in power by means of the army must therefore be counted as the greatest amongst Cromwell's difficulties. To what extent Puritanism blocked his way it is not so easy to decide. That Puritanism, regarded as an extreme expression of Protestantism and as upholding the rights of the individual conscience against authority, did not perish at the Restoration is beyond all reasonable doubt. It ceased not to find worthy champions to uphold its banner, and by penetrating and informing its conquerors, it became the most precious possession of the nation. Nor is there any convincing reason to suppose that hostility to Puritanism of this kind had much to do with the overthrow of Cromwell's system. The revival of interest in the system of teaching and organisation which had endeared itself to Laud's[3] comrades and disciples was mainly confined, as far as the somewhat scanty evidence in existence reaches, to the Cavalier country gentlemen, and the scholars expelled from the universities, together with those who fell under their influence. There is nothing to show that if the nation at large had been freely consulted on the religious question alone the Restoration would have been accompanied by a violent ecclesiastical reaction, still less that the absence of the ceremonial introduced or restored by Laud was unpopular at any time between the execution of Charles I and the Restoration of Charles II.

In speaking of Puritanism, however, as has been already said, we usually mean something different

[1] In the battle of Evesham (1265), Edward, future king of England, defeated a baronial alliance led by Simon de Montfort and restored King Henry III to power. In the battle of Falkirk (1298) Edward III put down a Scottish uprising led by William Wallace. [Editor's note.]

[2] A treaty of 1697 ending the War of the League of Augsburg. [Editor's note.]

[3] William Laud, Archbishop of Canterbury and one of Charles' chief advisers. [Editor's note.]

from this. It implies a system of doctrine and a system of discipline, though prominence was given unequally to these in various parts of the Puritan world. It was in fact a necessity that Protestantism should be systematised in one way or another. Without discipline, intellectual or physical, it would soon have drifted into anarchy, and into all the weakness that is the inevitable result of anarchy. As long as the struggle with Rome and her continental champions was kept up, so long did the systematising instinct prevail. In those years the Calvinist belief rooted itself even in episcopal minds, and found its strongest expressions in the Lambeth articles.[4] At the same time the propensity towards the Calvinistic Presbyterian discipline was highly developed, not merely amongst the religious clergy, but amongst the religious Protestant laity as well.

When the days of storm and stress were over, and the defeat of the Armada had demonstrated that England had power to defend its own nationality, and with that its own national religion, against the forces of Spain and Rome, it was but natural that the spiritual armour in which militant Englishmen had fought should appear heavy to the weary combatants, now anxious for rest, and that an opposition should spring up against the Calvinistic doctrine and discipline, which appeared to straiten rather than to support the free action of individual minds. On the one hand the opposition came from men who, like Bancroft, proclaimed the divine right of Episcopacy against the divine right of Presbytery, or, like Andrewes,[5] attached themselves to external rites as influencing the spiritual conscience and mellowing the ironclad reasoning of the Calvinistic preacher. The strongest attack, however, and one far more difficult to meet, proceeded from the growth of that mundane spirit which, without in any way pandering to the lower passions, reveals itself in the great writers of the later years of Elizabeth and the early years of James I. It was the part of these writers, whatever their personal creeds may have been, to recall to their generation the complex nature of man, and to ask that either religion should broaden itself out, or at least that it should not stand in the way of the development either of man's intellect or

of his physical independence. It was this opposition which eventually prevailed, not indeed against the spiritual and moral instincts, whether of Puritanism or of any other form of religion, but over the contraction of the Puritan creed and of the Puritan organisation. From this point of view the Puritanism of the seventeenth century may fairly be regarded as a backwater, taking its course in a contrary direction to the general current of national development.

Like all backwaters the Puritan stream was deflected by an obstacle in its way, the obstacle of Laudian ceremonialism. In the first Parliament of James I the House of Commons had distinctly asserted, "We are no Puritans." In the third Parliament of Charles I. it sought to restrain all preachers from declaring anything in opposition to the Calvinistic doctrine. In the Long Parliament the authors of the "Grand Remonstrance"[6] made the most of their determination not "to let loose the golden reins of discipline and government in the Church, or to leave private persons or particular congregations to take up what form of Divine service they please." It was inevitable that when once the fear of Charles and Laud was withdrawn, these pretensions should be somewhat abated. The only question was whether they should be modified from within the Puritan ranks, or battered down from without.

The change so far as it was directed from within was to be directed by Cromwell and by Cromwell's Independent allies. By them the doctrine of religious liberty was preached, and by them was upheld within the limits of practical statesmanship. Cromwell's first task was to preserve liberty of thought that the "people of God" might be shielded thereby. It was this that made Milton his warm ally, because with Milton liberty was not the negation of restraint, but the condition upon which high design and high achievement depends. Nor was Milton alone in pointing in this direction. It is significant that the one important religious body which originated in the seventeenth century—that of the Society of Friends—owed its strength on the one hand to that extreme individualism which marks its doctrine as the quintessence of the higher Puritanism, but on the other hand to its unshrinking opposition to the Calvinistic discipline and the Calvinistic doctrine. No wonder Cromwell was drawn to its founder. "If thou and I," said the Protector, "were but an hour of the

[4] The Lambeth articles of 1595 translated Calvin's teachings on grace and predestination into English prose. They stressed the need for a learned and active clergy.

[5] Richard Bancroft (1544–1610) was Archbishop of Canterbury from 1604 to 1610. Lancelot Andrewes (1555–1626) was successively bishop of Chichester, Ely, and Winchester. Both were strong supporters of Anglicanism. [Editor's note.]

[6] A summary of grievances presented to the king by Parliament in 1641 [Editor's note.]

day together, we should be nearer one to the other."

Yet it was not Cromwell who founded religious liberty in England. His system perished at the Restoration, and when the idea was revived under the guise of toleration it came from another quarter altogether. It was not from Puritanism, high or low, that the gift was received, but from the sons of those Cavaliers and Presbyterians who had been Cromwell's bitterest enemies.

What, then, was the secret of Cromwell's failure to establish — not his dynasty, for that is of little importance — but his ideas? First, amongst the causes of failure must be reckoned his dependence on the army. The master of 30,000, or rather of 57,000, men could not win over a spirited nation which abhorred the rule of the soldiery, however veiled, and no less abhorred the taxation necessary for their support. It was all the more difficult to reconcile the nation and the army because that army had not won its renown in combat with an alien foe. Unlike the soldiers of Napoleon, the men of the New Model had no Marengos or Jenas[7] to boast of, victories which went to the heart of the French citizen as well as of the French soldier. Their laurels had been gathered in civil wars, and whilst the conquered ascribed to them the diminution of their estates, those who had formerly applauded the conquerors forgot their services in their more recent pretensions. Cromwell, who could not dispense with the army, was pushed on to give it popularity by launching it against foreign nations. It was all in vain. Englishmen refused to regard that army with pride and enthusiasm, as their descendants regarded the army that stuck down Napoleon at Waterloo, or that died at its post before the beleaguered fortress of Sebastopol.

Indirectly, too, the military rule which Cromwell was never able to shake off endangered the permanence of his system, and must have endangered it even if, as his unreasoning worshippers fondly urge, his span of life had been prolonged for twenty years. It is the condition on which all strong intellectual and spiritual movements rest that they shall be spontaneous. They win their way by force of inward conviction, not by the authority of the State. How earnestly Cromwell desired to set conviction before force is known to all. He had broken the

[7] In the battle of Marengo (1800) Napoleon defeated the Austrians in Italy. At the battle of Jena (1806) he routed the Prussian army. [Editor's note.]

Presbyterian and Calvinistic chains, and had declared his readiness to see Mohammedanism professed in England rather than that the least of the saints of God should suffer wrong. Yet he dared not give equal liberty to all. To the Royalists his person was hateful alike as the murderer of the King, as the General whose army had despoiled them of their property, and as the violator of "the known laws" of the land. How, then, could he tolerate the religion of the Book of Common Prayer, which had become the badge of Royalism? It is true that the tide of persecution rose and fell, and that it was never very violent even at its worst; but it is also true that it could never be disowned. There was to be complete freedom for those who were Puritans, little or none for those who were not. Liberty of religion was to be co-extensive with the safety of the State. It was a useful formula, but hardly more when the safety of the State meant the predominance of an army, and the head of the State dared not throw himself on a free Parliament to give him a new basis of authority.

Nor was Puritanism itself, even after it had been cleansed in the waters of liberty, fitted to hold the directing power in the State. Though the checks which it placed upon worldly amusements have been over-estimated, it certainly did not regard such amusements with favour. Like all great spiritual movements, it was too strenuous, too self-contained to avoid drawing the reins over tightly on the worldling. All that was noblest in it would be of better service when it was relegated from the exercise of power to the employment of influence.

What, then, is Cromwell's place in history? If we regard the course of the two centuries which followed his death, it looks as if all that need be said might be summed up in a few words. His negative work lasted, his positive work vanished away. His constitutions perished with him, his Puritanism descended from the proud position to which he had raised it, his peace with the Dutch Republic was followed by two wars with the United Provinces, his alliance with the French monarchy only led to a succession of wars with France lasting into the nineteenth century. All that endured was the support given by him to maritime enterprise, and in that he followed the tradition of the Governments preceding him.

Yet, after all, the further we are removed from the days in which Cromwell lived, the more loth are we to fix our eyes exclusively on that part of his work which was followed by immediate results. It may freely be admitted that his efforts to establish the national life upon a new basis came to nothing, without thinking any the worse of the man for making the attempt. It is beginning to be realised that many, if not all the experiments of the Commonwealth were but premature anticipations of the legislation of the nineteenth century, and it is also beginning to be realised that, whatever may be our opinion of some of Cromwell's isolated actions, he stands forth as the typical Englishman of the modern world. That he will ever be more than this is not to be expected. Even if Scotchmen forget the memories of Dunbar and Worcester, it is certain that Drogheda and Wexford will not pass out of the minds of Irishmen.[8] It is in England that his fame has grown up since the publication of Carlyle's monumental work, and it is as an Englishman that he must be judged.

What may be fairly demanded alike of Cromwell's admirers and of his critics is that they shall fix their eyes upon him as a whole. To one of them he is the champion of liberty and peaceful progress, to another the forcible crusher of free institutions, to a third the defender of oppressed peoples, to a fourth the asserter of his country's right to dominion. Every one of the interpreters has something on which to base his conclusions. All the incongruities of human nature are to be traced somewhere or other in Cromwell's career. What is more remarkable is that this union of apparently contradictory forces is precisely that which is to be found in the English people, and which has made England what she is at the present day.

Many of us think it strange that the conduct of our nation should often appear to foreign observers in colours so different from those in which we see

[8] At the battles of Dunbar and Worcester (1650) Cromwell inflicted defeats on forces seeking to restore Charles II. In the battles of Drogheda and Wexford (1649) Cromwell crushed an Irish uprising in the name of Charles. [Editor's note.]

ourselves. By those who stand aloof from us we are represented as grasping at wealth and territory, incapable of imaginative sympathy with subject races, and decking our misconduct with moral sentiments intended to impose on the world. From our own point of view, the extension of our rule is a benefit to the world, and subject races have gained far more than they have lost by submission to a just and beneficent administration, whilst our counsels have always, or almost always, been given with a view to free the oppressed and to put a bridle in the mouth of the oppressor.

That both these views have truth in them no serious student of the present and the past can reasonably deny. Whatever we may say, we are and have been a forceful nation, full of vigorous vitality, claiming empire as our due, often with scant consideration for the feelings and desire of other peoples. Whatever foreigners may say, we are prone, without afterthought, to place our strength at the service of morality and even to feel unhappy if we cannot convince ourselves that the progress of the human race is forwarded by our action. When we enter into possession, those who look on us from the outside dwell upon the irregularity of our conduct in forcing ourselves into possession; whilst we, on the contrary, dwell upon the justice and order maintained after we have once established ourselves.

With Cromwell's memory it has fared as with ourselves. Royalists painted him as a devil. Carlyle painted him as the masterful saint who suited his peculiar Valhalla. It is time for us to regard him as he really was, with all his physical and moral audacity, with all his tenderness and spiritual yearnings, in the world of action what Shakespeare was in the world of thought, the greatest because the most typical Englishman of all time. This, in the most enduring sense, is Cromwell's place in history. He stands there, not to be implicitly followed as a model, but to hold up a mirror to ourselves, wherein we may see alike our weakness and our strength.

SIR ERNEST BARKER

THE DICTATOR

Sir Ernest Barker, former principal of King's College, London, and professor of political science at the University of Cambridge, is the author of books on such varied subjects as the European inheritance, the growth of the civil service in Western Europe, the British Empire, the political ideas of Aristotle, John Locke, and Jean-Jacques Rousseau. His work on *Oliver Cromwell and the English People* appeared in 1937 at the height of Adolph Hitler's popularity in Europe. And although Barker remarks that "historical parallels are often dubious," he nevertheless juxtaposes Hitlerian Germany and Cromwellian England. The comparison between the two nations and their leaders is pushed to the extreme: for example, Barker likens Cromwell's idea of the "chosen people of God" to Hitler's belief in the *Volk*; he underscores the religious or spiritual foundations of both movements; and he views both leaders as the living symbols of their cause. Above all, Barker believes that both men were joined in their desire for the unification of their nations.

In Germany to-day the figure of Oliver Cromwell stands massively present in the mind and imagination of many. He has become the type of English character and achievement. He is "the founder of the English fleet" and "the author of the expansion of England." These are exaggerations or misconceptions. The herrings of the North Sea had more to do with the founding of the English fleet than any man: if any man can be credited with its founding, the man was Henry VIII rather than Oliver Cromwell; and so far as the navy was cherished and extended in Oliver's time (as it was in the years which immediately followed the death of Charles I), the merit was not his, but belonged to the Presbyterian Parliament, which encouraged the more innocuous sailor as a counterblast to the Independent soldier. The expansion of England owes more to Cromwell; but his conquest of Jamaica was a much smaller factor in that expansion than the earlier Puritan colonization of New England, and Cromwell's policy of encouraging the Puritan settlers in New England to move southwards again to Jamaica was a policy calculated rather to hinder than to help the growth of his country's colonial power. He was more true to the natural genius of English expansion when he himself thought, as a good tradition suggests that he

did, about 1630, of emigrating to New England in the wake of the East Anglian exodus which had begun about 1628.

But there is a deeper reason why Cromwell should present himself to Germany to-day as a remarkable and arresting figure. Historical parallels are often dubious; and to draw a parallel between an Englishman, living in a period and a century of the dominance of the religious motive, and a German who lives and moves in a period and an epoch of the dominance of social and economic motives, is especially difficult and especially dubious. But to draw an historical parallel is itself an historical fact, which may have historical influence; and whatever the justice or the propriety of the parallel, the fact and the influence must be taken into our reckoning. There *is* a sense in which the English Puritan Revolution of the seventeenth century and the German National Socialist Revolution of recent years have their analogies. Cromwell came upon an England which was bitterly divided in regard to the ultimate foundations of national life. Monarchism quarrelled with parliamentarianism; both of them quarrelled with incipient democratic doctrines of the sovereignty of the people, and even with incipient com-

From Sir Ernest Barker, *Oliver Cromwell and the English People* (Cambridge, England, 1937), pp. 71–96. Reprinted by permission of Cambridge University Press.

munistic doctrines of the ownership of the people's land: Anglicanism, Presbyterianism and Independency jostled together. For a time, if only for a time, Cromwell gave unity: he drew his country together, in a common "assimilation" to a dominant trend: he insisted on a common foundation of common "fundamentals." In the same way, it may be said, the leader of National Socialism came upon a Germany which was equally divided: in the same way he drew his country together: in the same way he insisted on a unity of fundamentals.

The parallel may be carried further. If we look at the field of foreign relations, we may say that Cromwell, succeeding to the vacillating policy of the Stuart kings, gave England a new self-respect and a new prestige in the councils of Europe; and we may equally say that the leader of National Socialism, also succeeding to a previous period of vacillation, gave the same gifts to his people. But perhaps the parallel is closest when we turn to the field of what Cromwell called "the reformation of manners." This was the field in which, above all, he felt himself called to labour. His last prayer was a prayer that his people might have "consistency of judgment, one heart and mutual love": a prayer to God to "go on to deliver them, and with the work of reformation." The leader of National Socialism has equally looked to the work of reformation. At its worst, reformation has meant for him anti-Semitism, the isolation of opponents in concentration camps ("a keeping of some in prison," as Cromwell put it), and the sharp and terrible purge of the midsummer of 1934. But there is a speech of 28 March 1936 which looks deeper and further. "My German compatriots, there is very much which we have to make good before our own history and before our Lord God. Once His grace was upon us; and we were not worthy to keep it. Providence withdrew its protection from us, and our people were put down, put down deeper perhaps than any people before. In this dire need we learned to pray once more. We learned to respect one another: we believed again in the virtues of a people: we tried again to be better. So there arose a new community; and this people of to-day can no more be compared with the people that lies behind us. It has become better, decenter, nobler. We feel it: the grace of the Lord now turns again at the last towards us, and in this hour we fall on our knees and pray to the Almighty to bless us, and to give us strength to endure the struggle for the freedom and the future and the honour and the peace of our people. So help us God."

II

Carlyle interpreted Cromwell as a hero. He was interpreting him in terms of the German Romanticism with which he was imbued—a Romanticism inspired with the idea of a pantheistic universe, which sees in the people an incarnation of God, and in the hero or leader the incarnation of the people. A Cromwell so interpreted has his analogies with the modern leader, similarly exalted, and similarly idealized, by the permanent German spirit of Romanticism. The leader to-day can also appeal to the "evidences" of Providence. He can also regard himself—or rather, will he, nill he, he can be regarded by others—as sent by a foreseeing Power. "Among us Germans," the German Church Minister said, on the eve of the Christmas of 1936, "a man has arisen who has given renewed direction and steadiness to our life, in that he has brought us once more into the Divine order." That Divine order, the Minister went on to say, "was the community ordained by God, and decided by blood . . . the people; and to serve it was to offer real service to God Himself. . . ." This is Romantic heroism *in excelsis*. But has it, when it is analysed, any real bearing on the historic interpretation of Cromwell? Does it represent, in any respect, the mind of Cromwell and his contemporaries?

Cromwell himself, as has already been said, never thought of himself as a leader or hero. He was simply a constable, keeping the peace in his little parish. Nor was he regarded as a hero or leader by his contemporaries, even when they stood at his side and belonged to his following. There was a time when John Lilburn, the Leveller, spoke of him as "the most absolute single-hearted great man in England." But Lilburn turned, and accused him of high treason; and there was no jury in England which would ever convict honest John for the contumacy of his free speech. No sweeping enthusiasm ever surrounded Cromwell: the gusts of opinion beat steadily on him during his life, as gusts of wind shook the house in which he lay dying during his last stormy days. In the divided and tumultuous England in which he lived he was a great and elemental force; but he was surrounded by other forces, and he was never an engulfing vortex. He was not a sole and accredited leader; and he led no sole accredited party. Parties, in any sense in which they are known to us, were still unknown in his days. There were only trends of opinion, mainly religious, but partly (and consequentially) political.

The Early Modern Era

A dominant trend of Independent opinion, expressed in the army of which he was General, carried Cromwell along—sometimes struggling, and always seeking for a general healing and settling—on the current of its tide. But there were also other trends and other tides; and in the swirling eddies in which they met he felt himself battered and buffeted, sighing to "have lived under his woodside . . . rather than undertook such a government," or attempted so arduous a work of steering.

If there was something heroic in this, it was the ordinary workaday heroism of doing a job; preventing men from "running their heads one against another"; keeping things going; getting the business of the country done. It was something in the ordinary tradition of England, before his time and afterwards: the Duke of Wellington, if he had lived in Cromwell's day, would not have done very differently, nor would Cromwell, if he had lived in the days of Wellington, have done very differently from the Duke. The heroic interpretation of Cromwell must condescend to an ordinary level of heroism: if he was *fortis Agamemnon*, others had been brave before, and others were also to be brave afterwards. But there remains, in the general quality and temper of those times—not in him only, but in the general body of the Puritan cause—a bravery and a heroism which cannot but seem exceptional. Was the English people, for once at any rate in its history, transfigured? Did it become a people of one heart—an incarnation, in its own view, of the purpose of God; brought once more into the Divine order, with all its members serving God because they served the community ordained by God? If Cromwell himself was not a hero in the Romantic sense, was the people he governed a people, for the time being, in that sense?

Cromwell, as we have seen, had a doctrine of the two peoples. One was "the people of England"; the other was "the people of God" in England—"a people that are to God as the apple of His eye." By the people of God he meant the Puritans; and the Puritans were, in his view, the leaven that could stir the English people to be what he called "the best people in the world." This doctrine and this view demand close consideration. Here, if anywhere, the analogy between Cromwellian England and the Germany of National Socialism exists; and if it does not exist here, it is not a true and essential analogy.

The core of Cromwell's doctrine of the nature of the people is a religious core. It is belief in God, through Jesus Christ, which makes the people of God; and it is the people of God who make a whole people good, because they make it serve the purposes of God. There is nothing physical in this conception. There is no belief in blood or race. Cromwell is thinking entirely in terms of the mind ("truly, these things do respect the souls of men, and the spirits, which are the men"); and thinking in those terms he can welcome into the core and central leaven of the people all who are of the right mind—" Scots, English, Jews, Gentiles, Presbyterians, Anabaptists, and all." It is true that Cromwell and his Puritan contemporaries cherished a sort of nationalism; but the community or nation for which they cherished this feeling was a community decided not by blood but by faith. The English nation for which they were passionate was a nation by adoption and grace, after the manner of the Old Testament—"a new Israel, a chosen people, directly covenanted with God." This may be called a religious nationalism. It is a form of nationalism in which the nation is not a religion, or the object of a cult, but, on the very contrary, religion and cult are the nation, and *they* constitute the foundation of its being. It is therefore a nationalism which runs easily and naturally into internationalism. There is nothing exclusive in the conception of "a people of God" forming the core and leaven of a whole nation. The chosen people of one nation, and the whole of that nation through them, have a community and a fellowship with the chosen peoples of other nations, and with other nations through them. Cromwell himself and the Puritans generally were good internationalists. He could tell his Parliament himself that "all the interests of the Protestants . . . all the interests in Christendom, are the same as yours." Religion might constitute a chosen people; but it also constituted an international community of chosen peoples. It is true that this international community was itself exclusive. Cromwell could not transcend, on the premises from which he started, the idea of an international community limited to the Protestant world. Nor could he transcend, on the same premises, the idea of a martial and militant internationalism, engaged in a natural and providential enmity with the Roman Catholic world gathered under the leadership of Spain. But if his internationalism was exclusive, and even militant, his nationalism had never an exclusive quality. It was based too much on religion to exclude from its generous pale any man or body of men who professed that sovereign cause.

His nationalism was the less pronounced because,

such as it was, it was always combined with a stern and rigorous sense of the direct and immediate responsibility of each individual to God. Deeper than the internationalism of the Puritan lay his individualism. He might serve the chosen people, and through the chosen people he might serve the nation; but the service of which he always thought was the ultimate and lonely service which he owed directly to God. Community was not a word which bulked largely in his vocabulary; and he would never have said that service to the community was service to God Himself. Cromwell, essentially an Independent, and by the cast of his own mind an individual Seeker as well as an Independent, had no conception that even "the people of God," though they might be of "one heart and mutual love," were a uniform community, gathered in a single order or inspired by a corporate devotion. "When I say the people of God, I mean the large comprehension of them *under the several forms of godliness* in this nation."

III

All periods of revolution have naturally a certain similarity. They all carry with them an exhilarating sense of entry into a new and regenerated life. They all involve a closing of the ranks around the ideal of the new life; and that involves in turn both internal and external consequences. Internally there will be an impatience with dissident and anti-revolutionary elements: the sense of *fraternite*, as it was called in 1789, or of *Volkstum* and *Volksgemeinschaft*, as it has been called since 1933, will be deeply felt; and in the strength of that sense there will be an insistence on unity, even at the cost of repression—on the republic one and indivisible; on the *Reich*, and on the *Volk* behind the *Reich*, which is one and undivided in blood and policy. Externally the glow of a new life and the sense of a new solidarity will exert an expansive force: the revolution will become militant: it will seek to assert itself in the world, and to vindicate its worth on the public stage of the nations.

The Puritan Revolution shares with the German Revolution of to-day (as it also shares with the French Revolution of 1789) these common characteristics. It also shares, or seems to share, another characteristic—the figure of the revolutionary leader, a basalt figure emerging among the fires and in the eruption, a column and a symbol of the movement of mind from which he has come. But though these are common characteristics of revolu-

tions, each revolution is essentially unique. It has its own spiritual foundations: they are its own peculiar property; and they vest it in turn with a property, or quality, which is particularly and peculiarly its own. The spiritual foundations of the revolution of Cromwell's day were religious. They were hewn from the common rock of European Protestantism, even if they were quarried in a particular English quarry. They were hewn in the seventeenth century; and they have the particular quality of an age in which the religious motive was still the dominant motive. The spiritual foundations of the National Socialist Revolution are different. They are hewn from the particular tradition of Germany. They go back to the Romantic exaltation of the *Volk* which became current at the end of the eighteenth century: they go back, behind that, to the *Urvolk* of the German woods. So far as religion is part of their foundations, it is a religion not of theism (in any form, Protestant or Catholic), but of pantheism—a religion of a universally immanent God, who, instead of being found and worshipped by "a people of God," finds himself, and incarnates himself, in a whole people, which in turn incarnates itself in the leader of the people. The God who becomes a people, and the people which becomes identified with its leader, are not the God and the people which presented themselves to the mind of Cromwell. They are not the God and the people who present themselves to the minds of most modern Englishmen. The community "ordained by God and decided by blood" does not belong to our way of thinking. It belongs to tribalism—even if tribalism wears the mantle of a pantheistic philosophy.

All revolutions exaggerate. At any rate there are always revolutionary sections which exaggerate the tenets of revolution. It may be that the theory of tribalism goes far beyond the ideas of the leader of the German people, and far beyond the convictions of the great bulk of its members. There are utterances of the National Socialist party, and above all of its leader, which breathe the same spirit of religious conviction, and show something of the same instinct for religious liberty, which inspired the speeches of Cromwell. One of the "points" of the original party programme, of February 1920, proclaims: "We demand the liberty of all religious confessions in the State, so far as they do not imperil its stability, or offend against the sentiments of the German race in matters of social ethics and private morality." Here there is an ideal of religious liberty—qualified, it is true; but then it was also qualified in the ideas and practice of Cromwell. When the party eventually came into power, its leader, speaking as Chancellor, on 23 March 1933, went even further. "The national government," he said, "sees in the two Christian confessions the most important factors for the maintenance of our people's life. . . . The fight against a materialist conception of life, and for the restoration of a real community of the people, serves the interests of the German nation equally with those of the Christian faith." Here, in the spirit of Cromwell, and almost in his words, the leader of National Socialism connects "the Interest of Christians" with "the Interest of the Nation." But a little later, in a speech of 30 January 1934, he has already parted from Cromwell. The one thing which Cromwell firmly believed was that political uniformity did not require, or involve, religious uniformity. On that belief, like the rest of the Independents, he took his stand equally against Anglicans and Presbyterians. The leader of National Socialism, on the contrary, urges that a new system of political uniformity requires and involves, from the Protestant Churches of Germany (still organized in separate territorial bodies, which reflect the disintegration of the past), a corresponding new system of religious uniformity. "We all live in the expectation that the union of the Evangelical territorial churches and confessions in a German *Reichskirche* will give a real satisfaction to the longing of those who believe that they are bound to fear, in the disintegration of Evangelical life, a weakening of the strength of Evangelical faith. Since the National Socialist State has this year shown its respect for the strength of the Christian confessions, it expects the confessions to show the same respect for the strength of the National Socialist State." Here the proviso originally attached to religious liberty—that it should not imperil the stability of the State—shows its cutting edge. To Cromwell "the Interest of the Nation" was subordinate to "the Interest of Christians." To the leader of National Socialism "the Interest of the Nation" has become dominant.

But these comparisons only lead us down a blind alley. We come out again at the same door at which we went in. Our parallels show us mainly difference, with occasional glimpses of likeness; and to compare two things which are partly alike, but differ even more than they agree, may make even more bewilderment than it does for enlightenment. But it is one of the habits of men in revolutionary times, when they have broken loose from their moorings, to comfort themselves by thinking

that they are only engaged in the restoration of their own past, or that they have a precedent and an example in the past of some other country. It has been said that "restoration is always also revolution"; it may also be said that revolution is often also restoration—and sometimes imitation. The German revolution of our days proceeds on the idea of the restoration of the German past: it also proceeds—or some of its thinkers proceed—on the assumption of analogy and precedent in the English past. It is true that there is a sense in which Germany (and, we may also add, Italy) is going through a stage of development through which we went some centuries ago. It is the stage of unification; of the acquisition of national homogeneity; of the attainment of a sure and tranquil basis of national life, on which men are agreed, and in the strength of which they can quietly pass on their ways upon their lawful occasions. One of the observations which every visitor to England naturally and inevitably makes is the observation of the fact of national homogeneity and a generally agreed basis of national life. Such homogeneity, and such an agreed basis, have to be won, and have been won, by an effort.

Tantae molis erat Romanam condere gentem.

But it was not in the days of Cromwell that homogeneity and an agreed basis were first, or finally, won in England. If any man "imposed the yoke of peace" in England, it was Henry VIII rather than Cromwell; and it is Henry VIII rather than Cromwell who is the precedent and example for the totalitarian leader. If any Revolution ended by assuring to England an agreed basis of national life, it was the Whig Revolution of 1688, rather than the Puritan Revolution of the previous generation; and it is the Whig Revolution (with its prosaic sobriety, its compromises and its common sense), rather than the Puritan Revolution, which is the natural analogy and precedent for those who desire to achieve a permanent political settlement.

Cromwell had indeed a genuine passion for healing and settling; for unification: for an England settled within on the rock of religious liberty and reformation of manners, and great and glorious without because she was great and glorious within. But it was not given to him, or to those who thought with him, to achieve these things. Theirs was the triumphant but temporary explosion of a minority; and it passed. They left indeed a permanent legacy to

England—the legacy of an ineradicable Nonconformity: the legacy of the Free Churches: the legacy of a permanent idea of liberty, political as well as religious and civil, but pre-eminently and particularly the latter. But because they used force in the service of liberty (disbelieving in the force by which they acted, and yet acting by force in spite of their disbelief), they also left another legacy—the legacy of hatred of a standing army; the legacy of a rooted dislike of compulsory godliness; the legacy of contempt for the paradox of their cause, which could be, and was, interpreted as cant and hypocrisy. Yet their work was not unaccomplished. When they turned, as they did after 1660, from a victorious minority into a minority struggling for the just rights of minorities (toleration; liberty of worship; equality of access to education and civic rights), they came into their own, and they gave to England a great gift, essential and indispensable to her genuine tradition—the gift of the still small voice (after wind and earthquake and fire) of human liberty. The defeated Cromwells of hundreds of town and village chapels, scattered over England, carried on the heart of the cause of the victorious Cromwell, purged and purified; and the dust that lay in his unknown and unregarded grave still lived. So his actings fulfilled the good pleasure of God, and served their generations; and his rest was durable.

G. M. TREVELYAN

THE FOUNDER OF PARLIAMENTARY GOVERNMENT

Like his great-uncle Lord Macaulay, George Macaulay Trevelyan, the late master of Trinity College, Cambridge, was a brilliant stylist, an articulate historian, and a confirmed Whig. As a Whig historian, Trevelyan believes that Cromwell served both as the champion of Parliamentary supremacy and of religious toleration, thus personifying "the fusion of political and religious motives." Without him the English Revolution would, quite simply, not have succeeded. Trevelyan, however, balances his portrait by underscoring Cromwell's weaknesses, particularly his complicity in the judicial murder of Charles I, which, he says, was not only impolitic but a "crime against England." Moreover, the memory of this "crime" reinforced the conservative reaction of the Restoration (1660–1688).

It was agreeable to the nature of things that Cromwell's statue was not hidden away during the Second World War, but remained under fire, guarding the entrance of the House of Commons, with Bible and with Sword. It was equally appropriate that Charles I's statue was put away as a work of art too precious to be exposed to the chances of battle.

It is often remarked that some of our London statues are oddly chosen or curiously placed. The Duke of York, who deserves a bust in the War Office for the good work he did there, is set on the top of a column that rivals Nelson's, as though he meant as much in our military history as Nelson in our naval.

Meanwhile the Duke of Cambridge rides for ever outside the War Office! But Charles I and Cromwell are "just right." There they both are, in the heart of our capital, each statue symbolizing aspects of England's life once in mortal conflict, now reconciled, and making up together the best part of what we now are. What is less good in us to-day is neither Roundhead nor Cavalier.

The Nineteenth Century was agitated by the question—"Should Cromwell have a statue?"—and settled it in 1895 in a characteristically English way. Thornycroft's fine statue of him was placed at Westminster, but was not paid for out of public

From G. M. Trevelyan, *An Autobiography & Other Essays* (London, 1949), pp. 158–162, 164–175, 178. Reprinted by permission of Longmans, Green & Co.

funds. The Liberal government of that day wished to pay for it, but the proposal was vetoed by their political allies from Ireland. For in those old days England had to consult Ireland about English affairs, as the price of governing Ireland against her will. The great Unionist (or Conservative) party, to whom this arrangement about Ireland seemed to be the very palladium of the Constitution, was itself in two minds about Cromwell's statue: on the one hand he was a Dissenter and a Radical; on the other hand he was a Patriot and an Imperialist. So a compromise was agreed to, by which Lord Rosebery, the Liberal Prime Minister, paid out of his own pocket for the statue, which was set up outside the entrance to the House of Commons.

The position is excellently chosen. For one thing, it arouses question. "Who is this?" says the casual visitor to the Houses of Parliament, "Cromwell here? He of all people! Why, he marched his troopers into the House of Commons and took away the bauble!"

Nevertheless my opinion is that the statue is well placed—as well placed as the statue of Richard I, a hundred yards further on, is ill placed. What indeed is that levanting knight-errant doing outside the Houses of Parliament? No King had less concern with the development of our Constitution, or even with the government of England. Why not put Richard Lionheart in front of the War Office instead of the Duke of Cambridge?

But Oliver is well placed at the entry of the House of Commons, because without him we should not have become a nation governed by Parliament—not at any rate in the Seventeenth Century. For the King would have won the Civil War, and Parliament would have been put back into the position it occupied under the Tudors, or would have gone under as completely as the Estates of France and the Cortes of Spain. If our training in Parliamentary government had thus been delayed until the Industrial Revolution was upon us, we should have fared as badly as other lands that postponed their rebellion against monarchical power,—as badly as France, Italy, Spain, Germany and Russia.

We have now been so long accustomed to government by the House of Commons, that we find it difficult to imagine what an original and bold thing it was of Pym and Hampden[1] to embark on governing the country through a debating assembly, especially in an age when the whole tendency of things

outside England was moving rapidly to Monarchical Despotism. In England the King's power was indefinite, so he thought it was infinite. But Parliament's power also was indefinite, and might therefore be regarded as infinite. Hence the Civil War. The idea taught to the English Parliamentary chiefs by Coke[2] and the black-letter lawyers, that they were only defending their ancient privileges, was perhaps half true. But it was wholly useful, because the English like to think they have law on their side, even when they are making revolutions. Charles I attacked their ancient privileges, and the only way to save *privileges* which were legally theirs was to seize *power* which was not theirs by law. They claimed practical sovereignty for the House of Commons. It could not have been won except by war. And the war could not have been won without Cromwell. That was the real English Revolution. The Revolution of 1688 was only a conservative and official confirmation of the issue decided at Marston Moor and Naseby.

One often hears people who are devoted to our present free Constitution blame Pym and Cromwell for their violent courses. Such strictures are in some respects valid. No one to-day approves the whole Roundhead programme of 1641, especially as to religion; and the Regicide of 1649 still holds its place among the world's worst mistakes. But historical characters and historic policies must be judged in their totality. And I think England was better served by these rough fellows than Germany by her Liberals who could never say boh to a goose, either in 1848 or since, who always wilted before efficient ruffians like Bismarck or Hitler. In Germany the coarse-grained men of action who "deliver the goods" have always, with the exception of Luther in the matter of religion, been on the side of authority. In England they have been more equally divided,—Strafford[3] for instance on one side, but

[1] John Pym (1584–1643) was one of the leaders in the Parliamentary opposition to James I and Charles I; he was instrumental in securing the passage of the Petition of Right in 1629 and in enacting the program of the Long Parliament in 1640–1641. John Hampden (c. 1595–1643) was also an important Parliamentary leader opposing Stuart policy in the same period. [Editor's note.]

[2] Sir Edward Coke (1552–1634) was an English judge who was a strong defender of the common law against royal prerogative; as a consequence he was an opponent of the Stuarts. [Editor's note.]

[3] The Earl of Strafford (Thomas Wentworth) (1593–1641) was one of the chief advisers of Charles I in the years prior to 1640. When the Long Parliament met in 1640 the pent-up wrath of the Parliamentary forces was direct against him; as a consequence, a bill of attainder was passed against him and he was executed in 1641. [Editor's note.]

The Founder of Parliamentary Government

Pym and Cromwell on the other. If the Prussian Parliament had cut off Bismarck's head in 1860 as ours cut off Strafford's in 1640 the world would be a happier place to-day. But the Germans have never been as ready to fight for their own liberties as they have always been ready to fight against the liberties of other nations. It has been very different with the English-speaking peoples.

The amazing adventure of seizing "the empire and the rule" for the House of Commons in place of the King, would scarcely have been undertaken, and most certainly would not have succeeded, but for the question of religion. The notion of tolerating more than one kind of religion within the borders of a state was alien to the thought of the time. Intolerance was the accepted doctrine not only of priests and presbyters, but of politicians. It was regarded by the pious as a duty to God. "The abomination of toleration" was equally odious to most Anglicans and to most Puritans. Charles, being an Anglican with a Roman Catholic wife, was determined to put down all forms of Puritanism, both the narrow Presbyterianism of the Scots and of Prynne, and the less orthodox sectarianism and individualism dear to men like Cromwell and Milton, John Bunyan and George Fox. It was a dangerous undertaking, for Puritanism of one sort or another was then the prevalent inspiration and interest in life of the most active minded of the middle and lower orders of society, to say nothing of a very large section of the squirearchy of that day. However, Laud and the Bishops, under the Royal protection, were busy hunting all that down. Puritans of all kinds,—and there were many very different kinds,—must conform to the Anglican worship, or go to America,—or fight. At first they tried going to America. But after some years they found an opportunity to stay at home and make a bid for power,—the only way in those days to obtain toleration. The first of these movements founded the United States: the second founded English Parliamentary Government.

The reason why the Puritans were able to fight instead of continuing to go to America, was that from 1640 onwards Parliament, so long in abeyance, was again sitting, supplying them with a ground of authority on which to stand, and a flag round which to rally. They could fight for "the Houses," more particularly for the House of Commons. The political and religious issues ran together so precisely that it is often difficult to say whether a man chose his side for religious or for political reasons,—Hyde[4] for

instance, and Cromwell. Cromwell, in the middle of the Civil War (September 5, 1644), could write

We are said to be "factious," to "seek to maintain our opinions in religion by force,"—which we detest and abhor. I profess I could never satisfy myself of the justness of the War, but from the Authority of Parliament, to maintain itself in its rights.

Cromwell indeed represents the complete fusion, on equal terms, of the political and religious motives. It is impossible to imagine him as a supporter of the Court and the higher nobility; it is no less impossible to imagine him as a Catholic, either Roman or High Anglican. He was a man of the people, and he was a Protestant, standing at the junction of all those classes that opposed the Court, and of all those religionists who opposed the Bishops.

Presbyterians, Independents, all have here the same spirit of faith and prayer; the same presence and answer; they agree here, and have no names of difference: pity it is it should be otherwise elsewhere.

he wrote to the House of Commons from the Army in September 1645.

So, too, he represented the union of classes,—gentry, yeomen, shopkeepers,—who stood together for "the Houses and the Word." In September 1643 he wrote:

I had rather have a plain russet-coated Captain that knows what he fights for, and loves what he knows, than that which you call "a gentleman" and is nothing else. I honour a *Gentleman* that is so indeed!

On these principles he built up first his own Troops of Ironsides, who cleared the Royalists out of East Anglia, and then the New Model Army that won the war. It was a long, hard struggle to create such a force, always against Presbyterian and aristocratic intolerance, and at first against financial difficulties also. Here in his letter to Oliver St. John in the early stage of the process, September 11, 1643:

I am not ready for my march towards the enemy; who hath entrenched himself against Hull, my Lord Newcastle having besieged the town. Many of my Lord of Manchester's Troops are come to me: very bad and mutinous, not to be confided in; *they* paid to a week almost; *mine* noways provided-for to support them, except by the poor Sequestrations of the County of Huntingdon. My Troops increase.

[4] Edward Hyde, 1st Earl of Clarendon (1609–1674) was an important supporter of the episcopal establishment and of the royal cause during the Civil War and the Restoration; he became one of the chief ministers of Charles II after the Restoration. [Editor's note.]

I have a lovely company; you would respect them did you know them. They are no "Anabaptists," they are honest sober Christians; they expect to be used as men!

Cromwell, as we noticed, in September 1644, had written that he and his friends, "abhorred" the idea of maintaining their "opinions in religion by force," and that he considered the war was only justified by the Authority of Parliament . . . yet three years later he participated in the coercion of Parliament by force, in order to win the religious toleration that he and his friends demanded. Was he therefore a hypocrite? No more than other people who have changed their minds or their methods with changing circumstances. He was indeed, as we all know, a great "opportunist." That is to say he had a wonderful instinct for the need of the moment, and held no rigid theories about Church or State. Only he sought freedom of religion for Puritans of all sorts, and the government of the country by the House of Commons. But the two objects became incompatible after the war was won, because the House of Commons, egged on by the City of London, would tolerate no one but strict Presbyterians; he had therefore to choose, and after long hesitations he chose to secure religious freedom for himself and his fellow soldiers who had trusted him in war and in peace, at the expense of the liberties of the House of Commons. The House that had already "purged" itself of Cavaliers was now forcibly purged of the Presbyterian leaders.

This action deprived England of even the semblance of lawful government, and led through Regicide to the "forced power" of the Council of State and the Protectorate. But the blame for creating the chaos that Oliver Protector had ultimately to control by despotic rule, seems to me to rest much less with Cromwell and the Army than with the House of Commons and the City of London for their action in 1647. They had, very wisely, determined in the winter of 1644–45 to create the New Model Army on a basis of toleration in its ranks for all Puritans, and had thereby won the war against the King. But as soon as the war was won they proposed to cheat the men who had saved them in the field, by refusing to them religious toleration, and by setting up a narrow Presbyterian tyranny, a religion which, as the future showed, was alien to everything English,—Anglican and Free Church alike. At the same time the House of Commons failed to pay the arrears due to the New Model, though it had found money for the purpose fast enough so long as the

war lasted. The soldiers were to be demobilized unpaid, and as soon as they got back to civil life they were to be persecuted for their religion by Presbyterian Ministers whom they detested and despised. How could Cromwell consent to see his old comrades in the field, many of whom had enlisted because of their faith in him, thus defrauded at once of everything, mundane and spiritual, for which they had fought? When human folly reaches a certain point it has to be paid for, and that point was reached by the policy of Parliament and the City of London in 1647.

Cromwell's good faith and patriotism must be judged by the prolonged and earnest efforts which he made to prevent this fatal breach between Parliament and Army. For he knew that it would be fatal. In the course of these long negotiations, he and Ireton put forward the best of the various schemes suggested,—The Heads of the Proposals— which extended religious toleration to all Protestants, even permitting the use of the Prayer Book to those who wished. This was far more liberal than anything Parliament could swallow. He tried also to bring the King into the arrangement. But King and House of Commons were equally recalcitrant. It must never be forgotten in judging Cromwell's character and alleged schemes of personal "ambition," that he tried long and earnestly to bring about an agreement by consent which would have reconciled all parties and all Protestant congregations under Charles as constitutional monarch. He failed. Chaos ensued. And it was only to control chaos that he usurped the rule, to save England and the Empire from disruption.

This, so far as it goes, is a true statement of the case. But taken by itself it is too favourable to Cromwell: for one must add that after the failure of his earnest efforts to secure agreement, and after King and Presbyterians had raised a second civil war against the Army and the Sects, Oliver lost his temper and cut off the King's head. Thereby he added fuel to the flame of conflicting passions which he had so long and so vainly striven to reconcile. Yes, he lost his temper. I can indeed understand anyone losing his temper with King Charles; the combination of high-minded obstinacy with deceptiveness and intrigue, the refusal to understand that the defeat in war meant anything, was vastly irritating to those who earnestly endeavoured to bring him to some agreement. And the Second Civil War (1648) which Royalists and Presbyterians raised against the Army and the Sects was a very real provocation to the soldier "saints." It is not wonderful that, at their famous Prayer-meeting at Windsor, before they marched off to the Preston campaign, they came to the conclusion that it was "our duty, if ever the Lord brought us back again in peace, to call Charles Stuart, the man of blood, to an account." One can hardly blame those soldiers: but the world will always debate how far Cromwell can be forgiven for agreeing with them.

It is not so much the personal injustice to Charles that condemns the act, though of course it was utterly illegal, like most acts in time of Revolution. But it was impolitic in the long run, even if convenient at the moment. It was a crime against England, even more than against Charles. For it outraged the feelings of the immense majority of the English people, and in particular it rendered impossible the reconciliation of the Cavaliers. It alienated almost the whole of the squirearchy, who had been almost half Puritan. It ruined, in the end, the Puritan cause, by associating Puritanism with a deed which the English people was taught for generations to abhor. When Carlyle wrote that

this action of the English Regicides did in effect strike a damp like death through the heart of Flunkeyism universally in this world, whereof Flunkeyism . . . has gone about incurably sick ever since,

I think he was mistaken. In England at least, what Carlyle calls "Flunkeyism" got from the scene before Whitehall a new lease of life for centuries to come. The pity men felt for Charles became one of the strongest factors in English politics and religion, with results good and bad.

The Regicide ruined what chance Puritanism had of becoming the principle of the established Church, or the religion of any important section of the governing class. But even the reaction of 1660 could not eliminate Puritanism as a great factor in English life. For Cromwell's rule gave the Sects a decade of protection during which they struck deep roots in English soil, — ineradicable by later persecution. To Cromwell's protection we owe the survival of George Fox and his Quakers; Bunyan and his Baptists; Independents, Congregationalists and so forth. It was these Sects who survived the Restoration, very much more than the orthodox Presbyterians, in spite of the fact that the Presbyterians had opposed the Regicide and the Sects were mainly responsible for that permanently unpopular deed. The heart of English Puritanism down the ages has proved to be sectarian and individualist, not Presbyterian: there Cromwell was right and his work outlived him.

But, to go back to the Regicide, Cromwell, as I say, lost his temper and cut off the King's head. Here we come to grips with the very complicated question of Oliver's character, psychology and nervous system, — for though his nerves were of iron in battle, he had "nerves." His mind and character were a mosaic of contradictory elements, — love of field sports and "innocent jests," followed by groaning in conventicles; championship of liberty, and determination to enforce order; long periods of doubt and hesitation, breeding at the end fierce, immutable resolve; tearful pity and implacable anger; long patience with fools as in 1647, and gusts of fatal impatience next year. Walter Scott, who in *Woodstock* made the first effort since Cromwell's death to depict the real man, has emphasized and even exaggerated the temperamental element in Oliver's changing moods. Gusts of passion are particularly dangerous in a statesman, for he does in his wrath things which men remember when they have forgotten his long patience and good will. As Protector he earnestly tried to work with Parliaments of which he well knew the necessity and the value. But being provoked he could be flint, and his passion exploded in the "bauble" scene, which, in the eyes of half-informed posterity, has damned him as the enemy of Parliaments no less than of Kings.

Now in the matter of the Regicide, how did these psychological peculiarities work? In 1647 he had been striving with care and good temper to reconcile Parliament, Army and King, — Presbyterian, Independent and even Anglican. His word to his impatient soldiers had been "What we and they gain in a free way is better than thrice so much in a forced way, and will be more truly ours and our posterities. That you have by force I look upon as nothing." A wise word surely, and strangely pathetic as his honest opinion, when we consider all that was to come. His efforts at peace-making broke down, through no fault of his own; Presbyterian and Royalist joined to make a new war on the Army. The fury of Oliver's rebound was proportionate to the length and patience of his frustrated efforts for peace. In terms of his religion he believed that he had sinned in striving to effect a settlement with the ungodly, though in fact that effort is one of his clearest claims to honourable fame. During the

Prayer-meeting at Windsor before the Preston campaign, he and his fellow soldiers wept in repentance of their recent falling away, though in fact it was into statesmanship and common sense that they had then fallen. They groaned over their "carnal consultations with our own wisdoms, and not with the word of the Lord," though in fact their own wisdoms were all that they or any man ever had to consult, and "the word of the Lord" was merely another (and in this case less wise) mood of their own. A strange sight to modern eyes, Oliver and his strong comrades, the finest soldiers in the world, proved on a hundred stricken fields and stormed breaches,—sitting round bathed in tears. We cannot now quite understand it; we need not, with Carlyle, wholly admire it, but considering what manner of men these warriors were, we must reverence it,—reverently perhaps avert our eyes from that strange display of emotion, the more so as its outcome was a terrible mistake. Hypocrites? No. But earnest, well-meaning mortals, subject like all men to error.

Next winter the dread resolve to execute the King was put into effect, under the active leadership of Cromwell. It was, I think, this religious or fanatical element, exacerbating his temperamental human passions, that blinded him on this great occasion to a realistic consideration of the public interest, usually uppermost in his mind. In his passionate human resentment at having been tricked, and his mistaken "sense of sin" where there had been no sin, he failed in his duty to remember that the people of England regarded the Regicide with horror. And so, in a dangerous mood of exaltation, he crossed the Rubicon, a stream that should be traversed only in cold blood. He dug a gulf between himself and kindly English good sense, of which he had in his simpler and more usual moods more than an ample share.

But while we condemn the Regicide, it is only fair to remember the extreme difficulty of knowing what to do with Charles, as he would come to no agreement and would not let any of his sons take his place. There was no William III handy to solve England's problem, as forty years later. What they ought to have done with Charles, I confess I do not know. Men sometimes have the misfortune to be faced by problems actually insoluble. As Charles would not come to terms with the victors, he had to be deposed, and that necessarily involved either exile, imprisonment—or death. There were grave difficulties and dangers in each of these courses. I think

they chose what proved in the long run the worst. But at least they did not degrade our history by assassinating him in prison, as had been done under similar circumstances with Edward II, Richard II and Henry VI.

What then was this religion of Oliver's which proved both his strength and his weakness? It supported him through life, inspired him to action, and strengthened him to bear intolerable burdens which other men refused to shoulder. But sometimes it blinded him, by making him think his own passion was God's will. In the words of Hudibras it was

A dark lantern of the Spirit
Which none see by but those who bear it.

To think that God has given you victory in battle is modest in one sense, arrogant in another. It is certainly dangerous to suppose, as Oliver constantly supposed and said, that his victories were the direct work of God, and betokened the divine approval of some particular line of policy. The assumption was highly irritating to opponents, who called Cromwell a hypocrite. He was not that, but he was claiming what no mortal man has a right to claim. Were the Roman Catholic victories in the French Wars of Religion and the Thirty Years War acts of God, one would like to have asked him. The Jesuits thought so.

On the other hand this perfect faith that God was on his side enabled him to endure, never to lose heart and hope either in war or in peace, although he was by nature subject to melancholy and to long periods of hesitation and doubt before taking his great resolutions, and in the latter part of his life was friendless enough on his barren eminence of power. But he felt that God was beside him, a present help in trouble.

His religion was as little doctrinal as the religion of any man of that day, except perhaps some of the Quakers, to whom he showed a sympathy then very unusual. As he wrote to his son Richard "The true knowledge is not literal or speculative; but "inward, transforming the mind to it." The doctrinal and ecclesiastical questions about which the religious parties were quarrelling so fiercely, frankly bored him. Therefore he was perfectly ready to treat Presbyterians and Sectarians as friends on equal terms, and to tolerate Anglicans. Within those limits, which excluded Roman Catholics, he was an early Apostle of the principle of Toleration. If he had not so fatally turned all Anglicans into life-long enemies by the execution of the King, he would as Protector have tolerated their worship as he had suggested in the Heads of the Proposals.

His religious belief and practice may be summed up with the utmost brevity:—a sense of sin and of his own human worthlessness, save when redeemed by God's grace; a continual communion with God, through Christ, in the sanctuary of his own mind and heart. This personal intercourse with God is the essence of religion, stripped bare of all its trappings which to many mean so much but to the Puritan seemed impertinent and even impious. When freshly and sincerely felt this personal communion with God is a mighty power, and in those days it wrought mightily. But it was too assiduously cultivated and too perpetually talked about—even by Cromwell. When, in men less sincere, the wellspring was really dry and the words were repeated artificially as the shibboleth of a sect or party, nothing could be more odious. In this dual aspect of the Puritan religion we have the key to the successful Revolution of 1642 – 48, and also to the Restoration of 1660.

John Buchan has written in his Life of Cromwell:

He had the same power as Caesar and Napoleon, the gift of forcing facts to serve him, of compelling multitudes of men into devotion or acquiescence. But it is on that point alone that he is kin to those cyclopean architects and roadmakers, the world's conquerors. Almost without exception they were spirits of an extreme ambition, egotism and pride, holding aloof from the kindly race of men. Oliver remained humble, homely, with a ready sympathy and goodwill. For, while he was winning battles and dissolving parliaments and carrying the burdens of a people, he was living an inner life so intense that, compared with it, the outer world was the phantasmagoria of a dream. There is no parallel in history to this iron man of action whose consuming purpose was at all times the making of his soul.

The position in which the members of the Council of State found themselves on the morrow of the King's execution was appalling, and would have unnerved weaker men. Ireland and Scotland in their enemies' hands; the sea no longer in their obedience, for a portion of the fleet turned against them, under Prince Rupert;[5] the English people divided into factions, bitterly hostile to one another, but all

from different points of view hostile to the self-appointed Government; the House of Lords abolished, and the House of Commons a mere "rump," pruned so often that it no longer represented any large body of opinion; the Powers of Europe, Protestant as well as Catholic, regarding the regicides with horror and contempt. If the government was to obtain any semblance of authority, it had first to reconquer Ireland and Scotland and the sea, while enforcing order in England. If it failed in this task, nothing like the happy Restoration of 1660 could have taken place, for as yet no such agreement of parties existed. England would have foundered in blood and chaos, and her future destiny at home and overseas would have been fatally compromised. But she was saved by the courage and ability of the men who had usurped power, chiefly by means of their servant Blake[6] and of their colleague and master Cromwell.

Blake recovered the sea by his victories first over the Cavaliers, then over the Dutch and finally over the Spaniards. The great Admiral and the series of Republican governments that employed and supported him, raised the naval power of England to a permanent level, that had been touched but not maintained under the pacific and parsimonious Elizabeth. Cromwell conquered Ireland and Scotland and held the State together by force. Between them, Blake and Cromwell raised the prestige of England in the world to a point from which it had declined under James and Charles I, and which it lost again under Charles and James II, so that, half a dozen years after the Protector's body had been gibbeted, Samuel Pepys noted "It is strange everybody do nowadays reflect upon Oliver and commend him, what brave things he did and made all the neighbour princes fear him." Then, once more England's proper place in the world was secured by the Revolution of 1688, and was rendered permanent that time by its connection not with a military Dictatorship but with a free constitution and an agreement of parties that had been impossible in Oliver's day.

As an imperial statesman, he had an outlook far broader than that of subsequent Parliaments, Whig or Tory, who sacrificed the "Protestant interest" in Ireland to the jealousy of English clothiers and cattle breeders. Oliver's capacious mind regarded all English-speaking Protestants in the British Isles as citi-

---

[5] Prince Rupert (1619 – 1682), Count Palatine of the Rhine and Duke of Bavaria, was a nephew of Charles I; he played a key role as the commander of the Royalist forces during the early stages of the Civil War. After the battle of Naseby (1645) he broke with the king. Later a reconciliation occurred and Rupert was given command of the Royal navy. [Editor's note.]

[6] Robert Blake (1599 – 1657) was first a military commander for the Roundheads in the Civil War and then after 1649 the chief naval commander, an office which he filled successfully during the Cromwellian era. [Editor's note.]

zens with equal rights. In the end, all that was bad in his Irish settlement, the treatment of the native Roman Catholics, was confirmed, and all that was good in it was destroyed. Indeed his settlement of Ireland was not allowed a chance after his death because the "Protestant interest" there was undermined by economic restrictions, and the exodus of Irish Protestants to America was set going. So, too, his government of Scotland was wholly generous and wise in its treatment of Scottish religion and Scottish trade. Only, as his settlement of Scotland was imposed by the sword, not in "a free way," it was, to use his own language "not truly ours and our posterities." It was undone at the Restoration. But in 1707 Great Britain, after many bitter experiences, freely agreed to the policy of a just Union, such as Oliver had conceived and forced upon the recalcitrant island.

He never solved his English domestic problem. During the decade that elapsed between the King's death and his own he failed to win an agreement of parties to any new form of government, and failed to work with any of his Parliaments. The deep shadow of the Regicide still lay between him and his countrymen, so that he could not appeal to the Cavaliers or to moderate men in general against the uncompromising Republican idealists who more and more outraged his practical instincts as the governor of England, but to whom he was fatally committed by his past.

The same arts that did gain
A power must it maintain.

He could not disband the army, for it was almost the sole basis of his government, except in so far as people put up with the Protectorate as the only means by which they could enjoy order and domestic peace. But the necessary maintenance of a great military and naval establishment, and the war with Spain on which Oliver had chosen to embark, were financially ruinous. The country needed a period of economy and lower taxation which it could not get from the Protector. His death in September 1658 was probably fortunate for himself and his reputation; it was certainly fortunate for his country, because he had held the ring until time and opinion were ripe for the agreed Restoration of King, Law and Parliament.

Was then Cromwell's career either a misfortune, or a failure on the whole? I think not. It is true that the institutions he set up did not survive. But he saved the country from a number of great evils—first from absolute monarchy, then from Presbyterian tyranny, and finally from chaos and dismemberment. "I am a man standing in the place I am in," he said in 1657, "which place I undertook not so much out of hope of doing any good, as out of desire to prevent mischief and evil, which I did see was imminent on the nation." So then he himself was conscious that his work was mainly negative, like half the great and good things that are done in this world—England's wars against continental militarist Empires for instance.

If Cromwell had not won the Civil War for Parliament, King Charles and his Roman Catholic children after him could have done what they liked with England. They would certainly have set up such a royal despotism as was already the fashionable model on the continent. England would have forgotten Magna Carta and Edward Coke's black letter liberties, and become spiritually an apanage of continental Europe. We should not have had our peculiarly English and Conservative Revolution of 1688, but haply have been long afterwards whelmed in some European convulsion more like that of 1789.

But this did not happen, for Charles II was restored not by Cavalier conquest but by Parliamentary vote, and the great work of the first session of the Long Parliament continued at the Restoration still to be the law of the land. Moreover England had undergone the unforgettable experience of twenty years of Kingless rule, first by Parliament, then by Republican soldiers. That period is only an interlude in our history, but it is an interlude of which, in spite of its own characteristic crimes and follies, Englishmen have no need to be ashamed, for it brought to England prestige and independent power in the family of nations, such as neither the earlier nor later Stuarts were able to maintain.

The defeat of royal absolutism in war, and the control of the chaos that threatened to engulf the Parliamentary victory, were both the personal doing of Oliver Cromwell. And the position that Republican England so unexpectedly maintained in face of the scandalized Powers of Europe, was his doing also. Indirectly and in the long run our national liberties are based upon these events. And therefore Cromwell's statue is well placed, defending the entry of the House of Commons.

So much for his work. What of the man himself? He was loved and hated in his life-time. After his death a simulacrum or false image of him was set up by his enemies as a butt for popular reprobation for nearly two centuries. Now that the truth about him is known, he is once more loved and hated, as in his own life, but since the issues of these old days are now buried deep beneath the leaves of many years, most Englishmen now take a more unprejudiced view of the man.

The finest of modern lyric outbursts about him is that of Carlyle in the last paragraph of *Historical Sketches*.

I confess I have an interest in this Mr. Cromwell; and indeed, if truth must be said, in him alone. The rest are historical, dead to me; but he is epic, still living. Hail to thee, thou strong one; hail, across the long-drawn funeral aisle and night of Time! Two dead centuries, with all that they have born and buried, part us; and it is far to speak together; how diverse are our centuries, most diverse, yet our Eternity is the same; and a kinship unites us which is much deeper than Death and Time. Hail to thee, thou strong one, for thou art ours, and I, at least, mean to call thee so.

Well, very few of us are big enough to talk on equal terms with Cromwell across the centuries. Carlyle was so, no doubt, though I suspect Oliver might have been a little puzzled by him. But "Mr. Cromwell," as Carlyle says, is "ours" and not merely Carlyle's, and there are many things in him besides his rugged strength and mastership, which endear him to more homely English folk, of whom in some

respects Cromwell is the finest representative before mankind. His very uncertainty "whither he was going" which eventually carried him so far; his dislike of theory and dogma; his eye for the crisis of the moment; his long periods of brooding uncertainty; his fundamental modesty and refusal ever to regard himself as a "superman," are all good English traits. So are his affectionate family life; his good comradeship and feeling for men of all classes; his love of field sports and "innocent jests"; his pity and generosity when he was not in one of his black rages (though these must not be forgotten in judging the man); his growing awareness of the interest of England in the overseas world though he had risen as the leader of a party; his constant reference of all he did to a tribunal higher than human, though this also had its dangers; his sympathy with the despised and eccentric Quakers when all others in authority detested them. . . .

. . . The world honours England the more because Cromwell was an Englishman. If he is not the typical Englishman, he is as near to it as Wellington or Dr. Johnson. Certainly none of those three could have been produced by any other land. A French, a German, even a Scottish Cromwell is unthinkable. And so let his statue stand, firmly planted on his own high-booted legs, on guard over us in the heart of our political and governmental life, with the book and the sword, his head slightly bent in a brooding study of the insoluble problems of the government of men, and the no less insoluble problems of man's relation to God.

2

THE SCIENTIFIC REVOLUTION OF THE SEVENTEENTH CENTURY: A QUESTION OF CAUSES

Perhaps the greatest of the seventeenth-century revolutions was the scientific. After a century of debate, lasting from the 1540's to the 1640's, the Moderns, or proponents of the Copernican-Galilean explanation of the universe, routed the Ancients or defenders of the older Aristotelian-Ptolemaic world system.

The roots of this scientific revolution were embedded in the fourteenth and fifteenth-century quarrels of the latter-day scholastics. Their squabbles were transformed into modern terms with the appearance of Nicholas Copernicus' great work *On the Revolution of Heavenly Bodies*, published in the *annus mirabilis* of modern science, 1543. Copernicus (1473–1543), who based his work on a combination of mathematical reasoning, textual criticism, and observation, challenged the authority of Aristotle and Ptolemy by predicating the hypothesis that the sun rather than the earth is the center of the universe. At the same time, following the maxim that "simplicity is the seal of truth," Copernicus reduced the number of cycles and epicycles in the Ptolemaic universe from 77 to 34. Although the great astronomer's work was presented to the world in the guise of an hypothesis, its implications were revolutionary. In displacing the earth as the center of the universe, Copernicus obliquely asked: Was man to be left alone, an atom in the midst of a great solar machine? Was man bereft of imminent divine intervention? Was he no more than an "ant in the face of the infinite"? These questions caused both Protestant and Roman Catholic critics to condemn Copernicus' writings as pernicious.

After fifty years of bitter controversy, the Moderns found a champion in the eminent Italian mathematician-astronomer Galileo Galilei (1564–1642), whose book, the *Sidereal Messenger*, published in 1610, clearly questioned the Aristotelian concept that heavenly bodies were perfect spheres. He did so by noting that the Earth's moon had an irregular surface made up of high mountains and deep valleys. In the same work Galileo espoused the Copernican conclusions concerning the passage of the moon around the Earth by citing as proof (by analogy) the orbit made by the moons of Jupiter around that planet. Despite bitter clerical criticism of his book, Galileo continued to defend Copernicus in his later works, *Il Saggiatore* (*The Scales*, 1623) and the *Dialogue concerning the Two Chief Systems of the World* (1632).

Galileo was not alone in his struggle with the Ancients. His findings were supported by the work of the great German astronomer Johannes Kepler (1571–1630) and the Englishman Francis Bacon (1561–1626). Kepler defied Aristotle and Ptolemy by declaring that the planets followed an elliptical orbit not, as they had thought, a circular one. Bacon, though not a strikingly original thinker, popularized the findings of the New Science in his books: the *Advancement of Learning* (1605), the *Novum Organum* (1620), and the *New Atlantis* (1624). Bacon's insistence on the experimental method deeply influenced the thinking of the next two generations of English scientists, who in their zeal to support the "New Learning" helped found one of the great academies of Western Europe, the Royal Society for Improving Natural Knowledge, incorporated in 1662. The purpose of the Society was "to examine all theories, principles, hypotheses, elements, histories, and experiments of things natural, mathematical, and mechanical, invented, recorded, or practiced by any considerable author, ancient or modern." So great became the reputation of the Royal Society that scientists from all over Europe clamored for admission. By 1686 the Society had an active membership list of 309. Truly, as Richard Foster Jones points out in the selection reprinted below, the mid-seventeenth century was the product of a "Bacon-faced" generation.

On the European continent the Moderns were supported by such distinguished scientist-philosophers as René Descartes (1596–1650) and Christiaan Huygens (1629–1695) and by an array of scientific academies, led by the Academy of

Lynxes (or Lynx-eyed) in Italy; the College of Natural Curiosities in Germany; and the *Académie des Sciences* in Paris. Thus by the mid-seventeenth century the tide was running strongly against the Ancients. The final blow to the concept of the Aristotelian world picture was delivered by the great English physicist Isaac Newton, who was born in the same year Galileo died, 1642, and died in 1727. Newton published his great work *The Philosophiae Naturalis Principia Mathematica*, commonly known as the *Principia*, in 1687. In that work he proved, by means of elaborate geometric formulae and by the use of his own invention, differential calculus, that all bodies—earthly or celestial—had gravitational attraction for one another and that their attraction "varies inversely as the square of the distance between the two bodies." Newton, using his inverse square law and his findings concerning centrifugal force, constructed a universe held together by the immutable law of celestial mechanics. The universe had indeed—as many critics had a century before feared—become a vast, perpetual motion machine, appropriately termed the Newtonian World Machine. Thus by the end of the seventeenth century Newtonianism had replaced Aristotelianism as the reigning scientific dogma.

The "facts" of the great seventeenth-century scientific revolution are fairly well established. The interpretation of these facts—three of which are given below—are still open to debate.

ROBERT K. MERTON

THE MERTON THESIS

Robert K. Merton, whom the author of a recent *New Yorker* profile termed "Mr. Sociology," is a professor at Columbia University and the author of numerous works on sociology, among them his early monograph on *Science, Technology and Society in the Seventeenth Century* (1938), which is cited by both Professors T. K. Rabb and A. R. Hall (contributors to this section on science) as a pioneering effort in the fields of the history and sociology of science. In the article printed below, which preceded the monograph by two years, Merton postulates the thesis that the presence within English society of a Puritan "value-complex" did substantially aid in the genesis and development of the scientific movement in seventeenth-century England. In his study Merton evokes, as does Hall in the succeeding selection, the spirit of the Protestant Ethic, which, says Merton, "canonized and beatified" empiricism and rationalism.

It is the thesis of this study that the Puritan ethic, as an ideal-typical expression of the value-attitudes basic to ascetic Protestantism generally, so canalized the interests of seventeenth-century Englishmen

From Robert K. Merton, "Puritanism, Pietism, and Science," *The Sociological Review*, XXVIII (1936), 1–14, 29–30. Reprinted by permission of *The Sociological Review*.

as to constitute one important *element* in the enhanced cultivation of science. The deeprooted religious *interests* of the day demanded in their forceful implications the systematic, rational, and empirical study of Nature for the glorification of God in His works and the control of the corrupt world.

It is possible to determine the extent to which the values of the Puritan ethic stimulated interest in science by surveying the attitudes of the contemporary scientists. Of course, there is a marked possibility that in studying the avowed motives of scientists we are dealing with rationalizations, with "derivations," rather than with accurate statements of the "actual motives." In such instances, although they may refer to isolated specific cases, the value of our study is by no means vitiated, for these conceivable rationalizations themselves are evidence . . . of the motives which were regarded as socially acceptable, since, as Kenneth Burke puts it, "a terminology of motives is moulded to fit our general orientation as to purposes, instrumentalities, the good life, etc."

Robert Boyle was one of the scientists who attempted explicitly to link the place of science in social life with other cultural values, particularly in his *Usefulness of Experimental Natural Philosophy.* Such attempts were likewise made by John Ray, whose work in every branch of natural history was path-breaking and who was characterized by Haller as the greatest botanist in the history of man; Francis Willughby, who was perhaps as eminent in zoology as was Ray in botany; John Wilkins, one of the leading spirits in the "invisible College" which developed into the Royal Society; Oughtred,[1] Wallis,[2] and others. For additional evidence we can turn to the scientific body which, arising about the middle of the century, provoked and stimulated scientific advance more than any other immediate agency: the Royal Society. In this instance we are particularly fortunate in possessing a contemporary account written under the constant supervision of the members of the Society so that it might be representative of their views as to the motives and aims of that association. This is Thomas Sprat's widely read *History of the Royal-Society of London,* published in

1667, after it had been examined by Wilkins and other representatives of the Society.

Even a cursory examination of these writings suffices to disclose one outstanding fact: certain elements of the Protestant ethic had pervaded the realm of scientific endeavour and had left their indelible stamp upon the attitudes of scientists toward their work. Discussions of the why and wherefore of science bore a point-to-point correlation with the Puritan teachings on the same subject. Such a dominant force as was religion in those days was not, and perhaps could not be compartmentalized and delimited. Thus, in Boyle's highly commended apologia for science it is maintained that the study of Nature is to the greater glory of God and the Good of Man. This is the motif which recurs in constant measure. The juxtaposition of the spiritual and the material is characteristic. This culture rested securely on a substratum of utilitarian norms which constituted the measuringrod of the desirability of various activities. The definition of action designed for the greater glory of God was tenuous and vague, but utilitarian standards could easily be applied.

Earlier in the century, this keynote had been sounded in the resonant eloquence of that "veritable apostle of the learned societies," Francis Bacon. Himself the initiator of no scientific discoveries; unable to appreciate the importance of his great contemporaries, Gilbert, Kepler, and Galileo; naively believing in the possibility of a scientific method which "places all wits and understandings nearly on a level"; a radical empiricist holding mathematics to be of no use in science; he was, nevertheless, highly successful as one of the principal protagonists of a positive social evaluation of science and of the disclaim of sterile scholasticism. As one would expect from the son of a "learned, eloquent, and religious woman, full of puritanic fervour" who was admittedly influenced by his mother's attitudes, he speaks in the *Advancement of Learning* of the true end of scientific activity as the "glory of the Creator and the relief of man's estate." Since, as is quite clear from many official and private documents, the Baconian teachings constituted the basic principles on which the Royal Society was patterned, it is not anomalous that in the charter of the Society the same sentiment is expressed.

Boyle, in his last will and testament, echoes the same attitude, petitioning the Fellows of the Society in this wise: "Wishing them also a happy success in

[1] William Oughtred (1574?–1660) was an important mathematician. [Editor's note.]

[2] John Wallis (1616–1703) was also a mathematician and long-time professor at Oxford. [Editor's note.]

their laudable attempts, to discover the true Nature of the Works of God; and praying that they and all other Searchers into Physical Truths, may Cordially refer their Attainments to the Glory of the Great Author of Nature, and to the Comfort of Mankind." John Wilkins proclaimed the experimental study of Nature to be a most effective means of begetting in men a veneration for God. Francis Willughby was prevailed upon to publish his works—which he had deemed unworthy of publication—only when Ray insisted that it was a means of glorifying God. Ray's *Wisdom of God*, which was so well received that five large editions were issued in some twenty years, is a panegyric of those who glorify Him by studying His works.

To a modern, comparatively untouched by religious forces, and noting the almost complete separation, if not opposition, between science and religion to-day, the recurrence of these pious phrases is apt to signify merely customary usage, and nothing of deep-rooted motivating convictions. To him these excerpta would seem to be a case of *qui nimium probat nihil probat*. But such an interpretation is possible only if one neglects to translate oneself within the framework of seventeenth-century values. Surely such a man as Boyle, who spent considerable sums to have the Bible translated into foreign tongues, was not simply rendering lip service. As G. N. Clark very properly notes in this connexion:

There is . . . always a difficulty in estimating the degree to which what we call religion enters into anything which was said in the seventeenth century in religious language. It is not solved by discounting all theological terms and treating them merely as common form. On the contrary, it is more often necessary to remind ourselves that these words were then seldom used without their accompaniment of meaning, and that their use did generally imply a heightened intensity of feeling.

The second dominant tenet in the Puritan ethos designated social welfare, the good of the many, as a goal ever to be held in mind. Here again the contemporary scientists adopted an objective prescribed by the current values. Science was to be fostered and nurtured as leading to the domination of Nature through the facilitation of technologic invention. The Royal Society, we are told by its worthy historian, "does not intend to stop at some particular benefit, but goes to the root of all noble inventions." But those experiments which do not bring with them immediate gain are not to be contemned, for as the noble Bacon has declared, experiments of Light ultimately conduce to a whole troop of inventions useful to the life and state of man. This power of science to better the material condition of man, he continues, is, apart from its purely mundane value, a good in the light of the Evangelical Doctrine of Salvation by Jesus Christ.

And so on through the principles of Puritanism there was the same point-to-point correlation between them and the attributes, goals, and results of science. Such was the contention of the protagonists of science at that time. Puritanism simply made articulate the basic values of the time. If Puritanism demands systematic, methodic labour, constant diligence in one's calling, what, asks Sprat, more active and industrious and systematic than the Art of Experiment, which "can never be finish'd by the perpetual labours of any one man, nay, scarce by the successive force of the greatest Assembly?" Here is employment enough for the most indefatigable industry, since even those hidden treasures of Nature which are farthest from view may be uncovered by pains and patience.

Does the Puritan eschew idleness because it conduces to sinful thoughts (or interferes with the pursuit of one's vocation)? "What room can there be for low, and little things in a mind so usefully and successfully employ'd [as in natural philosophy]?" Are plays and play-books pernicious and flesh-pleasing (and subversive of more serious pursuits)? Then it is the "fittest season for Experiments to arise, to teach us a Wisdome, which springs from the depths of Knowledge, to shake off the shadows, and to scatter the mists [of the spiritual distractions brought on by the Theatre]." And finally, is a life of earnest activity within the world to be preferred to monastic asceticism? Then recognize the fact that the study of natural philosophy "fits us not so well for the secrecy of a Closet: It makes us serviceable to the World." In short, science embodies two highly prized values: utilitarianism and empiricism.

In a sense this explicit coincidence between Puritan tenets and the qualities of science as a calling is casuistry. It is an express attempt to fit the scientist *qua* pious layman into the framework of the prevailing social values. It is a bid for religious and social sanction, since both the constitutional position and the personal authority of the clergy were much more important then than now. But this is not the entire explanation. The justificatory efforts of Sprat, Wilkins, Boyle, or Ray do not simply represent opportunistic obsequiousness, but rather an earnest attempt to justify the ways of science to God. The Reformation had transferred the burden of individual salvation from the Church to the individual, and it is this "overwhelming and crushing sense of the responsibility for his own soul" which explains the acute religious interest. If science were not demonstrably a "lawful" and desirable calling, it dare not claim the attention of those who felt themselves "ever in the Great Taskmaster's eye." It is to this intensity of feeling that such apologias were due.

The exaltation of the faculty of reason in the Puritan ethos—based partly on the conception of rationality as a curbing device of the passions—inevitably led to a sympathetic attitude toward those activities which demand the constant application of rigorous reasoning. But again, in contrast to medieval rationalism, reason is deemed subservient and auxiliary to empiricism. Sprat is quick to indicate the pre-eminent adequacy of science in this respect. It is on this point probably that Puritanism and the scientific temper are in most salient agreement, for the combination of *rationalism and empiricism* which is so pronounced in the Puritan ethic forms the essence of the spirit of modern science. Puritanism was suffused with the rationalism of neo-Platonism, derived largely through an appropriate modification of Augustine's teachings. But it did not stop there. Associated with the designated necessity of dealing successfully with the practical affairs of life within this world—a derivation from the peculiar twist afforded largely by the Calvinist doctrine of predestination and *certitudo salutis* through successful worldly activity—was an emphasis upon empiricism. These two currents brought to convergence through the ineluctable logic of an inherently consistent system of values were so associated with the other values of the time as to prepare the way for the acceptance of a similar coalescence in natural science.

Empiricism and rationalism were canonized, beatified, so to speak. It may very well be that the Puritan ethos did not directly influence the method of science and that this was simply a parallel development in the internal history of science, but it is evident that through the psychological compulsion toward certain modes of thought and conduct this value-complex made an empirically-founded science commendable rather than, as in the medieval period, reprehensible or at best acceptable on sufferance. This could not but have directed some talents into scientific fields which other-wise would have engaged in more highly esteemed professions. The fact that science to-day is largely if not completely divorced from religious sanctions is itself of interest as an example of the process of secularization.

The beginnings of such secularization, faintly perceptible in the latter Middle Ages, are manifest in the Puritan ethos. It was in this system of values that reason and experience were first markedly considered as independent means of ascertaining even religious truths. Faith which is unquestioning and not "rationally weighed," says Baxter, is not faith, but a dream or fancy or opinion. In effect, this grants to science a power which may ultimately limit that of theology.

Thus, once these processes are clearly understood, it is not surprising or inconsistent that Luther particularly, and Melanchthon less strongly, execrated the cosmology of Copernicus and that Calvin frowned upon the acceptance of many scientific discoveries of his day, while the religious ethic which stemmed from these leaders invited the pursuit of natural science. In so far as the attitudes of the theologians dominate over the, in effect, subversive religious ethic,—as did Calvin's authority in Geneva until the early eighteenth century—science may be greatly impeded. But with the relaxation of this hostile influence and with the development of an ethic, stemming from it and yet differing significantly, science takes on a new life, as was indeed the case in Geneva.

Perhaps the most directly effective element of the Protestant ethic for the sanction of natural science was that which held that the study of nature enables a fuller appreciation of His works and thus leads us to admire the Power, Wisdom, and Goodness of God manifested in His creation. Though this conception was not unknown to medieval thought, the consequences deduced from it were entirely different. Thus Arnaldus of Villanova,[3] in studying the products of the Divine Workshop, adheres strictly to the medieval ideal of determining properties of phenomena from *tables* (in which all combinations are set forth according to the canons of logic). But in the seventeenth century, the contemporary emphasis upon empiricism led to investigating nature primarily through observation. This difference in interpre-

[3] Arnaldus of Villanova (1235?–1312) was a physician and alchemist who taught medicine at Barcelona and Paris. [Editor's note.]

tation of substantially the same doctrine can only be understood in the light of the different values permeating the two cultures.

For a Barrow,[4] Boyle, or Wilkins, a Ray or Grew,[5] science found its rationale in the end and all of existence: glorification of God. Thus, from Boyle:

. . . God loving, as He deserves, to be honour'd in all our Faculties, and consequently to be glorified and acknowledg'd by the acts of Reason, as well as by those of Faith, there must be sure a great Disparity betwixt that general, confus'd and lazy Idea we commonly have of his Power and Wisdom, and the distinct, rational and affecting notions of those Attributes which are form'd by an attentive Inspection of those Creatures in which they are most legible, and which were made chiefly for that very end.

Ray carries this conception to its logical conclusion, for in Nature is the manifestation of His power, then nothing in Nature is too mean for scientific study. The universe and the insect, the macrocosm and microcosm alike, are indications of "divine Reason, running like a Golden Vein, through the whole leaden Mine of Brutal Nature."

Up to this point we have been concerned in the main with the directly felt sanction of science through Puritan values. While this was of great influence, there was another type of relationship which, subtle and difficult of apprehension though it be, was perhaps of paramount significance. It has to do with the preparation of a set of largely implicit assumptions which made for the ready acceptance of the scientific temper characteristic of the seventeenth and subsequent centuries. It is not simply that Protestantism implicitly involved free inquiry, *libre examen*, or decried monastic asceticism. These are important but not exhaustive.

It has become manifest that in each age there is a system of science which rests upon a set of assumptions, usually implicit and seldom questioned by the scientists of the time. The *basic* assumption in modern science "is a widespread, instinctive conviction in the existence of an *Order of Things*, and, in particular, of an Order of Nature." This belief, this faith, for at least since Hume it must be recognized as such, is simply "impervious to the demand for a

consistent rationality." In the systems of scientific thought of Galileo, Newton, and of their successors, the testimony of experiment is the ultimate criterion of truth, but the very notion of experiment is ruled out without the prior assumption that Nature constitutes an intelligible order, so that when appropriate questions are asked, she will answer, so to speak. Hence this assumption is final and absolute. As Professor Whitehead indicated, this "Faith in the possibility of science, generated antecedently to the development of modern scientific theory, is an unconscious derivative from medieval theology." But this conviction, prerequisite of modern science though it be, was not sufficient to induce its development. What was needed was a constant interest in searching for this order in nature in an empirico-rational fashion, that is, an *active* interest in this world and its occurrences plus a specific frame of mind. With Protestantism, religion provided this interest: it actually imposed obligations of intense concentration upon secular activity with an emphasis upon experience and reason as bases for action and belief.

Even the Bible as final and complete authority was subject to the interpretation of the individual upon these bases. The similarity in approach and intellectual attitude of this system to that of the contemporary science is of more than passing interest. It could not but mould an attitude of looking at the world of sensuous phenomena which was highly conducive to the willing acceptance, and indeed preparation for, the same attitude in science. . . .

There remains a supremely important part of this study to be completed. It is not sufficient verification of our hypothesis that the cultural attitudes induced by the Protestant ethic were favourable to science. Nor, yet again, that the consciously felt motivation of many eminent scientists was provided by this ethic. Nor, still further, that the cast of thought which is characteristic of modern science, namely, the combination of empiricism and rationalism and the faith in the validity of one basic postulate, an apprehensible order in Nature, bears an other than fortuitous congruency with the values involved in Protestantism. All this can but provide formidable evidence of a certain probability of the connexion we are arguing. The most significant test of our hypothesis, the *experimentum crucis*, as it were, is to be found in the confrontation of the results *deduced* from our theory with relevant empirical data. If the Protestant ethic involved an attitudinal set favourable to science and technology in so many ways,

[4] Isaac Barrow (1630–1677) was a mathematician; included among his students was Isaac Newton, who succeeded him as professor of mathematics at Cambridge. [Editor's note.]

[5] Nehemiah Grew (1641–1712) was an anatomist and physiologist. [Editor's note.]

then we should find amongst Protestants a greater propensity for these fields of endeavour than one would expect simply on the basis of their representation in the total population. Moreover, if, as has been frequently suggested,[1] the impression made by this ethic has lasted long after much of its theological basis has been largely disavowed, then even in periods subsequent to the seventeenth century, this connexion of Protestantism and science should subsist to some degree. The following section, then, will be devoted to an experimental test of our hypothesis. . . .

[*Merton then proceeds with a number of demonstrations to show the relationship between science and Puritanism. He examines certain key members of the Royal Society and finds them to be religious men of Puritan persuasion. He also finds many Puritans to have subscribed to an educational philosophy that was utilitarian and empirical. He studies in great detail educational institutions in seventeenth-century Europe and finds that "Protestants, without exception, for a progressively larger proportion of the student body in those schools which emphasize scientific and technologic training, while Catholics concentrate their interest on classical and theological training. . . ." He is thus led to the following conclusion. Editor's Note.*]

With the presentation of these data we close the empirical testing of our hypothesis. In every instance, the association of Protestantism with scientific and technologic interests and achievements is pronounced, even when extra-religious influences are largely eliminated. The association is largely understandable in terms of the norms embodied in both systems. The positive estimation by Protestants of a hardly disguised utilitarianism, of intra-mundane interests, of a thorough-going empiricism, of the right and even duty of *libre examen*, and of the explicit individual questioning of authority were congenial to the very same values found in modern science. And perhaps above all is the significance of the active ascetic drive which necessitated the study of Nature that it might be controlled. Hence, these two fields were well integrated and, in essentials, mutually supporting not only in seventeenth-century England but in other times and places.

THEODORE K. RABB

THE NOMINALIST APPROACH

Professor T. K. Rabb of Harvard University, author of articles on the Thirty Years' War and on England in the seventeenth century, asks his reader, as did Voltaire, to define his terms with care. What, exactly, do we mean, asks Rabb, by the term "Puritanism?" Was it a coherent doctrine or an aggregation of disparate ideas? What was meant in the seventeenth century by the words "science" and "scientist." And, above all, is it possible "to prove that religious sanctions preceded an individual's interest in science [?]" Rabb's nominalist approach serves as a welcome corrective to the broad sociological sketch offered by Merton.

Discussion of the relation between Puritanism and the growth of interest in experimental science in England can be regarded as an offshoot of the controversy over the Weber "thesis." In fact, it was with an obvious and explicit debt to Max Weber that one of the first and most persuasive cases was made during the 1930's for connecting Puritanism and science.[1] During the last twenty-five years this connection has been forcefully drawn and there have

[1] Professor Rabb is referring here to the work of Robert K. Merton, whose ideas we encountered in the previous selection. [Editor's note.]

From T. K. Rabb, "Puritanism and the Rise of Experimental Science in England," *Cahiers d'histoire mondiale*, VII (1962), 46–57, 65–67. Reprinted by permission of the author and the Commission internationale pour une histoire du developpement scientifique et cultural de l'humanité.

been but few and scattered murmurs of dissent. As a consequence of several articles by D. Stimson and of important major works by R. K. Merton and R. F. Jones, Puritanism has come to occupy a place of considerable importance among the causes of the rise of science in XVIIth century England. So powerful was the impact of this hypothesis in the late 1930's that no full-scale refutation or qualification has yet been attempted.

At first the new hypothesis made moderate claims, but Puritanism rapidly came to hold a far more prominent place in the rise of science than had originally been suggested. This greater stress on religious factors began to appear in the works of Merton and Jones, and in reaction a few brief rejoinders rejected the hypothesis in its entirety. On the other hand G. Rosen stressed the idea even more strongly than its pioneers, when he declared that "it may be asserted without contradiction that Puritanism was one of the major motive forces of the new experimental science." A more balanced assessment has not been forthcoming, . . . Such an assessment is necessary if the problem is not to be left vaguely unresolved. Since the major treatments have all supported the link between Puritanism and science, a re-estimate is almost bound to be in reaction to that point of view. A reaction, however, need not be equal and opposite. The need seems to be for a strong qualification rather than a refutation.

Before discussing the literature, the basis of the dispute must be laid. The facts around which hypotheses can be constructed are simple to relate. The central event is the foundation of the Royal Society shortly after the Restoration of Charles II, and this event can be regarded as the climax of the growth of interest in science. The development of this interest was steady from the late XVIth century onwards, but after 1640 an acceleration began that can be traced through the meetings of the "invisible" college, then the Wadham group at Oxford, and finally the foundation of the Royal Society. This acceleration was accompanied by the emergence of Sir Francis Bacon as the movement's guiding philosopher, and it was helped by the government's interest in educational reforms and by the appointment of scientists as government officials and as Oxford dons. After 1660 a reaction set in: educational changes were abandoned, the Universities and the "Establishment" in general returned to their old ways of thought, and interest in science slowly faded with the gradual exhaustion of the impetus that had been developed between 1640 and 1660. The Dissenting Academies now became the bastions of the "new philosophy," while the Royal Society, after its magnificent start, entered a period of long decline at the end of the XVIIth century. The half century after 1640 was a great age for English science, and its tone was set during the years of the Puritan Rebellion. The key period therefore lies in the fifth and sixth decades of the XVIIth century, a time of rapid developments which culminated in the foundation of the Royal Society.

Matters will also be clarified if two terms central to the whole problem are placed in their XVIIth century context, namely, science and Puritanism. The first was perhaps best clarified by the scientists themselves when they called their great institution "The Royal Society of London for improving natural knowledge by experiments." The "new learning," and what it meant to the scientists or "natural philosophers" of the time was thus succinctly defined. They were interested primarily in experiments, which would enable them to wrest new data from Nature. With Bacon as their inspiration, their aims were firmly practical; hence the word "improving" and their implicit belief in human progress. Their attitude lay somewhere between the virtuosi on one side and pure speculators on the other. The virtuosi, amateurs who were fascinated by experiments, were not scientists. Although they contributed vital support and interest to the growing discipline, they differed from the scientists in that they sought knowledge only for its own sake or for "delight." In the rise of science in England, which consisted of a growing interest in natural phenomena, experiments certainly occupied a vital place; but the scientists, unlike the virtuosi, never regarded experiments as an end in themselves. On the other hand they were different from the pure speculators, such as astrologers, in that they never encouraged abstract theorizing: conclusions were based firmly on experimental evidence and proof. The scientists' view of their subject in the period of gathering momentum after 1640 thus followed closely the guidance of Bacon, whose inspiration was openly acknowledged in the aims of the Royal Society.

Puritanism is far more difficult to understand, let alone define. If the term is to have any useful meaning, however, an attempt must be made at a brief, yet full and strict definition. Puritanism was above all a religious movement, and all non-theological beliefs that are attributed to it were subsidiary characteristics that had to remain in strict harmony with overriding religious considerations. Essentially, it was a movement of protest, whose reaction against Roman Catholicism was more pronounced than that of the Anglican Church, which it condemned as an institution insufficiently reformed. The true Puritan was so deeply imbued with his theological beliefs that, though eager to convert others, he rarely abandoned his own principles, and if he did, it was usually towards a more radical position. He was an ardent believer in scriptural writings, but he considered the individual capable of interpreting scripture and communicating in prayer without the intervention of a priest. He was anti-episcopalian, though not necessarily opposed to church organization, and he was a believer in predestination and the futility of this world. He was an extreme Sabbatarian, austere in his attitude to life, which he thought should be devoted to the glorification of God. Often he was obsessed with a dislike of idleness, but in his eyes idleness was almost equated with neglect of the duty to glorify God. And he tended to be intolerant of differing beliefs.

It is easy to say that Puritanism was an attitude of mind, and such a judgement may be accurate for its post-XVIIth century manifestations. But, until 1640 at least, it was only a theological position. The characteristics noted above were not, singly, unique to Puritanism. Nor were the people who exhibited some or all of these traits necessarily united in other attitudes or beliefs: they might easily have had incompatible ideas on other subjects. All the same it seems justifiable to regard as Puritans all those who could be embraced by the definition that has been given. After 1640, however, the character of the movement changed. It became identified with a revolution that attempted to change society as a whole. Puritans turned to reforms that bore little relation to their pre-1640 theological demands. Yet the predominant emphases, as we shall see, were still on religious issues, and the leaders of the Interregnum were Puritans because of their concern with these issues. When attempting an assessment of the influence of Puritanism on the rise of science, it is most important to realize the differences between the aims of a Baconian, a Puritan, and a revolutionary. Their attitudes were frequently similar, but the three terms are not synonymous or interchangeable.

A rapid review of the literature must start with the work of Dean Stimson, who was the first modern scholar to suggest a link between Puritanism and science. She saw significance in the backgrounds of the men who formed small scientific circles during the Interregnum and later founded the Royal Society. The evidence for the membership of what was supposedly the earliest of these gatherings is dubious, however, and it is hard to agree that seven of the ten men involved can be closely connected with Puritanism. College backgrounds are not certain determinants, and it is often more revealing to look at subsequent careers. For instance, it seems far more significant that Wilkins[2] later became a Bishop than that he married Cromwell's sister. However conformist a man was during the Interregnum, his Puritanism cannot have been deep enough to provide a motive force if he was capable of a rapid transformation after 1660. Mere contact or conformity are not enough to prove the existence of a strong influence. For this reason one needs more evidence than political affiliations or early training to prove that 62% of these original members of the Royal Society about whom information is available were Puritans; and particularly so, since "they later accepted the Book of Common Prayer along with the Restoration and were conforming to the Church of England."

Dean Stimson's thesis that there was a link between Puritanism and the rise of science was suggestive, and "namierization" of the scientists might well have provided simple proof of the connection. But she applied the label "Puritan" somewhat too readily, thus limiting its usefulness. Therefore when she came to the really important question, why Puritanism should have promoted interest in science, her explanation was unconvincing. For instance, she regarded the "moderates" as the Puritans who produced scientists, yet she defined none of her terms. Similarly, she failed to explain why the "refreshment, entertainment and keen intellectual delight" provided by experimental science should have been noteworthy attractions for these people. The word "Puritan" finally loses nearly all meaning when one is informed that theological discussions were forbidden by the members of the "invisible" college, who were supposedly under Puritan influence. Such an attitude marks them as single-minded Baconians rather than as Puritans. Neither in her analysis of the scientists' backgrounds nor in her statement of their attitudes did Stimson show that

[2] John Wilkins (1614–1672) was a clergyman and scientist who helped found the Royal Society. He became bishop of Chester in 1668. [Editor's note.]

Puritanism in any strict sense was a motive force in the rise of science.

Stimson's contribution was to raise in detail the question of the origins of the mid-XVIIth century interest in science. Her answer was unconvincing, but she did focus attention on the key period and some of its important characteristics and problems. At the same time two major works were being written on the subject: Jones' *Ancients and Moderns* and Merton's "Science, Technology and Society in Seventeenth Century England." Though both reiterated Stimson's emphasis on Puritanism, they did so for different reasons.

Jones' method was to examine the literature of the period, but this approach rested on shaky foundations. The opinions of some contemporaries, who saw or revealed connections between Puritanism and science, are possibly significant, but not in themselves conclusive. The fundamental weakness of Jones' position, however, became evident when he, like Stimson, attempted to answer the crucial question of whether there was anything inherent in the outlook of a Puritan that would turn him to science. For this a clear definition of "Puritanism" would appear indispensable, but Jones gave no definitions, only fragmentary, loose characterizations. The resulting image of Puritanism was too generously inclusive to be really useful in explaining interest in science. Terms other than Puritanism would frequently be more accurate or meaningful in a description of some of the attitudes discussed by Jones. Even if a man was a Puritan, some of his opinions may well have owed their origin to influences other than his religious beliefs.

It was the serious Baconian, and not the Puritan with his love of interminable sermons and learned preachers, who had the "distrust of language and hatred of words" which Jones regarded as "a unique characteristic of early modern science." It is also doubtful whether Puritans were "public-spirited and humanitarian," considering their stress on the individual and their attitude towards the poor, or whether they were "materialistic." Of the latter characteristic Jones was firmly enough convinced to state that "certainly, no part of the population was more interested in the increase of wealth and the improvement of their material welfare than the 'godly men'." Such certainty might be qualified by the typically Puritan stand taken by Cromwell when he disregarded trade interests in the war against

Spain, or by the existence of men such as Sir Thomas Smythe, Lionel Cranfield and the Duke of Buckingham,[3] who were neither Puritan nor godly, and whose interest in the improvement of their material welfare a contemporary Puritan would have found it difficult to exceed. Jones also suggested that the Puritans approved of activity of the mind only when associated "with physical energy or material objects." Given these conditions few preachers could have met with their approval. Furthermore, the attack on the Ancients was certainly not essentially a Puritan trait. Nor were anti-authoritarian and democratic ideals inherent in Puritanism: the Bible, the primitive Church or lay elders were the new authority, while ideas of predestination and the rule of saints were hardly conducive to democracy. Here Jones seems to have mistaken the revolutionary for the Puritan. Similarly, it was the Baconian rather than the Puritan who preferred artisans to scholars. In any case, this last characteristic and a democratic outlook would surely have tended to retard, not stimulate, the growth of closed, learned societies. Jones undoubtedly revealed some of the motives and attitudes of XVIIth-century scientists. He noted intellectual forces which were active in this period, and which encouraged an interest in science, but he did not show that they were necessarily inherent in Puritanism. Nowhere was this better revealed than in his treatment of education. He realized that interest in education was an important stimulant to science, and he tried to relate it to Puritanism. Yet he noted that "it was the . . . belief that secular learning was essential to the ministry that aroused the resentment of the Puritans," who disliked "humane" learning and "heathenish philosophy." This attitude was the reason why some among the extreme Puritans disliked the Universities. Jones regarded as "saner" men those who, on the contrary, wanted to "banish" Divinity. The latter, of course, were supporters of science, but surely the former were the uncompromising and therefore true Puritans. Thomas Hall and Edward Leigh, who attacked John Webster for advocating science, are clear examples of Puritans whose interest in education was not necessarily a stimulus to science.[4] A Puritan certainly tended to separate divine and secular

[3] Sir Thomas Smythe (1558?–1625) was the first governor of the East India Company and an active supporter of other mercantile and exploring ventures. Lionel Cranfield, 1st Earl of Middlesex (1575–1645) was a merchant and administrator under James I; he ultimately rose to the office of Lord Treasurer. The Duke of Buckingham (George Villiers) (1592–1628) was an important adviser to James I and Charles I, playing an especially crucial role in foreign affairs. [Editor's note.]

The Early Modern Era

learning, but he did so entirely to the advantage of the former. As the Ejectors demonstrated, piety came far ahead of learning, and Propagation of the Gospel long before the spread of science. Without reference to a solid definition or to religious aims, a typical Puritan attitude towards education cannot be found. Neither the suspicion of learning shown by some extremists, nor Webster's enthusiasm for science which led to an attack on the Universities, was representative of the whole movement. Webster may have represented the Barebones Parliament,[5] but that was a body which was hardly representative of Puritanism.

Jones was more persuasive when he suggested that educational developments were a factor in the rise of science. Where he failed to convince was in the attempt to show that there was anything essentially Puritan in the interest in education. The reason for this interest is most important for an explanation of the rise of science, but Jones neither identified the motives for the educational reforms, nor showed that such motives could be found in Puritanism. He also missed the full significance of the difference between the men who were concerned with education and many of the scientists who, as he himself noted, were "less interested in the teaching of the method than in its application to natural phenomena"—a characteristic fully confirmed by the aims of the Royal Society. This difference shows quite clearly that those whose interests helped to promote science did not necessarily have the same aims as the scientists.

To expect the term Puritanism to serve as the origin of attitudes as diverse as those which Jones discussed is to expect too much. For it becomes too loose, general and vague a term to have much value, and can help only when it is specific and rigidly defined. If as a result it does not cover all the features, then other terms must be employed before a full assessment of its importance can be made. However, Jones made a real contribution to the problem by pointing out features of the period, no-

tably the interest in education, which were highly conducive to the rise of science. Moreover, in seeking the origins of these features he was attempting to answer an important question. If his own answer was too simple or too inclusive, he nonetheless helped to point the way towards a more convincing assessment.

Merton presented the fullest and soundest argument for connecting Puritanism and science. More than a third of his major study was devoted to a demonstration of their compatibility. Whatever the shortcomings of his more positive claims, he clearly established, as did Stimson and Jones, that at least Puritanism and an interest in science were not mutually exclusive. But the real goal was a demonstrable positive link between the two phenomena. This link Merton sought in the Puritan system of values which, he suggested, encouraged an attitude favourable towards experimental science. Such an attitude helped to make the study of science socially acceptable and was therefore an important factor in the growth of interest in the subject. Merton's was an interesting treatment owing much to the Weber thesis, and he was also exceptional among the students of this problem in that he was very thorough when laying the foundation for his views.

He began with an elaborate numerical analysis of the fluctuations of interest in science during the XVIIth century. However, the evidence he used for his exhaustive and precise figures—the entries in the *Dictionary of National Biography*—may have been only the reflection of scholarly opinion. The entries were not necessarily independent and conclusive testimony for national trends, nor were the compilers of the *Dictionary* necessarily able to avoid including more scientists than before for a period known as a great age in English science. Scholarly opinion, therefore, may not have prevented emphases which, instead of corroborating, were actually responsible for Merton's figures. Preconceptions could have created variations of emphasis within the field of science just as easily as between science and, say, politics. Merton noted only the possibility of the latter effect. Consequently his conclusion, that there was a steady rise of interest in science till the middle of the century and a slow decline thereafter, confirmed and reflected but did not improve the generally accepted picture. His general outline was accurate, but the proof was open to question, and not all of the details were established. Interest may well have been at a height

[4] Thomas Hall (1610–1665) was a minister of Presbyterian learnings who wrote a considerable number of religious tracts. Edward Leigh (1602–1671) was a Puritan theologian who supported the Parliamentary cause during the Civil War. John Webster (1610–1682) was a Puritan writer, teacher, and physician who attacked university education in his day. [Editor's note.]

[5] The Parliament appointed by Cromwell after he dismissed the Rump of the Long Parliament in 1653, so named because of Praise-God Barebone, whose name was first in the list of members. [Editor's note.]

The Nominalist Approach

after 1640, but its growth was probably not as great or as rapid as he suggested. The rise of interest seems to have started some time before 1600, a possibility that Merton discounted by implication with minimal figures for 1601–1605.

Despite his thoroughness Merton, like Stimson and Jones, was hampered by an inadequate definition of Puritanism. Rather than starting with a full definition which could at least qualify judgments about the Puritan's attitude to life, Merton attacked the problem from another direction. In greater detail, but basically in the same fashion as Stimson and Jones, he listed supposedly Puritan attitudes that encouraged interest in science. The criterion for his choice seemed to be whether the attitude would help science, not whether it could be identified as something essentially Puritan. In other words, he approached the problem from the point of view of science, not of Puritanism. As a result, although he, too, described various influences which encouraged the rise of science, he could not establish their origin in Puritanism. Once again this pliable term covered too easily what some Puritans might even have considered a multitude of sins.

Instead of a definition, Merton chose the writings of one man, Richard Baxter, as the main source for his decription of the Puritan ethos. In so doing, he was following an honoured tradition, but it was a doubtful choice for two major reasons. First, Baxter lived and was influential rather late to be considered good evidence for the attitudes that formed men's minds when the founders of the Royal Society were young. Puritanism was a complex of ideas in constant flux, and in the search for basic attitudes an influential forerunner, such as Cartwright,[6] might have been a better choice than an influential contemporary.

Second, the choice was based on the assumption that Puritans were united by a "substantially identical nucleus of religious and ethical convictions." This was certainly true of religious convictions, as has been indicated by the definition proposed at the outset of this essay. But the social ethos described by Merton was not a self-evident consequence of these religious beliefs. Unless the religious nature of the movement is recognized as its basis, any isolation of the social implications of Puritanism will

tend to be arbitrary and distorted. For the materialism or utilitarianism of a Puritan was only a secondary feature of his attitude to life, and was probably tempered by long hours spent with his Bible or in Church. This alone would severely qualify the simple statement that Puritanism "actually imposed obligations of intense concentration on secular activity," while the mystic tendencies of the movement would balance its supposed "emphasis on experience and reason as bases for action and belief." Such qualifications did not emerge from Merton's treatment because he used as the basis of his presentation the ideas of only one, supposedly "typical" Puritan. Yet Baxter, as J. W. Allen noted, was "an Episcopalian," a minister of the Church of England after 1638, who "found no difficulty in conforming in almost all respects," and "a royalist, at least in theory" after 1649. If there was a social ethos common to all Puritans, then it must be found by a thorough examination of Puritan beliefs. The ideas of one man, and of Baxter in particular, are not sufficient basis for general conclusions.

It cannot be stressed too often that, in dealing with a phenomenon as complex as Puritanism, no one aspect can be treated without reference to the whole. The same is true of the "typical" Puritan, and it is illuminating to enquire as to exactly what Baxter considered "profitable." Allen suggested a convincing answer: "It was that only that seemed to tend to the salvation of himself and others. What profits is preoccupation with the next world, study of God's Word, effort for the enlightenment of souls in darkness, avoidance . . . of even the appearance of frivolity (where does Wilkins' talking statue fit in here?), faith and the love of God, sorrow for sin and effort to do better. Practically everything else, it seems, was to him unprofitable or worse." Against this background a social ethos must be placed. To take one example, the belief in progress may have helped the growth of science, but before it is labelled as a Puritan concept it should be reconciled with the Puritan's deep conviction of the futility of this world. Belief in progress was a characteristic common to all Baconians, but not to all Puritans. In other words, some of the attitudes noted by Merton were attributed too easily to the influence of Puritanism.

Merton also suggested that "the sciences became the foci of social interest" after the Restoration, when "the full import of the Puritan ethic manifested itself." Rather than the ethos of a largely discred-

[6] Thomas Cartwright (1535–1603) was a Puritan theologian and educator who carried on a vigorous attack against the Elizabethan Church of England. [Editor's note.]

The Early Modern Era

ited and unpopular movement, it was Charles II's patronage, the fame of the scientists and the interest of the virtuosi that now spread the interest in science. As we shall see, developments between 1640 and 1660 were undoubtedly vital, and it was certainly helpful that devout men could regard science as the search for God in Nature, but Puritanism and its ethic did not generate powerful social forces after 1660. The virtuosi, whom Merton chose to exemplify the shift to science, were usually swayed, even during the Interregnum, by an outlook very unlike that which resulted from Puritan beliefs. The true virtuosi sought knowledge for its own sake or for delight, and they were "never devoted to utilitarian ends." Theirs was a snobbish aristocratic movement, and its historian did not note any Puritan attitudes among its causes or motives. Seeking God in Nature was to these men at best "the common *apologia* for natural philosophy," and they were far more interested in His ingenuity than His wisdom. If the importance of Puritanism in the rise of science is to be found, then it must be sought among obvious Puritans in the vital period 1640–1660. It did have importance for later developments, such as the growth of the Dissenting Academies, but this must be clearly distinguished as a second phenomenon. As so often in the discussions of this problem it is the presentation or the method, not the idea itself, which is an easy prey for criticism.

One final assumption made by Merton requires examination. He stated quite simply that "Puritan principles undoubtedly represent to some extent an accommodation to the current scientific and intellectual advance . . . but to dismiss the relationship between Puritanism and science with this formula would indeed be superficial." Indeed, it may be, but further explanation is needed. In this and another place Merton merely rejected the view contrary to his own with a counter-claim. Nowhere did he attempt to prove his basic contention, "that religious convictions . . . . (change as) the outcome of inherent tendencies which are gradually realized in the course of time." The opposite view, that they "change only through external pressures," is not *a priori* "a grievous error" or a "fundamental shortcoming." In fact, it seems to be a fairly sound explanation of why the ethic was not there in Calvin, yet was supposedly there in Baxter. Calvinist theology could have approved as easily of the outlook of a mystic as of bourgeois or scientific attitudes: no inherent reason determined the outcome. Nor, for instance, was the doctrine of predestination any

more similar or reassuring to the scientist's belief in immutable laws than the Catholic belief in a precise, unvarying dose of purgatory for a given sin. The more open approval of science that can be attributed to Puritanism after 1640 seems far more the result of circumstances than of inherent tendencies.

Moreover, and this is the crux of the whole problem, it seems impossible to prove that religious sanctions preceded an individual's interest in science. Some scientists, such as Boyle, seem to have been genuinely seeking the greater glory of God. But this conscious association of religion with science rarely admits of proof, and it was often merely a pious formality. Frequently, as with the virtuosi, religion provided an apologia or a sanction, but not a motive. It was important to have a religion which could perform at least this negative service, but it is doubtful whether only Puritanism would have served. Merton himself noted that Sir Francis Bacon regarded science as the glorification of God and for the "relief of man's estate." Rather than seeing this as a link with Bacon's Puritan mother, this might be considered as evidence that a non-Puritan could also find these sanctions. Perhaps the word to be stressed is one that Merton himself used when he said that science was "*congenial* to Puritan tastes." To avoid the implication that Puritanism was therefore the motivating force, it might be more accurate to say that some Puritan tastes were congenial to scientists. . . .

The contribution of the Stimson-Jones-Merton thesis has been to isolate the attitudes which favoured science in England in the XVIIth century, and to give Puritanism at least a place in the story. This place is perhaps not the one they would have assigned, but all credit is due to them for drawing attention to the problem. If a "spirit" is to be given any part, however, then it must be the spirit of greater intellectual curiosity and awareness, a sort of "Renaissance" outlook, that was manifest in England from the late XVIth century, and whose outward signs could be seen in voyages of discovery and the first colonial ventures. This in turn was an expression of England's growing wealth and strength. Puritanism itself did not stimulate scientific activity. At most, a number of individual Puritans provided the important sanction of religion, and also incidentally encouraged scientific studies through their interest in educational reform, but even in education their main concern remained with matters of religion. If direct links are to be found anywhere, they are in the sanctions and

The Nominalist Approach

the reform of education. But even here the connections are tenuous, for they were restricted to the thought of only a few Puritans, who had an intellectual rather than a Puritan interest in new ideas in a time of revolution.

In the final reckoning, the Puritans were important because they led a twenty-year revolution, during which their benign approval, acquiescence and occasional but hardly conscious encouragement helped to spread more quickly the growing interest in science. Puritanism cannot be regarded as a main factor or a tangible cause. Yet it would be hard to deny that its indirect help played a part of considerable importance in the developments of the time. Without this encouragement and patronage the situation would probably not have been ripe for the foundation of the Royal Society until well past 1660.

In conclusion, one final effect of Puritanism's espousal of science might be noted. The Restoration unleashed a tremendous reaction against the Interregnum, the way of life it had promoted, and many of its ideals. Styles of literature, art, and living changed almost overnight. Among other results was the return of the Laudian spirit to the Universities. The Puritans' incidental approval of science and the appointments given to scientists during the Interregnum now proved to be a disadvantage. For the Universities, in reaction to the interference of the Interregnum government, returned to the pre-revolutionary situation in an attitude of determined conservatism. Educational reforms, both in theory and practice, were doomed. They were tainted, as surely as the Major-Generals, by the stigma of revolution. Interest in scientific studies was therefore greatly weakened. Almost two centuries were to pass before science could recover its full stature in the Universities and the English "Establishment." In the meantime another dreaded revolution, this time in France, further delayed the recovery because it also was associated with scientific ideals.

The section of English society for which the stigma was inoperative was, of course, the nonconformist community, which was directly descended from the Puritans. Excluded from the Universities, the non-conformists established their own Academies, where the study of science continued its natural development. From these institutions came the new achievements in science, and it was there that in the XVIIIth and early XIXth centuries many of England's leading scientists, such as Priestley and Dalton, taught. Cavendish, Davy, Faraday, Herschel and Rumford[7] were also among the great scientists who worked outside the Universities.

Meanwhile the Universities and the Royal Society passed through a dismal period. After the impetus that had been generated before 1660 died away, scientific studies and achievements lost their prominence. There were various reasons for the decline: England's XVIIIth-century complacency, the overawing stature of Newton, the changed interests of the virtuosi, and many more. But the reaction after the Restoration was among the most effective hindrances to the further rise of science in England after the age of Newton. Whether the apathy of the Universities and the Royal Society really harmed the development of science, since an alternative patron was found in the dissenting community, is open to question. What cannot be doubted is that the alienation of scientific study from the central academic tradition was in no small measure due to the reaction of the Restoration against the ideals of the revolutionaries. The alternative patronage provided by the Dissenting Academies in the two succeeding centuries was the final heritage of the Puritans' incidental approval of science during the years of the Great Rebellion.

[7] Joseph Priestley (1733–1804) was a chemist who carried on fundamental investigations concerning electricity and gases. John Dalton (1766–1844) was also a chemist and a physicist, significant for his work with gases and his statements on atomic theory. Henry Cavendish (1731–1810) was a chemist and physicist who did important experimentation with gases and electricity. Sir Humphry Davy (1778–1829) was a chemist who worked with gases. Michael Faraday (1791–1867) was a chemist and a physicist who made fundamental discoveries concerning electricity. Sir William Herschel (1738–1822) was an astronomer whose discoveries played an important role in establishing the scientific study of the stars. Benjamin Thompson, Count Rumford (1753–1814), was an American-born physicist who was a Loyalist during the American Revolution. He spent most of his life thereafter in Bavaria where he promoted scientific study and conducted experiments in heating and lighting. [Editor's note.]

The Early Modern Era

A. RUPERT HALL

THE MERTON THESIS EXAMINED

A. Rupert Hall, the professor of the History of Science at London's Imperial College of Science and Technology, poses this searching question: Was the growth of the scientific spirit in seventeenth-century England due to the internal logic of the sciences or to external forces? In other words, was its development *sui generis,*— what the sociologists call "inner directed"? Or was its development due to its extraordinary sensitivity to outside forces such as the royal government, the aristocracy, the Anglican church, or the sectarians both in- and outside of the Anglican Settlement? As a corollary to the last question, he asks: if science in the seventeenth century was peculiarly sensitive to outside influences, can we then say that Protestantism, as pictured by Professor Merton and others, encouraged "science in a greater degree than Catholicism"? In this last question Professor Hall implies a negative restatement of the Weberian thesis of the Protestant Ethic, *viz.,* that resurgent Catholicism of the Counter-Reformation did as much to inhibit science as Protestantism did to encourage it.

A quarter of a century ago a brilliant young scholar, who has recently been dignified by the *New Yorker* as "Mr Sociology," published a monograph with the title "Science, technology and society in seventeenth-century England." In this thorough, well-argued and closely written study Robert K. Merton presented with a wealth of documentary evidence the classical instance of the historical analysis of science as a social phenomenon. Merton conceived of science as a cultural artefact, a manifestation of intellectual energy that is stimulated, checked or modified by the structure, beliefs and aspirations of the society with which this scientific activity is associated. Put thus crudely the idea seems almost a truism; of course no one in writing the history of science would ever divorce it completely from society's beliefs and structure. Merton's monograph was far from being an exercise in the obvious, however, nor were the historiographical themes with which it was concerned trivial. It was Merton's contention that the historical study of a past society can provide principles of historical explanation which are complementary to, if they do not replace, those offered by the historian of science. Particularly, sociological history provides (if I follow Merton's view

of 1938 correctly) principles sufficing to explain that crucial event, the scientific revolution of the seventeenth century, even though the provision of such an explanation was not Merton's chief or explicit concern. In fact Merton may be said to have insisted that the major displacements in science do require sociological explanations.

Merton's challenge was not at once accepted and his study was greeted rather with the admiration it deserved than with argument or criticism. Looking back one can see why: Merton's work was the culmination of an established tradition, not the beginning of a new one. To say that it aroused no great astonishment does not detract from its importance, which lay in making a strong case for the sociological explanation in one country at one time. As Merton himself generously acknowledged, his thesis was not (in broad terms) singular to himself. But Merton could justly regard himself as offering clear ideas backed by massive evidence, where his predecessors had brought forward little more than intuitions.

A current of historiography that favoured "externalist" explanations — ones deriving from the general

From A. Rupert Hall, "Merton Revisited or Science and Society in the Seventeenth Century," *History of Science,* II (1963), 1–15. Reprinted by permission of *History of Science.*

cultural, economic and social state of a nation or community of nations — ran strongly in the nineteen twenties and thirties. It derived its ultimate strength from two majestic Victorian conceptions: Marx's observation that the character of a society is largely determined by its economy, together with the compatible though distinct discovery of the anthropologists that "culture" is a unity. Adding these two ideas together, one is led to conclude that a man's thoughts on any one topic — say, celestial mechanics — are not independent of his thoughts on all other topics, nor of the economic state of the society in which he lives. So far, if we allow that "not independent of" is by no means equivalent to "causally determined by," we have a historiographical notion that is, today, hardly open to dispute. Some thirty years ago, however, historians were more apt to regard the case as one of causal determinism and to suppose that any correlation between an intellectual event A and a social event B could be understood as justifying the view that B in some sense "caused" A, or at least was a necessary condition for the occurrence of A. Such interpretations of historical occurrences in the less fundamental realms of politics, religion and so on by reference to other phenomena in the more fundamental realms of economics seemed to promise escape from the general mistiness and subjectivism of historical explanation.

Social explanations in history appeared objective and certain because they avoid emphasis on individuality and the hazardous significance of the individual. Authoritative models were provided by (for example) Max Weber and R. H. Tawney, whose *Religion and the rise of Capitalism* was published in 1926. Merton refers to the latter five times; remarking that "It is misleading to assume that [the] foci of scientific interest are exclusively due to the intrinsic developments within the various sciences," he credits to Max Weber the observation that scientists commonly select for treatment problems which are vitally linked with the dominant values and interests of the day. . . .

There is no need now to go back beyond Merton's monograph. "Science, technology and society in the seventeenth-century England" is both more complete and more sophisticated than any of its precursors. Merton saw the problem he proposed to himself as consisting of two parts: (1) why did "scientific development in England become especially marked about the middle of the seventeenth century"? and (2) "why was there a strong preponderance of in-

terest, among those concerned, in the physical sciences"? That each part of the problem was real — that is, that the characteristic to be investigated was genuine — Merton established by quite elaborate statistical analyses, as well as by the independent testimony of historians of science.

To each part of the problem Merton devoted a distinct social explanation. In order to account for the increase of interest in science that took place in England, he argued that a distinct change in values associated with Puritanism favoured science; to account for the partiality of this interest towards physical science he instanced the problems of engineering, navigation, warfare and so forth that could be solved by means of physical science. I shall consider each of these explanations in turn, and then the general issue of the balance between social and other forms of explanation in the history of science.

I. SCIENCE AND THE PURITAN ETHIC

The argument here closely parallels Tawney's in *Religion and the rise of Capitalism*. Not only (according to Merton and others) did Puritanism — or rather not the Puritan theology but the Puritan spirit — encourage scientific investigation, but it stimulated precisely that kind of scientific inquiry that flourished most in England:

Experiment was the scientific expression of the practical, active and methodical bents of the Puritan. This is not to say, of course, that experiment was derived in any sense from Puritanism. But it serves to account for the ardent support of the new experimental science by those who had their eyes turned towards the other world and their feet firmly planted on this.

That Boyle and many others had justified their work in science as a kind of practical divine service — it glorified God's creation in men's eyes, and so forth — seemed at least to indicate a strong link between science and religion, even though (as Merton of course was aware) neither Bacon the father of empiricism, nor Boyle the Christian virtuoso, was himself a Puritan in any meaningful sense of that term. Somewhat more cogently, Merton pointed to a strong Puritan bias among the early Fellows of the Royal Society and to the explicit association of the Society with Puritanism urged by the Society's detractors. He also quoted, as further direct evidence of the Puritan spur to science, a passage

The Early Modern Era

from Richard Baxter's *Christian directory* written in 1664–5:

the very exercise of love to God and man, and of a heavenly mind and holy life, hath a sensible pleasure in itself, and delighteth the man who is so employed. . . . What delight had the inventors of the sea-chart and magnetic attraction, and of printing, and of guns, in their inventions! What pleasure had Galileo in his telescopes, in finding out the inequalities and shady parts of the moon, the Medicean planets [etc.]. . . .

On the other hand, Merton cited some evidence that the compatibility of science with those ideas of religion and virtue that he associated with Puritanism was not universal. Not to stress the Middle Ages, which he regarded as essentially antipathetic to science, he instanced the passivity or quietism associated with the teachings of the Jansenists. However, Merton was careful not to make the causal inference between science and religion too strong: particular discoveries are not, he declared, to be "directly attributed to the sanction of science by religion," while the peculiar distinction of Puritanism was that it made science "socially acceptable . . . a laudable rather than an unsavoury occupation" so that more men were enticed into it.

This summary does not do justice to Merton's qualifications and reservations any more than it does to the impressive amount of evidence he collected; nevertheless, a reader today will be bound to urge certain questions. Seeking to test the significance of the Puritan ethic, it will strike him that this is notably irrelevant to the efflorescence of medical science in sixteenth-century Italy, and no less to the successes of that brilliant group in France which preceded the Royal Society by a few years. Not only were Gassendi, Mersenne, Descartes, Pascal, Roberval, Bouillaud[1] and so on pious Catholics; several of them were priests. Even in England, it is trivially obvious that whatever the importance of events in the Puritan 1640s and 1650s, science actually flourished and achieved something under the roy-

[1] René Descartes and Blaise Pascal need no identification. Pierre Gassendi (1592–1655) was an influential French mathematician and philosopher who advocated the empirical method and severely attacked Aristotelanism. Marin Mersenne (1588–1648) was a French mathematician and theologian who was a close friend and defender of Descartes. Gilles Personne de Roberval (1602–1675) was a mathematician who taught for many years at the Collège de France. It is not exactly clear to whom the author is referring in the case of Bouillaud; the famous physician, Jean-Baptiste Bouillaud (1796–1881) seems too late to fit the case under discussion. More likely the reference is to Ismael Bouillaud (1605–1694), who was an astronomer of some note and a prolific writer on science. [Editor's note.]

alist, Anglican reaction from 1660 onwards. Clearly, the most that can be said is that in England (and some other Protestant countries) the ascendancy of a markedly radical wing of the faith seems to be linked with scientific vigour; the link is obviously not *essential* to science as such, for counter-instances are too numerous; it is therefore doubtful whether the statements about the deep, intrinsic bonds between the spirit of Puritanism and the spirit of science can be considered reliable. At least, one cannot give credit to them upon a simple inductive basis, for when one is contemplating the issue of principle the effect of Urban VIII's views upon (say) Galileo and Descartes is of no greater weight than the equally hostile opinions of Luther and Melancthon.

Iteration and exemplification cannot, in any case, make the proposition "many scientists are Protestants" equivalent to the statement "men are scientists because they are Protestants." If induction by enumeration fails, as it must in this instance, what permits the inference that the association of science and Protestantism is more than a temporal correlation? Not the argument that science is justified by religion in Puritan eyes: for Catholics and Anglicans use this justification also. In the presentation of *laborare est orare* Puritanism had some polemical advantages, certainly, but as Merton admitted the basic ideas were taken by Puritans from the Catholic tradition and they were, indeed, employed by such Catholic apologists of science as Gassendi and Malebranche. Conversely, there were extreme Protestant sects such as the Quakers who were as quietist as the Jansenists: in seventeenth-century religion it is difficult to find any characteristic of one party that does not have a mirror-image in the other. . . .

For reasons that will be considered later there has been during recent years little discussion of the role of religion in the scientific revolution. In 1958 one historian, R. S. Westfall, expressed himself cautiously:

The influence of Protestantism on natural science is nebulous and difficult to determine. It can be suggested, however, that Protestantism provided an atmosphere more conducive to scientific investigation as such than was Catholicism; perhaps also Protestantism was more conducive to the acceptance of the peculiar mechanical conception of nature which accompanied early modern science and to its reconciliation with religious beliefs.

Since development of this point lay outside the scope of Westfall's book he did not pursue the question of the causal relation further, and perhaps would be understood as indicating no more than a correlation between science and Puritanism in seventeenth-century England. His comment is of interest, however, in suggesting that extension of the question to a general debate between Catholic and Protestant that had been discussed some ten years earlier, and indeed by Merton. For it is not a great step from the idea of the "Puritan spur" to science in England to the view that Protestantism (whose scientific martyrs are somewhat less notorious than Bruno and Galileo) has invariably encouraged science in greater measure than Catholicism. Thus Merton:

Uniformly, then available statistics indicate the undue [i.e. greater than random] tendency, on the basis of proportion in the total population, of Protestants to turn to scientific and technologic studies. . . . What are the relevant frequencies of Protestants and Catholics among scientists? [With reservations], proportionately speaking, Protestants constitute an overwhelming majority of the leading scientists.

The causal inference which Merton does not draw here is firmly made by Jean Pelseneer: "nous croyons avoir établi le rôle primordial de la Reforme dans la génèse de la science moderne." [We believe that we have established the primary role of the Reformation in the genesis of modern science.] Again, in a general discussion of the history of the social relations of science S. Lilley warmly endorsed Merton's conclusions, describing the latter's monograph as "a direct and scientific discussion of cause and effect," from which it followed that "Puritanism in England in the latter part of the seventeenth century provided an ethic which encouraged the pursuit of science." Somewhat weakening his position Lilley then endorsed Merton's refusal to describe Puritanism as the "ultimate cause" of the scientific movement in England, and introduced a curious escape-clause: "Whatever the cause it could have been effective in that period only if it had found a religious means of expression." Now, if this means anything serious, it is that religion was but a "means of expression" for some effective cause (which was not Merton's view); that is to say—since any effective cause has ex hypothesi a religious expression—the analysis of religious expressions can tell us nothing about the nature of the true cause. For Merton and other Protestant exponents, however, Puritanism was if not a cause of the scientific revolution in England a necessary concomitant of it, and this was determined by considering the the religious expression.

If Lilley had stated more plainly that certain forms of religious expression and some of the language used about science in the seventeenth century were related products having a common intellectual parentage he would have made an important point, and one whose recognition has contributed to the failure of interest in the Puritan or Protestant explanation of science. The weakness was there from the first in (for example) the reluctance of Merton to declare precisely what the relation between religion and science was. If Puritanism was not the "ultimate cause" of (say) the *Principia*, was it a cause? Was the religious encouragement of science the decisive factor or not? If it was not, then the fact that men are Catholic or Protestant is about as significant in the history of science as whether they wear breeches or trousers. But if Puritanism or Protestantism made the decisive difference—as Pelseneer maintains— then massive proof and argument is required in demonstration. That, as Westfall pointed out, has still not been provided.

2. SCIENCE AND TECHNOLOGY

Merton linked the two parts of his sociological study with these words:

if this congeniality of the Puritan and the scientific temper partly explains the increased tempo of scientific activity during the latter seventeenth century, by no means does it account for the particular foci of scientific and technologic investigation. . . . Was the choice of problems a wholly personal concern, completely unrelated to the sociocultural background? Or was this selection significantly limited and guided by social forces?

Once more, Merton made a statistical analysis—this time of Birch's *History of the Royal Society*—in order to display the character of scientific work; he assigned about 40 per cent of it to the category of "pure science" and the greater part of the rest to the fields of sea-transport, mining and military technology. After further strengthening his case by a review of the activities and attitudes of individual scientists, Merton concluded that the seventeenth-century English scientists' choice of problem was much influenced by socio-economic considerations. Yet he was clearly far from supposing that science was *determined* by outside pressures, as Hessen had suggested, and lately he has made this point clearer still; for Merton technological considerations are not *all*, but neither are they *nothing*.

This opinion is unexceptionable. No one can deny that conceptual science, let alone experimental science, is shaped by the technological equipment of the time in some measure; but the interesting question is: how much and in what way? Is science (as it were) an unconscious as well as a conscious instrument of society, or is it not? To say merely, for example, that X was a scientist and X was also interested in practical problems of technology, is not really to tell us very much; the bare information certainly permits no inference about the relation between X's scientific and technological interests. If X is the Royal Society as depicted in Birch's *History*, Merton's analysis will tell us that many Fellows were more interested in craft problems than in scientific ones; that a Baconian view of the utility of science was commonplace; and that men had a naive view of the relationship between pure science and the mastery of nature. Equally, the observation of Walter Houghton:

it was primarily the acquisitive temper of the middle-class, building on the heritage of Bacon and the social reformers, that directed the virtuosi to the History of Trades

is readily justifiable: Houghton has not made the mistake of identifying science with either the concerns of the virtuosi or social reform. But from such information, valuable and interesting as it is, we do not learn what seventeenth-century *science* was, nor does it serve to answer Merton's question: why were people more interested in physics than in biology? Nor does it answer Hessen's. Such inquiries tell us nothing about Boyle, or Hooke, or Newton, that is significant to consideration of their work as scientists. It is really of little benefit to an understanding of the scientific revolution from Galileo to Newton that quite a lot of men were interested in ships, cabbages, and sealing-wax.

As with the religious issue, the matter must be clearly and definitely put if it is to have significance. When and in what circumstances is one entitled to infer that a particular piece of scientific work was done for some extra-scientific reason? Those who maintain that often or in some telling way this is the case should lay down their principles of inference. To consider a recent example: by 1940 many physicists knew that the release of nuclear energy was possible, and many worked on the problem during subsequent years. Does this mean—by inference—that all physicists working in atomic physics before 1940 did so because they believed that their work would lead to the technological use of nuclear energy? Of course not. What is the difference when Newton wrote in the scholium to Proposition XXXIV of Book II of the *Principia*: "This proposition I conceive may be of use in the building of ships"? Was Newton's interest in physics conditioned by the needs (in applied hydrodynamics) of the society in which he lived? It is trivially obvious that Newton could not have written these words if he had been unaware of things called ships, and indeed could not have written the *Principia* at all if he had not been aware of moving bodies, pendulums and so forth. It is perhaps a little more interesting that a mathematician should think such a remark worth making at a time when no master-shipwright employed mathematical theory or would have admitted the competence of a mathematical physicist to instruct him. Yet this statement of Newton's is quoted in a portion of Merton's monograph from which the conclusion is drawn:

In general, then, it may be said that the contemporary scientists, ranging from the indefatigable virtuoso Petty to the nonpareil Newton, definitely focused their attention upon technical tasks made prominent by problems of navigation and upon derivative scientific research.

To me, this makes Newton sound like a superior carpenter, cartographer, or compass-maker. . . . An analysis that confuses mathematical physics with mathematical technology in this way bewilders rather than assists the historian of science.

The question of economic influence has proved to be of far less interest in the last few years than it was in the nineteen thirties. Another major investigator of the sociology of science, Edgar Zilsel, was prevented by death from completing his work, which has never been further extended. Zilsel, whose main thesis it was that modern science originated in the injection of new ideas and ambitions from craft sources into the aridity of traditional scholarship, took a far more economically-determinist line than did Merton. This may be illustrated by one brief judgment upon Francis Bacon:

Manifestly, the idea of science we usually regard as "Baconian" is rooted in the requirements of early capitalistic economy and technology; its rudiments first appear in treatises of fifteenth-century craftsmen.

That is to say, Baconian science is the blind servant of economic purpose, of the capitalism whose requirements must be satisfied by appropriate intellectual manoeuvres. If this is so, then the scientist's sense of freedom, that he may choose to be either a Copernican or an Aristotelian for instance, is a mere illusion; society compels him to be progressive and to take the former alternative (which Bacon himself rejected!). So far as this view was related by Zilsel to Bacon specifically he was exaggerating a familiar emphasis on Bacon as the "philosopher of industrial science." That Bacon believed in the pursuit of science for its benefits to society there can be no doubt, just as there is also no doubt that he preferred luciferous to luctiferous experiments and regarded a reform of logic as the essential step towards sound science. Benjamin Farrington has expressed this utilitarian aspect of Bacon insistently but not unfairly; for example:

Bacon is not, like other scientists, working in a chosen field in the light of a long tradition. Rather he makes himself the herald of a revolution in the life of humanity, which he calls a birth of time.

What has been all too often forgotten (by the would-be friends as well as the enemies of Bacon) is that he was not so stupid as to suppose that a sound, verifiable science could be created merely by believing it to be desirable; one had to determine the intellectual structure upon which such a science could be framed.

In its crudest forms at any rate the socio-economic interpretation of the scientific revolution as an offshoot of rising capitalism and mercantile militarism has perished without comment. Its unilluminating conclusions rested on defective logic and improbable psychology; very often, as I myself have tried to reveal, the true situation is far too complicated to yield such simple generalisations as "mathematicians were inspired to seek solutions to gunners' problems." In fact the influence of the art of war on seventeenth-century physics was negligible though (remembering Merton's words) we must not say there was *no* such influence. Hence some of the strongest reasons for the decline of the economic hypothesis are well expressed in the words of one of the most distinguished of modern economic historians, John W. Nef:

If we examine the background of the intellectual revolution that is responsible for the industrial world in which we live today, we find little to support the view that modern science resulted from industrial progress in the north of Europe between the Reformation and the (English) Civil War. During these times of decisive change in rational procedures it was the mind itself, not economic institutions nor economic development, which called the new tunes and composed most of the variations which the greatest scientists were playing on them. The revolutionary scientific discoveries by Gilbert, Harvey, Galileo and Kepler, like the new mathematics of Descartes, Desargues, Fermat and Pascal, were of no immediate practical use. Freedom, rather than necessity, was the principal power behind the scientific revolution.

Thus, recent historians reverse the arrow of economic inference: social forms do not dominate mind; rather, in the long run, mind determines social forms.

3. THE ASCENDANCY OF THE INTELLECT

In 1939, one year after Merton's monograph, there appeared the *Etudes galiléennes* of Alexandre Koyré. No contributions to the history of science could be less alike. It is beside my purpose to develop the contrast, save by the obvious remark that as Merton summed up one epoch, that of the socio-economic historian, Koyré opened another, that of the intellectual historian. Of course Koyré was no more first in the field than Merton was; in their different ways Tannery, Duhem, Cassirer, Mach, Meyerson and Lovejoy had initiated the history of ideas long before. None of Koyré's predecessors, however, had begun that analysis of the scientific revolution as a phenomenon of intellectual history which Koyré has made peculiarly his own. Among the younger historians of science especially his has been the dominant influence through the last ten or fifteen years, and this influence has had a marked effect in withdrawing interest from externalist explanations; other factors have of course worked in the same direction.

Such externalist forms of historical explanation as the sociological tend to confine the intellectual development of science within rather narrow bounds; it is a fundamental hypothesis of this historiography that the gross character of the science of any epoch is shaped externally, the intellectual or internal structure of science effecting only the minutiae and technicalities. To summarise Merton's view, for instance:

short-time fluctuations of interest in mathematics are largely explicable in terms of the appearance of important contributions by individual mathematicians . . . the foci of interest within the general field are partially determined by the nature of the problems which have been explained or brought to light. [Further, the] conclusion that the minor, short-time fluctuations in scientific interest are primarily determined by the internal history of the science in question is borne out by other facts. [The influence of Gilbert and Harvey is discussed.] In a sense, then, the study of these short-time fluctuations would seem the province of the historian of science rather than that of the sociologist or student of culture.

Here, it is clear the "long-time" fluctuations are not assigned to the province of the historian of science. Such a view is consistent with a "ripeness of time" concept of discovery or originality: we cannot (according to this concept) attach any special significance to the work of Newton in 1687, Darwin in 1859, or Einstein in 1905 because the time was ripe on each occasion for the work and if Newton, Darwin or Einstein had not written as they did some one else (Hooke, Wallace) would have served the same function. Only in a shorthand way therefore did Newton and the others have a permanent influence on science. Merton did not teach this view, but he did write that

specific discoveries and inventions belong to the internal history of science and are largely independent of factors other than the purely scientific.

A true, but a curiously negative statement. Why should not the general development of (say) astronomy in the seventeenth century be "largely independent of factors other than the purely scientific" and not merely the discovery of a fifth satellite of Saturn? This latter opinion has indeed been adopted by those who have followed Koyré in opposing the endeavour to credit the strategy of the scientific revolution to nonscientific influences. In the *Etudes* Koyré himself renounced just that liaison between modern physical science and empiricism which was regarded as crucial in the early nineteen-thirties; he has rejected also the thesis that classical science is "active" in the way postulated by the Protestant historians. For Koyré and many others since—as earlier for Burtt—the scientific revolution is to be understood as a transformation of intellectual attitudes:

Aussi croyons-nous, que l'attitude intellectuelle de la science classique pourrait être caractérisée par ces deux moments, étroitement liés d'ailleurs: geometrisation de l'espace, et dissolution du Cosmos . . . cette attitude intellectuelle nous paraît avoir été le fruit d'une mutation décisive. . . . C'est qu'il s'agissait non pas de combattre des théories erronées, ou insuffisantes, mais de *transformer*

les cadres de l'intelligence elle-même. . . . [Thus we believe that the intellectual attitude of classical science could be characterized by these two thrusts, closely bound together in other respects: geometrization of space and dissolution of the Cosmos . . . that intellectual attitude appears to us to have been the fruit of a decisive mutation. . . . It was not a matter of combatting erroneous or insufficient theories, but of *transforming the framework of thought itself* . . .]

There is no suggestion here that the new intellectual attitude was generated by or dependent upon anything external to science, nor does Koyré ever contemplate such a thing. The intellectual change is one whose explanation must be sought in the history of the intellect; to this extent (and we need not pause now to expound all the obvious provisos about microscopes, X-rays, cyclotrons and so forth) the history of science is strictly analogous to the history of philosophy. It is no accident that Koyré himself is a philosopher, nor that an English philosopher-historian should have expressed in *The idea of Nature* a vision of the scientific revolution similar to his. When Collingwood wrote

the Renaissance philosophers enrolled themselves under the banner of Plato against the Aristotelians, until Galileo, the true father of modern science, restated the Pythagorean-Platonic standpoint in his own words by proclaiming that the book of nature is a book written by God in the language of mathematics

he asserted, as Koyré has asserted, that modern science is of its own intellectual right fundamental and absolute; it is not derivative from some other displacement in civilization such as the reformation or the rise of capitalism. The historians of religion have never claimed that the reformation "transformed the very structure of the intellect" and it would be indeed odd if someone holding this view of the transcendent significance of the scientific revolution should also consider it as a mere epiphenomenon. One who has written on the history of religion, Herbert Butterfield, put it no less strongly ten years later, declaring that the scientific revolution "outshines everything since the rise of Christianity and reduces the Renaissance and Reformation to the rank of mere episodes, mere internal displacements, within the system of medieval Christendom."

If modern science is the fruit of an intellectual mutation its genesis must be considered in relation to an intellectual tradition; to quote Butterfield once more, its sources stretch far "back in an unmistakably continuous line to a period much earlier" than the sixteenth century. Those who find the origins of science in the Puritan-capitalist complex, however, have no need for and see little value in the evidence for continuity in scientific thought. On the whole they have been empiricists rather than rationalists. Despite the scholarly researches of Duhem, Sudhoff, Little and many others, the Middle Ages did not get a good press from historians of science during the first two decades of this century; only after Sarton, Haskins, Thorndike and their generation had filled in many more details and suggested new interpretations did Duhem's thesis command widespread attention. . . .

. . . Most historians would nowadays emphasize the discontinuity between medieval and modern science much less strongly and in very different terms. Certainly dissent from Duhem's thesis does exist—that thesis has been firmly criticised by Anneliese Maier for instance—and some of the most effective of the intellectual historians, Koyré among them, are far from regarding the scientific revolution as fully prepared in the Middle Ages. Meanwhile, different forms of the case for continuity in dynamics, kinematics, optics, epistemology and so on have been prepared by Marshall Clagett, A. C. Crombie, E. A. Moody and J. H. Randall; even if their work is not considered conclusive in every respect it is far from being negligible. In fact the intellectual historians are by no means divided among themselves on the issue of continuity in the way that they, as a group, are divided from the socio-economic historians. All are agreed, for example, that early modern science was in some measure indebted to medieval science; and that if seventeenth century concepts are not identical with those of the fourteenth there is an intellectual connection between them.

Even without making a detailed review of the work of other historians of science active at the present time it is clear that the trend towards intellectual history is strong and universal. Since the journal Centaurus published in 1953 a special group of articles on the social relations of science no single article that can be judged to represent the sociological interpretation of history has appeared in that periodical, or Isis, Annals of science, Revue d'histoire des sciences, or the Archives internationales. There has been little discussion of the historiographical issue: indeed, it sometimes seems that the case for setting the development of scientific thought in its broader historical context is con-

demned before it is heard, though one knows from personal conversations that this is not neglected in pedagogic practice. Clearly, externalist explanations of the history of science have lost their interest as well as their interpretative capacity. One reason for this may be that such explanations tell us very little about science itself; about the reception of Newton's optical discoveries, or the significance of Galileo's ideas in mechanics, or about concepts of combustion and animal heat. Social and economic relations are rather concerned with the scientific movement than with science as a system of knowledge of nature (theoretical and practical); they help us to understand the public face of science and the public reaction to scientists; to evaluate the propaganda that scientists distribute about themselves, and occasionally—but only occasionally—to see why the subject of scientific discussion takes a new turn. But to understand the true contemporary significance of some piece of work in science, to explore its antecedents and effects, in other words to recreate critically the true historical situation, for this we must treat science as intellectual history, even experimental science. A sociologist like Merton understood this, of course; what he doubted was the significance of such intellectual history divorced from the social context which was, naturally, his main focus of interest.

Profoundly different historical points of view are involved. It is not enough to suggest, as Lilley modestly did, that there is a bit of truth in both of them so that

the development of science can be fully understood only if the internal and external types of influence are considered together and in their mutual interaction.

(The suggestion that the very stuff of science, that which it is at any moment, should ever be considered as an internal influence, is rather curious.) To suppose that it is not worth while to take sides or that the determination of the historian's own attitude to the issue is not significant is to jeopardise the existence of the historiography of science as more than narration and chronicle. For example: how is the historian to conceive of science, before he undertakes to trace its development; is he to conceive it as above all a deep intellectual enterprise whose object it is to gain some comprehension of the cosmos in terms which are, in the last resort, philosophical? Or as an instruction-book for a bag of tricks by which men master natural resources and each other? Is a scientific theory a partial, temporally-limited vision of nature or a useful message printed on a little white card that pops out of a machine when the social animal presses the button — different cards for different buttons, of course? I have deliberately given an exaggerated emphasis to these rhetorical questions in order to indicate the violent imbalance between two points of view that one simply cannot ignore nor amalgamate. In the same way the historian's concept of the scientific revolution of the seventeenth century is historiographically dependent. One issue between the externalist and the internalist interpretation is this: was the beginning of modern science the outstanding feature of early modern civilisation, or must it yield in importance to others, such as the Reformation or the development of capitalism? Before 1940 most general historians and many historians of science would have adopted the latter position; since 1940 nearly all historians have adopted the former one. Why this change should have come about it is not hard to imagine.

By this I do not mean to suggest that the problems raised by the sociologists of science are obsolete; on the contrary, as some scientists like J. D. Bernal have been saying for a long time and many more are saying now, they are immensely real and direct at this moment. Consequently the historical evolution of this situation is of historical significance too, and I believe we shall return to its consideration when a certain revulsion from the treatment of scientists as puppets has been overcome when (if ever) we are less guiltily involved in the situation ourselves so that we can review it without passion, and when a fresh approach has been worked out. This will not, I imagine, take the form so much of a fusion between two opposite positions in the manner of the Hegelian dialectic, as the demarcation of their respective fields of application with some degree of accuracy. There may also develop a socio-techno-economic historiography whose study will be the gradual transformation of society by science and not (as too often in the past) the rapid transformation of Science by society. All this will require a fine analysis, a scrupulous drawing of distinctions and a careful avoidance (except under strict controls) of evidence drawn from subjective, propagandist and programmatic sources. A true sociology of science will deal with what actually happened and could happen, not with what men thought might happen or should happen.

RICHARD FOSTER JONES

INDIVIDUAL GENIUS AND THE ORIGINS OF SCIENCE

Richard Foster Jones's work on the quarrel between ancients and moderns was hailed as an epoch-making book when it appeared in 1920. As Majorie H. Nicholson said, it awakened the interest of an entire generation of scholars to the impact that scientific ideas had generally on the evolution of thought and specifically on the development of literary criticism. In 1936 Professor Jones continued his study of "the rise of the scientific movement" by publishing a detailed study of *The Ancients and Moderns*, from which the present selection is taken. As Jones says, he wishes to be "objectively historical, but if a thesis can be discovered [in my work], it is that Sir Francis Bacon bears the same relationship to the early scientific movement . . . as for example Karl Marx bears to the development of Communism. . . ." In other words Jones sees Bacon as the prophet and the "human center of the scientific movement of the seventeenth century." Jones thus espouses the great-man thesis, or what recent critics call the role of the individual genius in history.

. . . The present study strives to be objectively historical, but if a thesis can be discovered in it, it is that Sir Francis Bacon bears the same relationship to the [early scientific] movement . . . as for example, Karl Marx bears to the development of Communism, but, of course, to much better purpose. It is that type of relationship in which a leader becomes the human center of a movement, to whom men can feel and pay loyal allegiance in the spirit of discipleship. The encouragement and stimulation derived from this attitude is by no means a negligible factor in the development of science during the mid-seventeenth century, though obscured by more tangible evidences of Bacon's influence.

Sir Francis both expressed and molded his age. Before his scientific writings appeared, not only had significant discoveries been made, but also important elements of the movement itself had taken form, such as hostility to the authority of the ancients, and the importance of experiments, yet in England it was indeed moving slowly until he rang his bell, and as the century advances it assumes more and more a Baconian complexion. Some of the most influential ideas in the current of scientific thought are too uniquely his to render any other source credible. An outstanding example is his idea of the necessity of an universal natural history drawn from authentic records of the past as well as from contemporary observations and experiments, one wide enough indeed to cover all nature. Upon this material his inductive method was to be employed for the purpose of discovering the fundamental laws of nature, knowledge of which would enable men to use them, singly or in combination, to secure all the effects of which nature is capable. Bacon cheerily announced that this happy event would follow soon after the ages required for the compilation of his history. The unquestioning acceptance of this impossible idea by the best scientific thinkers of the day may be termed one of the marvels of history, which only Bacon was capable of bringing about. He inspired in his followers such complete confidence in his ideas that they were stimulated and incited to carry on experiments with an intensity hitherto unknown, so much so, in fact, that Sprat was moved to call his times "this age of experiments." It is hardly an exaggeration to say that the compilation of this history was the conscious goal of most of the scientific activities of the day.

Another unique element is the emphasis which Bacon placed upon experimentation, for the latter, though by no means new, had never been accorded the absolute authority and exclusive role upon which he insisted. This attitude is to be associated with his attack on the authority of antiquity, to which men had for ages largely turned for knowledge of nature. In experiments he had an alternative to offer men whom he would turn from the ancients, and whom he thus brought to nature herself. He and the age he influenced never tired of contrasting the two sources of information, as the antitheses which the contrast suggested testify: nature versus books, works versus words, laboratories versus libraries and closets, industry versus idleness. At times it seems as if men were charmed by the magic word "experiment" itself, and it must be confessed that in general no great progress was made in penetrating deeply into the true nature of experimentation. A few like Boyle and Hooke, it is true, were inquiring into the characteristics of truly scientific experiments and the proper method of making them, but some let the word rather than the proper conception serve their purpose. Even the physical exertion required by experimental research assumes an aspect of virtue, and the physical inactivity of reading becomes nothing more than sloth. Sometimes the contrast comes perilously near that between doing and thinking. The science of the day was most frequently called "the experimental philosophy," though other adjectives, "new," "free," "solid," "useful," "real," find expression. And finally faith in experimentation influenced the Baconians in their attitudes toward other types of science. It softened their criticism of the bragging chemists, and rendered suspect, to a certain extent, the mechanical philosophy of matter, motion, and mathematics, which under the influence of Descartes and the atomic philosophers was slowly establishing science on the firmest foundation it had ever possessed, but which at the time was criticized as being a theory only and not based on a sufficient number of experiments.

There was one other characteristic of seventeenth-century science for which Bacon was largely, if not entirely, responsible, namely, its pronounced utilitarianism. The purpose of his *Magna Instauratio* was to enable man to know nature in order to command her. It is true, Bacon divides experiments into two

From Richard Foster Jones, *Ancients and Moderns. A Study of the Rise of the Scientific Movement in Seventeenth-Century England*, 2nd edition. (Berkeley, 1965), pp. vii–xii, 268–272. Reprinted by permission of the University of California Press.

The Early Modern Era

groups, those that give light and those that bear fruit, but the purpose of the first was to enlarge man's knowledge so that he might thereby enjoy more fruit. Bacon feared that in observing and experimenting, men would gain bits of knowledge which they could immediately turn into material benefits, and thus be tempted to abandon further investigation; so he cautioned them not to be diverted by such opportunities from a goal larger but not different in kind. The utilitarian spirit is everywhere evident in the twenty years preceding and following the Restoration, that is, among the Baconians, not among the atomic scientists. The effects of it are seen in the attitude of the age toward what we call pure science. The satisfying of intellectual curiosity through scientific inquiry is regarded as a legitimate activity, but it is associated with the proud speculative man in contrast to the humble experimenter working for the good of mankind. The utilitarian spirit is also revealed in the interest shown by scientists in agriculture and in the "mechanical" arts and manual trades. Both Bacon and his followers looked upon these as able to furnish much valuable information to investigators, but they also stressed the great contribution which experimental science could make to them, and through them to the world.

A number of other characteristic values and attitudes of the age find in Verulam[1] their most likely source, such as the need to develop a critical mind, which would be slow and cautious in accepting any proposition not thoroughly proved by experiments. This attitude led directly to a distrust of reason and an antipathy to systems, which were regarded as the product of the mind and not of experiments and observations. The attack on the ancients was partly inspired by the conviction that reason played a more important part than sensuous observations in their philosophy, which for this reason comprised abstract generalities derived from the mind and not from nature. The relegation of reason and learning to a position subordinate to the senses, together with the large number of men requisite for the compilation of the natural history, was responsible for lowering the intellectual qualifications required for scientific work to such extent that anyone who had hands and eyes was thought capable of performing experiments. Bacon, however, found another reason for the low qualifications he established for scientific brains, and that was the need to remove the despair

[1] Bacon was made Baron Verulam in July, 1618. [Editor's note.]

which the moderns felt of ever equalling the ancients in mental powers because of the widespread belief in the decay of nature, an hallucination which rendered modern inferiority inevitable. In England the great lord chancellor came to be regarded as the champion of modernity against the ancients, and he had much to do with the intellectual independence of his followers, but he never tried to equate modern and ancient genius. Instead he offered the world his method as requiring a minimum of intellectual power, and yet as more than offsetting the advantage of better brains enjoyed by antiquity. It is hardly too much to say that during this period reason and mind were somewhat suspect in the domain of science.

There were also certain social correlatives of the scientific ideas mentioned above that, especially in the puritan era, receive vigorous expression because congenial with attitudes arising from other sources. These sprang almost entirely from the utilitarian element in scientific thinking and from the lowered intellectual gifts demanded of experimenters. The farmer, artisan, and mechanic, because they were in contact with natural things and were unhindered by any intellectual principle of exclusion, rise in importance and receive considerable recognition. The democratic implication in this situation can hardly escape notice, and indeed becomes conspicuous in what Sprat says about the liberal membership policy adopted by the Royal Society. Certainly science contributed something to that stream of democratic thought and feeling which, arising in the Reformation, was gathering force among the Puritans. The emphasis placed by Bacon upon the material benefits which his philosophy would bestow upon man could not but introduce or re-enforce the social motive of the public good, for this philosophy made such a goal seem quite feasible. A specialized version of this social conception is revealed in the appearance of a humanitarian spirit which found in the prospective blessings of science the hope and the means of bettering the condition of the poor. Bacon speaks of his philosophy as capable of relieving the miseries of man, and he describes the Father of Solomon's House, a scientific organization in the *New Atlantis*, as looking as if he pitied men. During the mid-seventeenth century the social utility of science is recognized; the beneficent results of scientific activity are contrasted with the evils of war; and the heroes of science supplant those robed in martial glory.

But Bacon did more than furnish ideas; he offered encouragement and hope to men oppressed by the subtlety of nature, for which the science handed down from antiquity was no match, and by the prevailing opinion of nature's decay. He eloquently and convincingly (for fortunately he had the power of convincing) held out his historical and inductive method as quite adequate to overcome those bugbears. Furthermore, the very title of his first scientific works displayed the promise of progress, and was adopted as a slogan by others. Today his experiments do not arouse much enthusiasm, but the numerous editions of the Sylva Sylvarum which appeared before the Restoration, and the frequent and approving references to it suggest the comfort which his example, as well as his philosophy, must have given his followers. In fact, he offered himself as an example of what one man, though beset by many duties, could achieve in the field of experimentation. The scientific spirits of that day vividly realized that they were carrying out his instructions, and this realization, supported by the hope of ultimate success, made them feel that they were living at a momentous time in history. "A universal light," says Sprat,[2] "seems to overspread this Age." They were also aware of the character which their own active pursuit of knowledge was imposing on their generation, as the terms they use to describe it make clear: "a learned and inquisitive age"; "a prying and laborious age"; "an age of industry and inquiry" marked by a "searching spirit" and an "affection to sensible knowledge." Bacon had made it plain that the "far-off divine event" toward which they were making their way was indeed far-off, yet occasionally we hear a confident voice proclaiming it just around the corner. Whereas Glanvill and Boyle had only seen in visions a future technological paradise, Sprat speaks of the "wonderful perfection" already achieved by the "mechanical Arts." The age needed no future historian to apprise it of its significance. . . .

The unceasing war which the Baconians waged against the ancients in the seventeenth century, as well as the obsequious submission to the authority of antiquity in the sixteenth, make it clear that the classical obstruction had to be removed before science could find a place in the sun. In his savage attacks on the ancients, Gilbert[3] plainly showed his realization that as long as freedom of thought was restrained by internal or external coercion, truth warred in vain against error. It is not strange that during the first forty years of the seventeenth century, when his influence was at its height, the ideal of liberty of thought and discussion made marked progress, and prepared the way for the fierce onslaught upon antiquity in the time of the Commonwealth. Bacon's influence, of course, re-enforced and later overshadowed his, but the part Gilbert played in vigorously asserting his right to disagree with the ancients is an important fact in the history of the liberation of the mind. In general, this ideal, which has been pursued so ardently by subsequent generations, received more powerful and consistent support from the scientific spirit than from any other source.

The chief foundation of the blind reliance upon antiquity was the debilitating theory of nature's decay. The antithesis of the idea of progress, which colored and brightened the thought of the last century, it laid its enervating hand upon human powers, and bred a despairing resignation to an apparently inexorable decree of fate. In the light of this theory, one can easily understand why Bacon considered it so important to instill courage and confidence in the hearts of men. But unlike Hakewill[4] he did not squarely meet the issue. He may have subscribed to the theory himself; thinking the obsession too deep to be eradicated, he may have considered a concession to his age expedient; or he may have made use of the idea to enhance the importance of his method. But the fact remains that he nowhere clearly states that the moderns equal the ancients in genius. On the other hand, he seems tacitly to admit the inferiority of the former. He justifies the confidence with which he wished to inspire his readers, in part, by the incremental nature of the growth of knowledge, which, together with his paradox that the moderns are the ancients, supported their claim to superiority in learning. But above everything else, it was his method which he impressed upon men as sinking the balance in the favor of modernity. He confidently opposed his method to the genius of the ancients.

The Commonwealth [1649–1658] was a very significant period in the history of science. It firmly

[3] William Gilbert (1544–1603) the famous Elizabethan physician and scientist. [Editor's note.]

[4] Geroge Hakewill (1578–1649) was an English divine and scholar who argued in some of his writings against the prevalent idea that the world and men were decaying. [Editor's note.]

[2] Thomas Sprat (1635–1713) was a clergyman and writer who compiled a history of the Royal Society. [Editor's note.]

The Early Modern Era

installed Bacon as the dominant influence of the day. The materialism, utilitarianism, democracy, social-mindedness, humanitarianism, and anti-authoritarianism, explicit or implicit in his writings, developed rapidly in the congenial atmosphere of Puritanism. Perceiving the practical worth of the experimental philosophy, the reforming Puritans seized upon it with eagerness, and made it the companion of their fanatical religion. At first sight this appears an odd couple, indeed, but upon closer scrutiny the strangeness disappears. Certainly no part of the population was more interested in the increase of wealth and the improvement of their material welfare than the "godly men." Bacon had pointed out only too clearly the relationship between his philosophy and such desirable benefits. Furthermore, there was nothing in his philosophical conceptions to antagonize the Puritans, for the potentialities which his views possessed for discrediting religion had not yet appeared, and he himself had clearly separated theology and science.

The Puritans chose what would seem to have been the most direct and fundamentally efficacious method of establishing the new science, namely, education. It is true that the first group of experimenters met in London, but before long its more important members were transplanted in Oxford, evidently for the purpose of introducing the experimental philosophy into the university, which thus remained for a decade the center of scientific activities in England. Most of the Puritan propaganda for Baconianism is found in educational treatises, which attack the established curriculum with virulence and support the new method with enthusiasm, and which gave rise to those values that have plagued our own educational world. In them professional, vocational, and scientific education is directly opposed to the study of subjects in part humanistic and cultural. Science and the classics fought their battle then as they did in the nineteenth century. Philistinism made its first appearance.

In the Restoration this attempt at educational reform retained its earlier associations more clearly, aroused more fear and animosity in conservative hearts, and suffered more from the general reaction against the Puritans than any other element in the scientific movement. The Puritan scientists as a whole made their way safely into the royalist camp, and science fortunately rested under the protection of a lenient King. Though the Baconians continued to manifest and recommend most of the values and attitudes of Commonwealth science, they carefully avoided advocating any disturbance in established academic subjects. Sprat, though personally approving a scientific education, disclaimed for the Royal Society any educational schemes. Glanvill[5] followed him in this respect, and when Casaubon, Stubbe, and others, with an eye on the earlier treatises, accused the Society of designs on the universities, he strenuously denied the charge. Many of the writers of these treatises were not received into the scientific fold. Hartlib drops suddenly and completely out of sight, and John Webster tones down his former scathing criticism of the schools to an innocuous proviso. Though Boyle remained at Oxford until shortly before the Restoration, and a definite attempt was made to secure support and sympathy for the experimental philosophy there, the reaction against the Puritan ideas was too strong, and the university, which had been staunchly royalist while Charles I was alive, ceased to play any significant part in the scientific movement. The characteristic feature of Baconianism in the Commonwealth was educational; in the Restoration this feature all but disappeared.

Another reason for the abandonment of the educational aspect of the new science is found in the demands of a universal natural history. In the intense propaganda for, and defence of, the experimental method which followed the establishment of the Royal Society, this conception of Bacon's rose to a pre-eminent position, and became almost the sole motive and goal of scientific activities. The task which confronted the virtuosi was the accumulation of as much data as possible through observation and experiments, and all their energies were concentrated on the work. This pressing demand caused them to be less interested in the teaching of the method than in its application to natural phenomena. Their chief concern was to defend their new philosophy against the upholders of antiquity, who still sought their knowledge in the lore of the past, and to incite as many men as possible to observe and carry on experiments. They were more interested in recruiting mature men to assist in carrying on the work than in teaching the new science to

[5] Joseph Glanvill (1636–1680) was an English philosopher who attached Aristotelianism and Scholasticism and favored an empirical approach. Florence Casaubon (1599–1671) was an important classical scholar of the English Civil War era. Henry Stubbe (or Stubbs, Stubbes) (1632–1676) was an English physician and author who often attacked the clergy, the universities, the monarchy, and most other things supported by the royalists; after the Restoration he became more moderate. [Editor's note.]

youths. Thus they were willing to relinquish that element in the scientific movement which had most outraged conservative thought.

But the naturalistic tendencies of the new science, which had lifted an ugly head in Sprat's *History*, together with the Philistinism of the Puritan treatises, intensified the opposition to experimentalism. The Stubbian period marks the first clear realization of the inevitable clash between naturalism and humanism and of Bacon's relation to it. Aside from the fact that conservative thought naturally viewed with concern the weakening of one element in the established social order, so that religion, education, government, and the professions seemed threatened, men began to sense clearly just what implications and potentialities lay in the experimental philosophy and its extravagant demands. The humanistic spirit was aroused, and engaged in an energetic defence of its creed, by which the world of man is sharply distinguished from, and opposed to, the natural world. And humanism planted itself squarely upon the classics. This fact, together with the association of the new science with the mechanical philosophy, which was falling more and more under the suspicion of atheism, presented the most formidable obstacle to science.

The reaction against the Puritans helped in keeping the universities humanistic, though the new science succeeded in getting a foothold in them, especially in Cambridge. Likewise, literature remained humanistic in theory if not always in practice. The influence of Ben Jonson and the French critics succeeded in establishing the ancients as literary arbiters, so that Aristotle, who had suffered badly at the hands of the scientists, maintained his prestige in criticism. Not that science did not exert influence on critical ideas. It was one of the chief liberalizing forces playing upon neo-classical dogma. Dryden's vacillation may in part be explained by the influence, on the one hand, of classical and neo-classical critics, and, on the other, of the new science, in which he was interested. It is true that other poets of the time were members of the Royal Society, but for the most part they were little influenced by it. Restoration comedy, containing a definite romantic element and reflecting a philosophy of life which had been determined to some extent by the materialism of the scientific spirit, clashed with neo-classical criticism and was defeated. Though Sprat had definitely tried to bring science and literature together, humanism won the day in the literary world, and later directed much of its satire against the "men of Gresham." So we have a neo-classical rather than romantic period in literature.

Thus science, having to thread its way between a humanistic literature and humanistic universities, found its growth retarded in spite of Newton's great discoveries, or perhaps partly because of them, but its values were by no means extinguished. They persisted especially in that element of the population which derived from the Puritans. When this class rose to greater power in the eighteenth century, and the dogma of neo-classical criticism began to disintegrate, partly owing to science, romanticism began to take form, and those attitudes which flourished in the third quarter of the seventeenth century—utilitarianism, humanitarianism, democracy, and the like—resumed their onward march.

HERBERT BUTTERFIELD

EVOLUTIONARY FACTORS IN THE ORIGINS
OF SCIENCE

The Master of Peterhouse in the University of Cambridge, Herbert Butterfield, supports not only what is called the "genius theory" of scientific development but also the evolutionary approach. In his provocative book on *The Origins of Modern Science*, which first appeared in 1950, Butterfield presents a comprehensive sketch of the progress of science in the modern world, in which he carefully blends the genius theory with a discussion of the Protestant ethic and its impact on seventeenth-century Europe. Butterfield's readers will be interested in his definition of the Renaissance and in his emphasis on the date 1660 as marking the watershed in the development of modern science.

A primary aspect of the Renaissance, however, . . . is the fact that it completes and brings to its climax the long process by which the thought of antiquity was being recovered and assimilated in the middle ages. It even carries to what at times is a ludicrous extreme the spirit of an exaggerated subservience to antiquity, the spirit that helped to turn Latin into a dead language. Ideas may have appeared in new combinations, but we cannot say that essentially new ingredients were introduced into our civilisation at the Renaissance. We cannot say that here were intellectual changes calculated to transform the character and structure of our society or civilisation. Even the secularisation of thought which was locally achieved in certain circles at this time was not unprecedented and was a hot-house growth, soon to be overwhelmed by the fanaticism of the Reformation and the Counter-Reformation. During much of the seventeenth century itself we can hardly fail to be struck, for example, by the power of religion both in thought and in politics.

People have talked sometimes as though nothing very new happened in the seventeenth century either, since natural science itself came to the modern world as a legacy from ancient Greece. More than once in the course of our survey we ourselves have even been left with the impression that the scientific revolution could not take place—that significant developments were held up for considerable periods—until a further draft had been made upon the thought of antiquity and a certain minimum of Greek science had been recovered. Against all this, however, it might be said that the course of the seventeenth century as we have studied it represents one of the great episodes in human experience, which ought to be placed—along with the exile of the ancient Jews or the building-up of the universal empires of Alexander the Great and of Ancient Rome—amongst the epic adventures that have helped to make the human race what it is. It represents one of those periods when new things are brought into the world and into history out of men's own creative activity, and their own wrestlings with

truth. There does not seem to be any sign that the ancient world, before its heritage had been dispersed, was moving towards anything like the scientific revolution, or that the Byzantine Empire, in spite of the continuity of its classical tradition, would ever have taken hold of ancient thought and so remoulded it by a great transforming power. The scientific revolution we must regard, therefore, as a creative product of the West—depending on a complicated set of conditions which existed only in western Europe, depending partly also perhaps on a certain dynamic quality in the life and the history of this half of the continent. And not only was a new factor introduced into history at this time amongst other factors, but it proved to be so capable of growth, and so many-sided in its operations, that it consciously assumed a directing role from the very first, and, so to speak, began to take control of the other factors—just as Christianity in the middle ages had come to preside over everything else, percolating into every corner of life and thought. And when we speak of Western civilisation being carried to an oriental country like Japan in recent generations, we do not mean Graeco-Roman philosophy and humanist ideals, we do not mean the Christianising of Japan, we mean the science, the modes of thought and all that apparatus of civilisation which were beginning to change the face of the West in the latter half of the seventeenth century.

Now I think it would be true to say that, for the historian, as distinct perhaps from the student of prehistory, there are not in any absolute sense civilisations that rise and fall—there is just the unbroken web of history, the unceasing march of generations which themselves overlap with one another and interpenetrate, so that even the history of science is part of a continuous story of mankind going back to peoples far behind the ancient Greeks themselves. But we cannot hold our history in our minds without any landmarks, or as an ocean without fixed points, and we may talk about this civilisation and that, as though they were ultimate units, provided we are not superstitious in our use of the word, and we take

From Herbert Butterfield, *Origins of Modern Science* (London, 1950), pp. 162–174. Reprinted by permission of G. Bell & Sons Ltd.

care not to become the slaves of our terminology. Similarly, though everything comes by antecedents and mediations, and these may always be traced farther and farther back without the mind ever coming to rest, still we can speak of certain epochs of crucial transition, when the subterranean movements come above ground, and new things are palpably born, and the very face of the earth can be seen to be changing. On this view we may say that in regard not merely to the history of science but to civilisation and society as a whole the transformation becomes obvious, and the changes become congested in the latter part of the seventeenth century. We may take the line that here, for practical purposes, our modern civilisation is coming out in a perceptible manner into the daylight.

In this period the changes were not by any means confined to France, though what we have hitherto studied has drawn our attention to certain aspects of the transition in the case of that country in particular. The movement was localised, however, and it is connected with the humming activity which was taking place, say from 1660, not only in England, Holland and France, but also actually between these countries—the shuttle running to and fro and weaving what was to become a different kind of Western culture. At this moment the leadership of civilisation may be said to have moved in a definitive manner from the Mediterranean, which had held it for thousands of years, to the regions farther north. There had been a pull in this direction on the part of the university of Paris in the later middle ages, and a still stronger pull after the Renaissance, when Germany had revolted against Rome and the north had taken its own path at the Reformation. In any case the Mediterranean had become at times almost a Mohammedan lake, and the geographical discoveries had been transferring the economic predominance to the Atlantic seaboard for a number of generations. For a moment, then, the history of civilisation was focused on the English Channel, where things were weaving themselves into new patterns, and henceforward the Mediterranean was to appear to the moderns as a backward region. Not only did England and Holland hold a leading position, but that part of France which was most active in promoting the new order was the Huguenot or ex-Huguenot section, especially the Huguenots in exile, the nomads, who played an important part in the intellectual exchange that was taking place. After 1685 —after the Revocation of the Edict of Nantes—the alliance between the French and the English Protes-

tants became more close, when Huguenots fled to England or became the intermediaries for the publication in Holland of journals written in French and communicating English ideas. As the eighteenth century proceeded, the balance in Europe shifted more definitely to the north, with the rise of the non-Catholic powers of Russia and Prussia. Even in the new world it was the northern half of the continent that came to the forefront, and it was soon decided that this northern part should be British not French, Protestant not Roman Catholic—an ally, therefore, of the new form of civilisation. The centre of gravity of the globe itself seemed to have changed and new areas of its surface found for a time their "place in the sun."

This new chapter in the history of civilisation really opened when in 1660, after a long period of internal upheaval and civil war, a comparative political stability was brought about not merely in France but in general throughout the continent, where on all sides the institution of monarchy had been gravely challenged but had managed to reassert itself and to re-establish a public order. In fact, what we have already noticed in the case of France was still more true in England and Holland in the seventeenth century—we see the power in intellectual matters of what, in spite of the objectionableness of the term, we must call the middle class. And just as the Renaissance was particularly associated with city-states (or virtual city-states) in Italy, South Germany and the Netherlands, where the commerce and economic development had produced an exhilarating civic life, so in the last quarter of the seventeenth century the intellectual changes were centred on the English Channel, where commerce had been making so remarkable a rise and so much prosperity seemed to have been achieved. The city-state disappeared from history in the first half of the sixteenth century; but on the wider platform of the nation-state the future still belonged to what we call the middle classes.

If we have in mind merely the intellectual changes of the period we are considering, they have been described by one historian under the title, *La crise de la conscience européenne*—a title which itself gives some indication of the importance of the transition that was taking place. What was in question was a colossal secularisation of thought in every possible realm of ideas at the same time, after the extraordinarily strong religious character of much of the thinking of the seventeenth century. John Locke

The Early Modern Era

produces a transposition into secular terms of what had been a presbyterian tradition in political thought, and in doing so he is not a freak or a lonely prophet—he stands at the pivotal point in what is now a general transition. This secularisation came at the appropriate moment for combination with the work of the scientific revolution at the close of the seventeenth century; yet it would appear that it was not itself entirely the result of the scientific achievements—a certain decline of Christianity appears to have been taking place for independent reasons. One is tempted to say on quite separate grounds that this period emerges as one of the lowest points in the history of Western Christianity between the eleventh century and the twentieth. If we look at the general moral tone of Charles II's reign after the period of the Puritan ascendancy and compare it with the extraordinarily parallel case of the Regency in France after the religiosity of the closing years of Louis XIV's reign, it is difficult to resist the feeling that in both cases a general relaxation in religion and morals followed periods of too great tension —these things were not the straight results of the scientific revolution taken in isolation. In any case it lay perhaps in the dialectic of history itself that in the long conflicts between Protestant and Catholic the secular state should rise to independence and should secure an arbitral position over what now seemed to be mere religious parties within it. The whole story of the Renaissance shows within the limits of the city-state how the exhilarating rise of an urban civilisation is liable to issue in a process of secularisation—the priest as well as the noble loses the power that he was able to possess in a more conservative agrarian world. Something parallel has happened over and over again in the case of nation-states when not only have towns become really urban in character—which is late in the case of England, for example—but when a sort of leadership in society has passed to the towns, and literature itself comes to have a different character.

There is another reason why it would be wrong to impute all the changes in thought at this time to the effect of the scientific discoveries alone. It happened that just at this moment books of travel were beginning to have a remarkable effect on the general outlook of men—a postponed result of the geographical discoveries and of the growing acquaintance with distant lands. Western Europe was now coming to be familiar with the widespread existence of peoples who had never heard of ancient Greece or of Christianity. When these were taken into one's larger survey, the European outlook came to be envisaged not as universal, not necessarily even as central, but somewhat as a regional affair. It became possible to look upon it as only the local tradition of a comparatively small section of the globe. So one could begin to regard one's own culture, even one's own religion, with a great degree of relativity. It was possible to look on each local creed as embodying one essential truth, but covering that truth with its own local myths, perversions and accretions. What was common to all was the universal irreducible truth—the principles of natural religion—and in French books of travel, therefore, you find the essential ingredients of Deism before John Locke had shown the way. Furthermore, you could feel that in western Europe Christianity had its basis in the same universal truth, but the principles had been covered (in Roman Catholicism, for example) by local accretions, revelations and miracles, from which it now required to be extricated. The results of all this harmonised with the operations of the new science, and strengthened the case for the kind of Deism which Newton's system seemed to encourage—a Deism which required a God only at the beginning of time to set the universe in motion.

From this period also there developed in a remarkable way and with extraordinary speed the tendency to a new type of Protestantism—the more liberal type which most of us have in mind when we are in controversy on this subject. It was a Protestantism married to the rationalising movement, and so different from the original Protestantism that it now requires an effort of historical imagination to discover what Martin Luther had in mind. Some remarkable developments in this rationalising tendency were only checked in England by the rise and the pervasive influence of John Wesley. On the other hand we have to note that if books of travel affected the attitude of western Europeans to their own traditions, the very attitude these people adopted (the kind of relativity they achieved) owed something to a certain scientific outlook which was now clearly becoming a more general habit of mind. Similarly, when in the 1660s a writer like Joseph Glanvill could produce a book on *The Vanity of Dogmatising*, insisting on the importance of scepticism in science and on the system of methodical doubt, it is impossible to deny that this critical outlook is an effect of the scientific movement. In general, we ought not to close our eyes to the extremely dislocating effects of that general overthrow of the authority of both the middle ages and antiquity which again had been produced by the scientific revolution. Either we may say, therefore, that a number of converging factors were moving the Western world in one prevailing direction, or we must say that there was one wind so overpowering that it could carry along with it anything else that happened—a wind so mighty that it gathered every other movement into its sweep, to strengthen the current in favour of secularisation at this time.

The changes which took place in the history of thought in this period, howevever, are not more remarkable than the changes in life and society. It has long been our tendency to push back the origins of both the industrial revolution and the so-called agrarian revolution of the eighteenth century, and though, as I have said, we can trace back the origin of anything as far as we like, it is towards the end of the seventeenth century that the changes are becoming palpable. The passion to extend the scientific method to every branch of thought was at least equalled by the passion to make science serve the cause of industry and agriculture, and it was accompanied by a sort of technological fervour. Francis Bacon had always laid stress on the immense utilitarian possibilities of science, the advantages beyond all dreams that would come from the control of nature, and it is difficult, even in the early history of the Royal Society, to separate the interest shown in the cause of pure scientific truth from the curiosity in respect of useful inventions on the one part, or the inclination to dabble in fables and freakishness on the other. It has become a debatable question how far the direction of scientific interest was itself affected by technical needs or preoccupations in regard to shipbuilding and other industries; but the Royal Society followed Galileo in concerning itself, for example, with the important question of the mode of discovering longitude at sea. Those who wish to trace the development of the steam-engine will find that it is a story which really begins to be vivid and lively in this period. Apart from such developments, the possibilities of scientific experiment were likely themselves to be limited until certain forms of production and technique had been elaborated in society generally. Indeed, the scientific, the industrial and the agrarian revolutions form such a system of complex and interrelated changes, that in the lack of a microscopic examination we have to heap them all together as aspects of a general movement, which by the last quarter of the seventeenth century was palpably altering the face of the earth. The hazard consists not in putting all these things together and rolling them into one great bundle of complex change, but in thinking that we know how to disentangle them—what we see is the total intricate network of changes, and it is difficult to say that any one of these was the simple result of the scientific revolution itself.

Embraced in the same general movement is that growth of overseas trade which we have already noticed in the case of France—and once again we find a remarkable postponed result of the geographical discoveries of a much earlier period, reminding us that the New World represents one of the permanent changes in the conditioning circumstances of the modern age, one of the great standing differences between medieval and modern times, its results coming in relays and reproducing themselves at postponed periods. In the England of Charles II's reign we begin to see that we are an empire; the Board of Trade and Plantations comes to occupy a central position in the government; it is after 1660 that the East India Company reaps its colossal harvests. We begin to hear much less in the way of complaint about the excessive numbers of the clergy—henceforward what we begin to hear are complaints about the growing number of customs officials, Treasury men, colonial officers, contractors—all of them subject to corruption by the government. This is the epoch in which, as historians have long pointed out, wars of trade—especially amongst the Dutch, the French and the English —succeeded the long series of wars of religion. In a similar way we must take note of the foundation of such things as the Bank of England and the national debt—a new world of finance that alters not merely the government but the very fabric of the body politic. We have seen how in France and England there already existed signs of that speculative fever which culminated in the scheme of John Law[1] on the one hand and the South Sea Bubble[2] on the other; while in Holland there had been a parallel financial sensation earlier still.

[1] John Law (1671–1729) was a Scottish financier and promoter, whose most famous venture was the "Mississippi Scheme," which he undertook while serving as French controller-general or finance in 1720. [Editor's note.]

[2] A term applied to the speculation engaged in by many Englishmen prior to 1720. The South Sea company was the center of speculation. It was expected that this company would gain important concessions in the Spanish possessions after the War of the Spanish Succession. This expectation led to wild speculation, but when the profits failed to materialize the expanded values of the stock fell and numerous investors were ruined. [Editor's note.]

For two thousand years the general appearance of the world and the activities of men had varied astonishingly little—the sky-line for ever the same—so much so that men were not conscious of either progress or process in history, save as one city or state might rise by effort or good fortune while another fell. Their view of history had been essentially static because the world had been static so far as they could see—life in successive generations played out by human beings on a stage that remained essentially the same. Now, however, change became so quick as to be perceptible with the naked eye, and the face of the earth and the activities of men were to alter more in a century than they had previously done in a thousand years. We shall see later, in connection with the idea of progress, how in general—and for effective purposes—it was in this period that men's whole notion of the process of things in time was thrown into the melting-pot. And the publication of a host of journals in France, England and Holland speeded up the pace of intellectual change itself.

A curious feature of seventeenth-century English life illustrates the growing modernity of the world, and throws light not only on social change but on a certain different flavour that is becoming apparent in the prevailing mentality. There is a foretaste of it in the debates of James I's reign when we find that certain people called Projectors are being attacked in parliament—the sort of people whom we might call company-promoters, and who devised schemes for making money. They developed very greatly after the Restoration, becoming a considerable phenomenon in William III's reign, and they culminated in the period of the South Sea Bubble, when companies were founded to execute all kinds of fantastic schemes, including a method of procuring perpetual motion. Just before the end of the seventeenth century Daniel Defoe—who emerges as a remarkably modern mind—produced an *Essay on Projects* in which he commented on the whole phenomenon, satirised the Projectors, but then produced many schemes of his own to swell the flood. It is curious to note that these Projectors provided another of what we should call the "mediations" which assisted the passage to the *philosophe* movement; for though some of them had schemes for getting rich quickly—Defoe had a scheme for improving trade by settling the problem of the Barbary pirates, for example—some others had wider views—schemes of general amelioration, schemes for tackling the problem of the poor, plans for female education,

devices for getting rid of the national debt. The famous socialistic system of Robert Owen was taken, as Owen himself explains, from John Bellairs, who produced the design of it in 1696 under the title of "a scheme by which the rich were to remain rich and the poor were to become independent, and children were to be educated." Bellairs had other proposals for general amelioration—for example in connection with prison-reform. Such things easily passed into projects for new forms of government, and curious mechanical schemes were put forward—the prelude to modern constitution-making and blue-prints for Utopia. They make it clear that the historical process is very complex; that while the scientific movement was taking place, other changes were occurring in society—other factors were ready to combine with it to create what we call the modern world.

It is always easy for a later generation to think that its predecessor was foolish, and it may seem shocking to state that even after the First World War good historians could write the history of the nineteenth century with hardly a hint of the importance of Socialism, hardly a mention of Karl Marx—a fact which we should misinterpret unless we took it as a reminder of the kind of faults to which all of us are prone. Because we have a fuller knowledge of after-events, we today can see the nineteenth century differently; and it is not we who are under an optical illusion—reading the twentieth century back unfairly into the nineteenth—when we say that the student of the last hundred years is missing a decisive factor if he overlooks the rise of Socialism. A man of insight could have seen the importance of the phenomenon long before the end of the nineteenth century. But we, who have seen the implications worked out in the events of our time, need no insight to recognise the importance of this whole aspect of the story.

Something similar to this is true when we of the year 1949 take our perspective of the scientific revolution—we are in a position to see its implications at the present day much more clearly than the men who flourished fifty or even twenty years before us. And, once again, it is not we who are under an optical illusion—reading the present back into the past—for the things that have been revealed in the 1940s merely bring out more vividly the vast importance of the turn which the world took three hundred years ago, in the days of the scientific revolution. We can see why our predecessors were less conscious of the significance of the seventeenth century—why they talked so much more of the Renaissance or the eighteenth-century Enlightenment, for example—because in this as in so many other cases we can now discern those surprising over-laps and time-lags which so often disguise the direction things are taking. Our Graeco-Roman roots and our Christian heritage were so profound—so central to all our thinking—that it has required centuries of pulls and pressures, and almost a conflict of civilisations in our very midst, to make it clear that the centre had shifted. At one time the effects of the scientific revolution, and the changes contemporary with it, would be masked by the persistence of our classical traditions and education, which still formed so much of the character of the eighteenth century in England and in France, for example. At another time these effects would be concealed through that popular attachment to religion which so helped to form the character of even the nineteenth century in this country. The very strength of our conviction that ours was a Graeco-Roman civilisation—the very way in which we allowed the art-historians and the philologists to make us think that this thing which we call "the modern world" was the product of the Renaissance—the inelasticity of our historical con-cepts, in fact—helped to conceal the radical nature of the changes that had taken place and the colossal possibilities that lay in the seeds sown by the seventeenth century. The seventeenth century, indeed, did not merely bring a new factor into history, in the way we often assume—one that must just be added, so to speak, to the other permanent factors. The new factor immediately began to elbow at the other ones, pushing them out of their places—and, indeed, began immediately to seek control of the rest, as the apostles of the new movement had declared their intention of doing from the very start. The result was the emergence of a kind of Western civilisation which when transmitted to Japan operates on tradition there as it operates on tradition here—dissolving it and having eyes for nothing save a future of brave new worlds. It was a civilisation that could cut itself away from the Graeco-Roman heritage in general, away from Christianity itself—only too confident in its power to exist independent of anything of the kind. We know now that what was emerging towards the end of the seventeenth century was a civilisation exhilaratingly new perhaps, but strange as Nineveh and Babylon. That is why, since the rise of Christianity, there is no landmark in history that is worthy to be compared with this.

3

MERCANTILISM: THE HISTORY OF AN IDEA

The first writer to use the term "mercantilism" was Adam Smith, who devoted the fourth book of his great work on The Wealth of Nations (1776) to a study of the pernicious effects of mercantilism on the European economy. Smith condemned mercantilism as a selfish program pursued by a small group of seventeenth- and early eighteenth-century merchants and manufacturers. These entrepreneurs, misunderstanding the true principles of the free flow of trade, said Smith, contrived to delude the statesmen of Western Europe into pursuing a false policy that emphasized the search for precious metals and reliance on a closed economic system.

Smith's attack on the so-called "mercantile system" was welcomed by many businessmen of the late eighteenth century who were eager to throw off the shackles of government control and to espouse the principles of laissez-faire or free trade. They, and the generation that followed them, not only eschewed the principles of mercantilism but ignored the very word itself. It was not until the late nineteenth century, when the world was once again entering upon an era of protectionism, that the German writer Gustav Schmoller revived the term in his famous book on The Mercantile System and Its Historical Significance (1884).

The Early Modern Era

Schmoller, who equated the mercantile system with the growth of the national state, asserted that "mercantilism . . . in its innermost kernel is nothing but state-making." Power and wealth, said Schmoller, were the twin pillars upon which the absolute monarch built his commonwealth. Thus Schmoller deftly countered Adam Smith's charge of mercantile selfishness by claiming that the system had been the creation of statesmen concerned to give their people security and prosperity.

The debate over the meaning of mercantilism continued in the writings of such eminent twentieth-century economists and economic historians as John Maynard Keynes, Herbert Heaton, Jacob Viner, and above all the distinguished Swedish historian, Eli F. Heckscher, whose great work on *Mercantilism* appeared in Swedish in 1931 and within the next four years was translated into German and English. Heckscher believed that there were two mercantile systems: one that existed in the minds of the theorists of the seventeenth and eighteenth centuries and the other that represented a codification of the practical experience garnered by the statesmen of the period. His ideas, particularly concerning the "unifying principle" of mercantilism, has been challenged by numerous critics.

For the student, the mercantile system, whether it be defined in the pages of Adam Smith, Gustav Schmoller, or Eli Heckscher may, in general terms, be described this way: the modern state, which in the sixteenth century emerged slowly from a static stage of development into a more dynamic, nation-building stage, became increasingly concerned with economic matters. Spurred on by a need to finance a burgeoning bureaucracy, larger armies and navies, and more elaborate building programs, the statesmen of Early Modern Europe inaugurated programs for state aid to industry, for the regulation of the medieval guild system, and for the stimulation of commerce. These statesmen, men like Cardinal Richelieu, Oliver Cromwell, and Louis XIV, believed—and were often reinforced in their beliefs by the writings of such great mercantilists as Barthélemy de Laffemas (1545–1641), Thomas Mun (1571–1641), and Jacques Savary (1622–1690)—that if the state encouraged its citizens to export more than they imported the wealth of the world would eventually be diverted into their own coffers.

The prototype of the mercantile "legislator" was Jean-Baptiste Colbert, Louis XIV's secretary of the marine and controller-general of finance for twenty years (1663–1683). Colbert's program, later termed by historians as "Colbertism," emphasized the expansion of bureaucratic controls, the codification of the laws, government regulation and protection of industry, careful administration of taxes, sponsorship of the arts and sciences, and control of imperial trade.

While Colbertism flourished in France, England instituted its own system of imperial controls through series of Navigation Acts (1651, 1663, and 1670) which regulated the carrying trade between the mother country and the empire. Under these laws, commonly known as the Old Colonial System, England, like France, required that goods be carried in the ships of the mother country, that the colonies import their manufactured products exclusively from England, and that colonial ports be closed to foreign commerce.

Hardly had the mercantile system reached its apogee in the early eighteenth century when decay set in. Plagued by the disruptions of intercontinental wars, by the demands of a restive merchant class, and by the stresses of the first phase of the Industrial Revolution, statesmen across Europe (with the exception of Prussia) began to relax controls over industry and commerce. They were supported in their attacks on "this monstrous mercantilism" by the writings of the Physiocrats in France and Adam Smith and his followers in England. Thus began a new stage in the economic history of Europe, the era of Free Trade.

Many of the key issues concerning the mercantile system are debated by Eli Heckscher and his critics in the following pages.

ELI F. HECKSCHER

A PHASE OF ECONOMIC POLICY
AND ECONOMIC IDEAS

For Eli F. Heckscher (1879–1952), the distinguished Swedish economist and economic historian, mercantilism was, as Herbert Heaton notes, "an instrumental concept which [Heckscher felt] should enable us to understand a particular historical period more clearly than we otherwise might." Heckscher, in the article reprinted below on "Mercantilism" written in 1936 for the *Economic History Review*, reasserts the importance of three of these instrumental concepts: namely, mercantilism as (1) an instrument for the unification of the state: (2) as a quest for political power and prestige; and (3) as a general conception of society. To his critics Heckscher concedes that he may have overemphasized the theme of state unification, which he notes was more conspicuous in its failure than its success. As to the mercantile quest for power, Heckscher modifies the position from that taken in his two-volume work on *Mercantilism* (1931; English translation, 1935) by stating that both "power and opulence"—Adam Smith's terms—were important "to economic policy of every description." Heckscher, however, holds that in the Early Modern period of European history (from the end of the sixteenth century to the mid-eighteenth century) the quest for power had an edge over the desire for opulence and that these goals were reversed during the *laissez-faire* era of the nineteenth century. Lastly, Heckscher maintains that the mercantilists envisaged a "general conception of society," which was not unlike that of its successor, the *laissez-faire* system, with certain notable exceptions. Withal, Heckscher presents an articulate summary and spirited reexamination of his concept of mercantilism.

The Editor of *The Economic History Review* has asked me to write a short article on Mercantilism in the series "Revisions in Economic History." This has proved a more difficult task than I had anticipated, first because it presupposes in the writer a definite conception of what the accepted doctrine is; and that is not at all clear to me. Secondly, the vastness of the subject makes it literally impossible even to mention, in the small space available to me, the many instances where I find a different relationship between different parts of the subject than that usually described; or, generally, a new point of view. And even with regard to the somewhat arbitrarily selected points raised here it is impossible to give chapter and verse for my conclusions.

The different treatment accorded to mercantilism by, say, Adam Smith, Schmoller, and Cunningham is principally rooted in insufficient attention to the difference between ends and means. The ends of statesmen in the economic field between, say, the beginning of the sixteenth and the middle of the eighteenth centuries were of course diversified; but I think it may be said that at least two tendencies played a very great part, *i.e.* that towards the unification of the territory of the State economically and the use of the resources of their countries in the interests of the political power of the State—more of this below. But important as this was in itself, it does *not* constitute the most characteristic contrast to what came later. An illustration may be found in the fact that the foremost, and by far the most intelligent, among German mercantilists, Johann Joachim Becher, gave his principal work a title which differed only very slightly from that of the *Wealth of Nations.* Consequently, the most important difference did not lie in the choice of ends, but in opinions as to the best way of achieving those ends, *i.e.* in the choice of means. Through this, mercantilism became not only a specific type of economic policy, but, even more, a characteristic body of economic ideas; for the views as to what constituted the best means were rooted in conscious or unconscious interpretations of the tendencies of economic life. Through this, mercantilism came to mean a discussion of the relations between causes and effects of economic factors; it paved the way to a theory of economics, in spite of having started from purely practical considerations. It is not, in this case, a question of a choice between theory and practice, but of practice leading unintentionally to theory. I do not think any student with a theoretical insight can fail to see, especially when studying the writers of the seventeenth century, how they came more and more, and almost in spite of themselves, to work out theories of the relation between causes and effects in the economic field.

Returning now to the ends pursued by mercantilist statesmen, opposite views have recently been expressed. A German scholar, Dr. Hugo Rachel, . . . has said—in strong opposition to his own teacher, Schmoller—that the important point of view of mercantilist statesmen was not the idea of economic unity, but that of economic power. Though some of the facts adduced for this contention do not appear to me at all convincing, I think there is something to be said for this criticism of my previous treatment of the subject. It is not only that the attempts at unity were, with few exceptions, failures—such was the result of the majority of mercantilist measures; even these attempts themselves were to a great extent half-hearted. It is difficult to find more than two bold attempts In this direction in the leading countries. One is the Statute of Artificers of 1563 in England, the other Colbert's tariff of 1664. Besides these two, the unifying measures in customs administration in Sweden in the seventeenth century were to a very great degree successful; but Sweden, like England, was a country where disintegration had been avoided in the earlier period, and consequently in Sweden the problem of unification was little more than a question of merging new territories into the body of the old. And that was effected without great difficulty.

This consideration gives rise to a suspicion that mercantilist statesmen did not take their unifying work seriously. They were, however, unable to shirk altogether the task of adapting the medieval framework of European society to new economic and social conditions. This task I have also interpreted, perhaps incorrectly, as part of the unifying work of mercantilism. It fell into two rather distinct categories. The one was concerned with "feudalism," *i.e.* the disintegration caused by more or less anarchical measures undertaken by the lawless or self-willed territorial lords and provincial nobles in their own interests. Briefly stated, there was little need for any activity against this tendency in England and Swe-

From Eli F. Heckscher, "Revisions in Economic History. V. Mercantilism," *Economic History Review,* VII (1936–37), 44–50, 52–54. Reprinted by permission of the publisher and of His Excellency Gunnar Heckscher, Ambassador of Sweden at New Delhi.

den. In Germany, on the other hand, the need for it was greater than almost anywhere else; but the efforts to overcome this anarchy came to very little. The country where both the need was great and something was done to satisfy it was France; the French monarchy was able to achieve some remarkable results of this field, though much of the old disorder was allowed to survive until the great revolution.

Even more important than "feudalism" was that particular type of disintegration which resulted from the independence of the towns; and in spite of some dissimilarities most European countries presented the same fundamental features in this respect. . . . The medieval towns had created the most consistent, vigorous and long-lived system of economic policy that has ever existed, the most important parts of which were the gild system and the internal regulation of industry in general, and the organisation of foreign trade and commerce. The fight against medieval municipal policy was most successful in the country in which it was least constructive—that is, England. There, after an attempt at a really constructive policy under the earlier Stuarts, the gild system was allowed to fall to pieces under the impact of new economic forces. When Cunningham gave the name of "Parliamentary Colbertism" to the policy pursued in the period after 1689, he should have added that it was Colbertism not only without Colbert, but also, which is even more important, without the vast administrative machinery created by Colbert—that it was, in fact, a system almost without any administrative machinery at all. On this point I think the views of Unwin[1] were almost entirely correct. How far this explains the fact that what is usually called the Industrial Revolution came to England first, instead of beginning in continental countries—which were probably less backward than England before that time—is of course impossible to decide with certainty. Many other factors made their contribution, and I can only record my personal impression that the absence of administrative control was one of the most important. The exigencies of space prevent me from going into the causes of the peculiar character of this disintegration of the old order of administration in England; but further researches have in my opinion decidedly strengthened the view put forward by

Professor Tawney, that the most potent force was the attitude of the Common Law courts.

In this respect France was the opposite of England; and continental developments were mostly of the French type, though much less advanced. French policy, like that of the rest of the continental countries, consisted in a sustained and very painstaking attempt at regulation; but it resulted in upholding, and greatly enlarging the sphere of, medieval methods, not in adapting them to a changing world. The great administrative power of the French monarchy enabled it to perpetuate the gild system and to spread it over a far greater area than it had regulated during the Middle Ages. Throughout the Continent the result was the same. Mercantilism made itself responsible for what bears the imprint of the Middle Ages, and carried the medieval system, especially in Germany, far down into the nineteenth century. Even the enlargement of the local organisations into national units—an important part of the policy of unification—remained for the most part on paper.

This policy was not altogether ineffective; and least of all in France. If European industry had continued on the lines of its earlier development, catering for the needs of the upper classes or the Church, France would have remained the leading industrial country in Europe. When, on the contrary, industry came to mean mass production for mass consumption, the old system of regulation had to disappear. It is therefore difficult to assign any important positive influence to mercantilism, as it worked out in practice, in the creation of modern industry, as contrasted to industry on the old lines. In foreign trade and business organisation the influence of mercantilism was much more complicated. The Dutch and English method of equipping trading companies with powerful privileges, not to say sovereign powers, certainly gave a great impetus to their development and was a characteristic example of western mercantilism. The initiative in these cases, however, was almost entirely private, and it is hard to say how far this policy, as embodied e.g. in the British Bubble Act of 1719,[2] retarded the spread of new forms of business organisation to wider circles. But this exceptionally interesting and important subject must now with reluctance be left aside.

[1] George Unwin (1870–1925) was an English economic historian whose works on medieval and early modern English economic history contributed much to developing economic history as a scholarly pursuit. [Editor's note.]

[2] An act which forbade the issue of shares by companies formed before 1718, ostensibly as a move to curb speculation. [Editor's note.]

The Early Modern Era

Summing up the results of mercantilism as a unifying system, there cannot be the slightest doubt that what it left unfulfilled was enormous when compared with its positive results. The real executor of mercantilism was *laissez-faire*, which did almost without effort what mercantilism had set out but failed to achieve. The most spectacular change in this respect was effected by the French *Constituante* in 1789–91; but English results were perhaps in the long run even more important, and in this case very little of what disappeared has so far come to life again.

The second of the aims of mercantilist policy emphasised by Cunningham—that of power—has met with a great deal of criticism from reviewers of my book, foremost among them Professor Viner . . . I agree with my critics on that point to the extent of admitting that both "power" and "opulence"—to make use of the terms employed by Adam Smith —have been, and must be, of importance to economic policy of every description. But I do not think there can be any doubt that these two aims changed places in the transition from mercantilism to *laissez-faire*. All countries in the nineteenth century made the creation of wealth their lode-star, with small regard to its effects upon the power of the State, while the opposite had been the case previously. I think Cunningham was right in stressing the famous saying of Bacon about Henry VII: "bowing the ancient policy of this Estate from consideration of plenty to consideration of power."

The most important consequence of the dominating interest in power, combined with the static view of economic life as a whole, was the incessant commercial rivalries of the seventeenth and eighteenth centuries, which degenerated easily into military conflict. One of the most serious mistakes of Sombart[3] in his treatment of mercantilism has been his iterated statements of the "dynamic" character of mercantilism, as contrasted with the "static" one of *laissez-faire*. It is true that mercantilists believed in their almost unlimited ability to develop the economic resources of their own country (a belief that was even more strongly held by nineteenth-century writers and politicians), but they only hoped to do so at the expense of their neighbours. That the wealth of the world as a whole could increase was an idea wholly alien to them, and in this they were "static"

[3] Werner Sombart (1863–1941) was a German economic historian who studied the history of capitalism—usually in a critical vein. [Editor's note.]

to a degree. The commercial wars were the natural outcome of this combination; they could not have played the same part either in the Middle Ages, when economic bias was truly "static," or in the nineteenth century, when it was "dynamic" throughout.

But all that has now been said of the aims of mercantilist policy is less significant to economists than the mercantilist attitude to *means*. It must also, I think, be admitted that mercantilism was more original in this latter field than in the field of economic unity and economic power. This aspect of mercantilism reveals itself most clearly in its relation to two distinct though closely allied objects, commodities and money. It goes almost without saying that the need for a theoretical treatment is particularly great in this part of the subject.

With regard to commodities, it is necessary to stress the fact that they can be, and actually have been, viewed from at least three mutually exclusive angles. In the eyes of the merchant, goods are neither welcome nor unwelcome; they form the basis of his transactions, to be both bought and sold; he does not want to exclude them, but neither does he want to keep them. The consumer, however, is a partisan of "plenty"; he is bent upon ensuring a large supply, while sales interest him much less. Lastly, to the producer under a system of exchange sales are everything; in his eyes an over-supply is the ever-present danger, while he sees nothing objectionable in keeping the market understocked. It might, no doubt, have been expected that these three aspects of commodities should have existed side by side, either blended judiciously in the minds of ordinary sane people or represented by different social groups. To some extent this was so; but much less so than might have been expected.

The merchant's point of view can never have prevailed throughout, for the number of merchants must always have been small in comparison with the whole population. Still, it played a very important part, especially in medieval and sixteenth-century towns like Hamburg, Antwerp, Amsterdam, etc., which were made "staple towns" for different commodities; and that type of policy may therefore properly be labelled "staple" policy. The citizens were afraid of their city being depleted of necessities by unlimited exports on the part of the merchants.

The dominating feeling throughout the Middle Ages, mostly in towns, which were almost the only repositories of medieval economic policy, was the one natural to consumers; they wanted to hamper or prevent exports but favoured imports; their tendency was a "love of goods"; their policy may be called one of provision. It is easy to show, even statistically, how measures directed against exports were predominant throughout the Middle Ages, and how difficult this tendency was to overcome, especially with regard to foodstuffs. But however long-lived the medieval view was, it did not prevent an opposite tendency from gaining ground, a "fear of goods," a policy directed against imports instead of exports —in one word: protection. This became the mercantilist policy when concerned with commodities as distinct from money; and I do not think there can be any doubt that it constituted the most original contribution of mercantilism to the development of economic policy. It became more and more all-pervading, carrying at last also the citadel of the "policy of provision," the encouragement of a great supply of foodstuffs; introducing in its stead import prohibitions or import duties on foodstuffs, as well as bounties on exports of food.

It is important not to overlook the fact that protection here does not mean simply interference with foreign trade. All the three policies now under consideration were in agreement about interference; none of them was anything approaching laissez-faire. The characteristic feature of mercantilism in this respect went much farther than that; it meant a particular attitude to commodities. The protectionist attitude may even be said to be natural to the man in the street in a money economy, where the connection between purchases and sales disappears, being concealed by the cloak of money. If so, the gradual advance of money economy during the later Middle Ages explains the likewise progressive spread of protection from the more to the less advanced countries.

It is well known from later discussions on commercial policy that one of the greatest difficulties of protection, from a political point of view, consists in the fact that the protection of one branch of production means an increased burden upon those branches which make use of its products. In other words, the question arises how the factors of production should be treated. This difficulty is insoluble in principle, but various practical solutions are always attempted. What is interesting from the present point of view is the solution found by mercantilism on two points which appear in modern eyes to be perhaps

the most important of all, those of foodstuffs and labour. With regard to agriculture, the European continent long continued to regard it simply as a prerequisite of industry and therefore to keep down the prices of its products; but the opposite tendency, that represented by England, triumphed in the nineteenth century in almost every country. With regard to labour the early attitude retained its influence; for labour was not at all "produced" and therefore the quantity of it could be kept down without any disadvantage to "production." The outcome was the "economy of low wages," which had a host of advocates among mercantilists and dominated actual policy almost throughout; this aspect of the subject has been studied (from a standpoint different from mine) by Edgar Furniss in his far too little-known but really brilliant treatise, The Position of the Laborer in a System of Nationalism. It should be added, however, that this view was not quite universal among mercantilist writers, because it clashed with some other tenets of their mercantilism; and especially noticeable is an utterance by Daniel Defoe, who is otherwise the reverse of profound; almost alone among mercantilist writers he stressed the view that it is meaningless to be able to sell goods if this means impoverishing those who are producing them. This paved the way for the position taken up by Adam Smith. . . .

Lastly, mercantilism had a side which has until now been mostly overlooked. That may be called its general conception of society. The remarkable feature of this conception was its fundamental concord with that of laissez-faire; so that, while mercantilism and laissez-faire were each other's opposites in practical application and economic theory proper, they were largely based upon a common conception of society. No less remarkable is the character of this common conception, which is one that has usually been considered typical of laissez-faire and appears to be almost the opposite of mercantilism, as usually understood. Especially noticeable is the likeness between writers like Sir William Petty and Thomas Hobbes on the one hand and the leaders of English utilitarianism, such as Bentham, Austin, and James Mill, on the other.[4]

From other points of view the existence of ideas

[4] Petty and Hobbes were seventeenth-century political economists and theorists who lived and wrote during the golden age of mercantilism. Jeremy Bentham, John Austin, and James Mill were all prominent in the early nineteenth century as advocates of laissez-faire. [Editor's note.]

The Early Modern Era

common to mercantilism and its successor ought to be less surprising, for they were in harmony with the general trend of thought dominating Europe since the Renaissance. Philosophically, their basis was the concept of natural law, and connected with that was a belief in unalterable laws governing social life in general, a growing tendency to stress social causality, and consequently to deprecate interference directed against effects instead of causes. On principle, mercantilist authors and statesmen not only believed in but actually harped upon "freedom," especially "freedom of trade"; the expression, *la liberté est l' âme du commerce*, occurs hundreds of times in the correspondence of Colbert. To some extent this was doubtless due to the influence of the merchant class, though that influence was much weaker in a country like France than in England and Holland; and the fundamental identity of outlook between these three countries shows the existence of other factors besides. The most important of these undoubtedly was the influence of what may be called, by a somewhat hackneyed word, emancipation — emancipation from belief in traditional political and social institutions, and the contrary belief in social change. Closely allied to this was the emancipation from religious and ethical ideas in the social field, a secularisation and an amoralisation. Mercantilists came more and more to recommend amoral means to amoral ends; their most typical exponent in that respect was the Dutch-English physician Mandeville,[5] but Sir William Petty belonged to the same category; both, it should be noted, were entirely unconnected with the merchant class. Non-religious and amoral views came to light in every direction, in the treatment of interest-taking, in the recommendation of luxury, in the tolerance of heretics and Jews as favourable to trade, in opposition to celibacy, alms-giving, etc.

As I said just now, the remarkable thing is not the existence of these views, but the fact that while they were common to both mercantilism and *laissez-faire*, mercantilist and *laissez-faire* policies were poles asunder. I think the explanation of this apparent antinomy is to be found in one fundamental difference, namely, in the mercantilists' disbelief and the liberals' belief in the existence of a pre-established harmony. In the eyes of mercantilists the desired results were to be effected "by the dextrous management of a skillful politician"; they were *not*

expected to follow from the untrammelled forces of economic life. And the result was remarkable. If I may be allowed to quote a previous conclusion of my own: it was precisely this general mercantilist conception of society which led statesmen to even greater ruthlessness than would have been possible without the help of such a conception; for though they had rationalised away the whole social heritage, they had not arrived at a belief in an immanent social rationality. Thus they believed themselves justified in their interference and, in addition, believed in its necessity, without being held back by a respect for such irrational forces as tradition, ethics and religion. The humanitarian outlook was entirely alien to them, and in this they differed fundamentally from writers and politicians like Adam Smith, Malthus, Bentham, Romilly, and Wilberforce.[6] Lastly, the influence of their social philosophy upon their actions was weaker than that of their other conceptions.

There remains the question, whether it is admissible to speak of mercantilism as a policy and as a theory governed by an inner harmony; this has often been denied in later years, ... As to those parts called, in my sketch of mercantilism, a system of protection, money, and society, it appears to me beyond doubt that such a harmony existed. This does not, of course, mean that all statesmen and all writers were in complete agreement in their arguments, and even less that they all advocated the same measures. In the choice of practical issues they were greatly influenced by personal and class interests; but what shows the fundamental unity of their underlying principles is that opposite measures were advocated on the basis of a common body of doctrine. Also the fact that writers outside the clash of commercial interests, such as Petty and Locke, argued on exactly the same lines as the protagonists as well as the opponents of powerful commercial interests like those of the East India Company seems to prove it.

Needless to say, the relation between opinions on economic means and those on economic ends — the latter identical with commercial and monetary pol-

[5] Bernard de Mandeville (1670?–1733) was a philosopher and satirist who argued that men's self-interest and not their higher nature was the driving force which led to progress. [Editor's note.]

[6] Thomas Malthus (1766–1834) was an English economist who developed an influential thesis stating that population always tends to increase to the limits of the food supply. Jeremy Bentham (1748–1832) was one of the major proponents of utilitarianism. Sir Samuel Romilly (1757–1818) was an English jurist who carried on a long campaign to bring about legal reforms, especially the cruelty of the criminal law. William Wilberforce (1759–1833) was an English clergyman who conducted a campaign, especially in Parliament, to abolish slavery. [Editor's note.]

icy as applied to a unifying system and a system of power—was less intimate. However, the connection with the power of the State was quite clear to numerous statesmen and pamphleteers when they advocated protection and an increase in the supply of money; colonial policy is particularly enlightening in this respect, as can be seen, e.g. from the books by G. L. Beer.[7] On the other hand, with regard to mercantilism as a unifying system, there is the difficulty that in England, where ideas on protection and money supply were for the most part elaborated, the unifying side of mercantilism was of small importance. On the Continent, however, Colbert presents a clear-cut expression of *all* sides of mercantilism as here understood; and he is not only

[7] George L. Beer (1872–1920) was an American historian who wrote on the relation of the American colonies to British foreign policy. [Editor's note.]

the one great statesman who completely adopted mercantilism, but he was also given to working out on paper the principles underlying his actions to an extent uncommon among practical politicians. I therefore think it admissible to consider all aspects of mercantilism, as defined here, as interconnected, while admitting that the unifying aspect was more independent of the rest than the others were among themselves. This, of course, does not mean that what has here been called mercantilism belonged in all its ingredients exclusively to the period between the end of the Middle Ages and the nineteenth century. Like all other historical realities, it drew largely upon ideas and external realities surviving from previous ages, and in its turn influenced later developments. Mercantilism is simply a convenient term for summarising a phase of economic policy and economic ideas.

HERBERT HEATON

HECKSCHER'S AGE OF MERCANTILISM

In his article written at the request of the editors of the *Journal of Political Economy*, Herbert Heaton, a well-known economic historian, now emeritus, of the University of Minnesota, takes Heckscher to task for "idealizing mercantilism," that is for giving the concept of mercantilism too prominent a place as a formative factor in the development of Western society. Moreover, Heaton claims, the "evidence presented by Heckscher raises more questions than it answers." For example: "Who are the parents of mercantilism?" Were they the rulers, publicists, merchants, or "society" itself? And just what were "classes" in society? And, did these so-called classes differ from country to country? What exactly were the historical antecedents of mercantilism? Heaton's questions—and he has many—are sharply searching in their focus.

To Heckscher, as to all other writers on the subject, mercantilism is not a compact, consistent *ism*. Rather it is "only an instrumental concept which, if aptly chosen, should enable us to understand a particular historical period more clearly than we otherwise might" (I, 19).[1] Its content is that "phase in the

[1] The citations in parentheses throughout this article refer to Heckscher's *Mercantilism* (2 vols. London: 1935); [Editor's note.]

history of economic policy" which lies between the end of the Middle Ages and the dawn of the age of laissez faire. The chronological boundaries vary from country to country, but the sixteenth to eighteenth centuries see the policy in its heyday. During that period mercantilism was the normal approach to "a common European problem" (I, 13). France and England provide the best examples and occupy most of the pages, but similar policies were pursued

Reprinted from "Heckscher on Mercantilism" by Herbert Heaton in *The Journal of Political Economy*, XLV (1937), 371–372, 378–387, 392–393, by permission of the University of Chicago Press.

(and are briefly considered) in Scandinavia, the German states, Italy, and Spain. Then, as later, statesmen were copycats and imitated each other either in flattery or retaliation. . . .

When Adam Smith reviewed and reviled "the mercantile system," he dealt chiefly with its monetary attitude and its protectionist policy. When Schmoller wrote about *The Mercantile System and Its Historical Significance* in 1884, he declared that its "innermost kernel is nothing but state-making . . . . the total transformation of society and its organization, as well as of the state and its institutions, in the replacing of a local and territorial economic policy by that of the state." To Schmoller's English contemporary, Cunningham, mercantilism was a "system of power," a policy pursued "so that the power of England relatively to other nations might be promoted." These three writers thus examined four different aspects—money, protection, unification, and power—but each concentrated on one or two items which seemed important to him. Heckscher embraces all four and adds a fifth, for through the welter of discussion and the smoke of controversy he is able to perceive the emergence of a "fairly uniform conception of general social phenomena in the field of economics" and a "mercantilist conception of society." . . .

While Volume I [of Heckscher's *Mercantilism*] is entirely devoted to the endeavor of the state to secure or to exercise its internal power against particularist institutions, Volume II begins with a discussion of the need for external power in relation to other states. The question is put: Was this power "conceived as an *end in itself*, or only as a means for gaining something else, such as the well-being of the nation in this world or its everlasting salvation in the next?" (II, 16). Heckscher's answer is that power was an end in itself, to which all other considerations must bow and to which all economic activities must be bent. The quest for plenty must be subordinate to the quest for power. . . .

For this description of the mercantilist viewpoint Heckscher has been forcefully taken to task by his critics, and has retreated so far as to admit that "both 'power' and 'opulence'—to make use of the terms employed by Adam Smith—have been, and must be, of importance to economic policy of every description." But he still insists that mercantilism put power above opulence, in contrast with laissez faire, which made the creation of wealth its lodestar, with

small regard to the effect on the power of the state. I think he might have avoided this criticism if he had stopped to consider whether his end was not in turn a means. What did the mercantilist state want to do with its power when it got it? Use it partly for dynastic, religious, or diplomatic ends, but also to advance economic aims. As Fay has pointed out, England fought its rivals for access to the New World and the high seas in the sixteenth century, for the carrying trade in the seventeenth century, and for an overseas empire, conceived as a source of raw materials and a market for manufactured goods in the eighteenth century. Mercantilism was not a gospel of states that were satisfied merely to defend themselves and keep what they had already; it was a weapon for aggression, for acquisition, for securing more political power *and* economic benefits. Further, Heckscher might have considered whether the silence of laissez faire exponents about power was not due to the fact that they happened to live in a powerful country which was in no danger of attack and in a world that somehow managed to escape a first-class continental war between 1815 and 1914.

Whether power was sought as a means or an end, and whether those who wanted it were monogamous or bigamous in intent, the wooing influenced the attitude of the state toward most forms of economic enterprise. Two methods were adopted. In the first place the state tried to insure that it had within reach the appropriate necessities for war —especially munitions, ships, naval stores, sailors, and money; it therefore forbade the export of some essentials, encouraged the import of others by low duties or premiums, ordered fish to be eaten in order to keep a plentiful supply of hardy seamen, insisted on the use of native ships in parts of foreign or colonial trade, tried to keep what bullion it had and attract more, restricted the cutting of trees, and, if it had colonies, formulated plans for imperial self-sufficiency. In the second place, the state sought to create "a reservoir of economic resources generally," to stimulate the general economic prosperity of the country, and thus build up a large national income as a guaranty for insuring a powerful state. . . .

. . . Instead of telling us what was done, Heckscher tells us that what men did was determined by the general ideas which they held on the working of the economic system. "Economic policy is determined not so much by the facts as by people's conceptions of these facts" (II, 59); mercantilist economic policy was determined by the prevailing economic ideal, and Heckscher therefore sets out to describe the conception of economic life on which that ideal was based.

This conception is described as a matter of attitudes toward commodities and money; the difference between medieval, mercantilist, and laissez faire policies was the result of different attitudes toward these two goods. Toward commodities three viewpoints can be held: (1) To the merchant, "goods are neither welcome nor unwelcome; they form the basis of his transactions, to be both bought and sold; he does not want to exclude them, but neither does he want to keep them." (2) To the consumer, goods are things that one should have in plenty and at a low price; the consumer has a "hunger for goods." (3) To the producer, goods are a menace if they are too plentiful; oversupply is the enemy, and an understocked market is best; the producer has a "fear of goods." While policies might be expected to effect a compromise between two or even three of these viewpoints, since producers were also consumers and each community contained two or three classes of interests, Heckscher maintains that this was "much less so than might have been expected"; policy was dominated by one or other of the attitudes. . . .

After the end of the Middle Ages the position was "completely changed." A new policy and a new attitude toward goods pushed the medieval view farther and farther into the background; "there was a break between the staple policy and the policy of provision on the one hand and protectionism on the other." The "fear of goods" gripped men's minds, stimulating a policy directed against imports and in favor of exports—or, in other words, a policy of protection. This policy, together with a new monetary policy, "represents the most important contribution of mercantilism to the history of economic policy" (II, 59). It became "more and more all-pervading, carrying at last the citadel of the 'policy of provision,' the encouragement of a great supply of foodstuffs; introducing, in its stead, import prohibitions or import duties on foodstuffs, as well as bounties on exports of food."

If we ask why medievalists were provisionists, why mercantilists were protectionists, and what caused the change of attitude, Heckscher's answer is strong and simple. The policy of provision was only partly due to fiscal or military needs or to diplomatic strategy. It was not due to any universal scarcity of goods, since it took shape just when the crusades were stimulating trade and transportation. It was only partly due to uncertainty concerning local supplies of necessaries. All these possible explanations "pass over the really vital fact," which was the *prevalence of a natural economy rather than a money economy.* So long as goods were exchanged for goods, the facts of economic life could be seen more clearly than when a "veil of money" was drawn over the interconnected factors in exchange. Even "the meanest intelligence" would be able to see that nothing was gained if the goods offered brought only a small amount of other goods in return, and that "exchange was the more favourable the larger the amount of goods which could be got in exchange for one's own" (II, 103). Hence there was an ingrained reluctance to let goods go except where those obtainable in return seemed a marvelous bargain. But with the spread of money economy, "the result of production, from the producer's standpoint, no longer consists in other goods, but in money, [and] the money yield appears as the only aim of economic activity." Plenty of goods in the home market is now a bane rather than a boon, since prices are pushed down; buying and importing take money out of one's pocket and out of the country, but selling and exporting put it there. Thus the transfer from provisionism to protectionism, from hunger for goods to fear of goods, is explained fundamentally by the change from natural to money economy.

I wish we could believe it was all as simple as that. Of course it is true that money conceals the barter nature of trade and makes short-sighted views possible; but so does the work of the middle-man, and so does every piece of specialization or additional complication or roundaboutness in economic life. We might let much light into discussions of trade policy if every farmer or manufacturer whose goods go abroad were forced to take foreign goods of equal value in return, or if every merchant who carries on an export business were also obliged to run an import trade as well. But does Heckscher establish firmly enough the correlation between economies and policies? He admits it is difficult, and that "it is not possible to provide a *proof* that this explanation is the right one." But he maintains it fits in with the temporal development, and insists it is established "if the results arrived at [by an economic analysis of the situation] are not contradicted by the known facts and if these do not admit of any

The Early Modern Era

other equally plausible interpretation" (II, 139). Well, let us see.

Even allowing for a good time lag of conceptions after facts, is the temporal relationship close enough? The time chart runs as follows: The policy of provision "may be said to have commenced after ancient times in various countries during the course of the 12th century and reached its culminating point in the 14th century" (II, 90–91). The protectionist policy began in the first part of the thirteenth century in northern Italy, "when money economy was making great progress"; then in the fourteenth century it spread to the Low Countries, "which were in an advanced state of economic development," then to England by the fifteenth century, and so to other countries. There is thus a gap of only a hundred years between the beginning of provision and the beginning of protection. Was the crucial change in that hundred years the emergence of money economy? Was twelfth century Italy, or thirteenth-century Flanders, in the grip of natural economy? Did the economies of these two countries change so markedly in such a short space of time that a fundamental change in attitude toward commodities was inevitable? Was the policy of provision as portrayed in the tenth-century *Book of the Prefect* of Constantinople due to the fact that the metropolis of the Eastern Empire was operating on a natural economy? Was fourteenth-century England, which supplies Heckscher with his statistics of export control, on a natural economy? Do we, in fact, know enough about the early economic history of Italy or western Europe to be able to say that a policy of provision *originated* at any date or period, or that a natural economy prevailed until a certain time? Heckscher has shown that natural economy existed in Sweden as late as the sixteenth century; but we need many intensive studies of other countries before we can make strong assertions about genesis or exodus. Certainly Mr. Salzman's microscopic study of *English Trade in the Middle Ages* presents no simple picture of set policy determined by this or that economy; rather it warns one against painting simple pictures, against postdating developments, and against minimizing the modernity of the medieval.

The evidence presented by Heckscher raises more questions than it answers. For no single country are we given an adequate account of the two policies or of the trend from one to the other. But three questions are worth putting. In the first place, are not the protectionist elements present in medieval urban policy during the period of provision too large to be dismissed as "historical antecedents" (II, 130); and are not the elements of provisionism present in the mercantilist period so important that the shift in emphasis is really slight? If we take such a classic case as the English grain trade, where Heckscher finds a "sudden change in policy," the medieval policy did not exclude export in good years, while the seventeenth-century laws looked after the consumer by suspending export bounties, banning exports, and welcoming imports in bad years. Professor Barnes, in his *History of the English Corn Laws*, has shown that these steps were taken with sufficient frequency to be regarded as an essential part of the policy, and were not occasional and exceptional.

In the second place, should not the nature of the export prohibitions, as well as their number, be explored? If this were done, I doubt whether the majority of the 102 prohibitions and 76 export licenses found in Rymer's *Foedera*[2] would be found capable of a provisionist explanation. They would—as Heckscher points out and then blunts the point—be found to have a fiscal bearing, to be revenue-raising devices, to prevent trading with the enemy, to exert diplomatic pressure, to give or sell a privilege to one group at the expense of the rest, to benefit a local industry by hitting a foreign one, and so on. They might reinforce an opinion based on other medieval decrees that in the Middle Ages one could not do anything without getting permission, while in the modern world one can do anything provided one is not expressly forbidden. A prohibition was an exercise of political power, a ban that could be lifted by paying for exemption. The medieval ruler obtained much of his income by saying "No, unless you pay me to say 'Yes.'"

In the third place, cannot the growth of protectionism be explained by the growing intensity of competition as medieval commerce extended its range and volume, by the increasing tendency to attach nationality (or urbanity) to inanimate things, by the desire of infant (or even prenatal industries to ward off competition from maturer producers, by the desire of old industrial centers to check the competition of young virile rivals, and by the desire to hit a political or economic enemy? I do not think it is anachronistic to suggest that economically backward states felt the urge of economic nationalism for

[2] A collection of documents relating to medieval English history. [Editor's note.]

much the same reasons as did Australia, Canada, and the United States in the nineteenth century, or that economically mature states felt the same dread of newcomers as the Chamberlains made England do in the twentieth.

If rulers did not feel that way of their own accord, the native merchant or manufacturing class did not need to be very old or big before it began to bring pressure to bear and to use the state as a weapon in fighting the foreign rival. This was especially true when the political center was also the trade center, when a wobbly throne needed financial, moral, or muscular support, or when the bourgeoisie ran the state. It was also the case when a depression hit the market or the price level, and sent the victims scurrying to the ruler with demands that something be done to relieve and protect them. I have long felt that a graph showing business fluctuations should be a compulsory frontispiece for every historical study of commercial policy, and even for every general history. The relationship between depression on the one hand, and discontent, drastic demands, concessions to the vociferous, and great changes in policy, on the other hand, is intimate.

The foregoing comments on external pressure on the state lead to the consideration of a question that recurs frequently as one travels through Heckscher. Who suggested or thought of this or that item of policy? Who were the parents of mercantilism? All too often the policy is regarded as having only one parent, the state; it is described as the child of a ruler who is wise and solicitous for the welfare of his subjects or who is greedy for power, prestige, and pennies. But it seems important to remember that, as is usual, there were two parents. If kings wished to make economic means serve political ends, individuals, groups, regions, and classes were equally willing to use political means to secure profitable economic ends. They would appeal to patriotic or social ideals, and point out the harmony between the expected enhancement of their own income and the furtherance of the national good or the swelling of the king's income; they would exploit the growing antipathy toward the foreigner; they would use their full weight in parliament or at court to drive a proposal through; or they would bribe courtiers, send gifts to the king, and offer to split the profits fifty-fifty. They had nothing to learn from any modern lobbyist.

The initiative rarely came from a whole class, for a class was too unwieldy, too class-unconscious, and too much torn by conflicting faiths or interests to have one will or voice. Action came from individuals or compact groups who saw an opportunity to profit by protection or promotion; by getting English tobacco cultivation suppressed for the benefit of the Virginia Company; by stopping the Merchant Adventurer's export of undyed cloth for the benefit of Alderman Cockayne and his Eastland Company; by attacking the London merchants' monopoly of cloth exports, as did the Exeter merchants, and then passing on to demand a ban on the export of Irish wool or woolens to any part except England in the interests of the Devon textile industry and in defiance of the wishes of the London merchants. The more we dig into the details of seventeenth-century history, the less startling becomes Unwin's contention that nine-tenths of the ingenuity of that period was engaged not in exploiting the powers of nature "but in the endeavour to manipulate the power of the state and the wealth of the community for the benefit of individuals" or special interests. For, let economic historians always try to remember, the aim of enterprise is to get an income; the end matters more than the means, and if the state was the fountain of valuable monopolies or privileges, why not go there for your drink? . . .

In concluding, it seems just to ask: "What, then, was mercantilism? Was there ever such a thing?" I was once informed that in the London School of Economics ordinary pass students are told there was an Industrial Revolution, but honors students are told there was not. Heckscher tilts hard at another stand-by of the economic history teacher; he protests against the merging of mercantilism into "that unwholesome Irish stew called 'modern capitalism,'" and lashes at those who treat "all sorts of disconnected tendencies, paving the way to modern conditions," survey the economic history of Europe since the end of the Middle Ages, and then call it a history of modern capitalism. But has he saved mercantilism from this lynching of labels, this chastising of chapter headings? Has he not done the same thing as the Sombartians: strung on a thread, at least as tenuous, "all sorts of disconnected tendencies" in governmental policy during several centuries and called the result an *ism*? An *ism* usually consists of a criticism of existing conditions, an outline of an alternative policy, a theory to justify the criticism and the alternative, and an agitation or movement to supplant the old with the new; or, to put it another way, it is a policy and a theory governed by an inner harmony and advocated or applied in a particular time or phase of development. Under fire from his critics, Heckscher seems willing to let two of his five aspects—unification and power—go, though by no means completely. In his three other aspects—protection, money, and conception of society—he stoutly insists the harmony of a system is clear. If the criticisms made in this review are valid, the clearness is somewhat muddied; and the trinity of situation, theory, and policy is not apparent. One reason for this is that he has sought for a general principle—the attitude toward goods, and sought to fit policy into it. Another reason is that he has taken some of his sources too seriously. A third reason is that he has all too rarely let his eyes wander to see what was happening to the state or to economic life. It might even have helped him greatly to let capitalism come in occasionally to play ball with his hungers, fears, and economies. One of our best American students of mercantilism is not afraid to do so, and is able to reach the following illuminating and realistic conclusion: "Capitalism, then as now, found certain types of governmental action useful for promoting its profit-making ends, and the special pleading found in mercantilism gives us an early illustration of the intensity with which capitalism sets about to achieve its pecuniary goals." Consideration of the political and economic forces that surged round the mercantilist might have made the result an Irish stew; but that would be fitting, for certainly the age of mercantilism was not clear soup.

JACOB VINER

HECKSCHER ON THE ENDS OF MERCANTILISM

The renowned economic theorist, Jacob Viner, of Princeton University, opens his article, written in 1948 for the first issue of *World Politics*, with the assertion—often forgotten—that Heckscher was a free-trader, an economic liberal; and, as such, his volumes on mercantilism represent a sustained attack on that system. Leaving this point, Viner concerns himself in the rest of the article with Heckscher's contention that mercantilism was a system designed to promote the power and prestige of the rulers of the dynastic states rather than to increase the wealth and opulence of those states. But was power, asks Viner, an end in itself? or was it a means to the creation of wealth? On the last page of this selection, Viner suggests an answer to this question.

Eli Heckscher, the great Swedish economic historian and the outstanding authority on mercantilism today, follows the standard interpretation of the mercantilist objectives, but clearly to add to their shame rather than to praise them. Heckscher is an outstanding liberal, an individualist, a free-trader, and clearly anti-chauvinist. When to the section of his great work dealing with the foreign policy of the mercantilists he gives the heading "Mercantilism as a System of Power," and applies it to mercantilism in general and not only to the mercantilism of the absolute monarchies or of the non-maritime countries, he is reinforcing the indictment of it which he makes on other grounds, for to him "power" is clearly an ugly name for an ugly fact. More systematically, more learnedly, and more competently than anyone else, he supports his thesis that the mercantilists subordinated plenty to power. His argument calls therefore for detailed examination if this proposition is to be questioned.

Heckscher really presents an assortment of theses, ranging from the proposition (1) that for mercantilists—whether for most, or many, or only some, not

From Jacob Viner, "Power Versus Plenty as Objectives of Foreign Policy in the Seventeenth and Eighteenth Centuries," *World Politics*, I (1948). Excerpted by permission of the editors of *World Politics*. pp. 4–11.

being made very clear—power was the *sole* ultimate end of state policy with wealth merely one of the means to the attainment of power through the "eclectic" thesis (2) that power and plenty were parallel ends for the mercantilists but with much greater emphasis placed on power than was common before or later, to the concession (3) that mercantilists occasionally reversed the usual position and regarded power as a means for securing plenty and treated purely commercial considerations as more important than considerations of power. His central position, however, and to this he returns again and again, is that the mercantilists expounded a doctrine under which all considerations were subordinated to considerations of power as an end in itself, and that in doing so they were logically and in their distribution of emphasis unlike their predecessors and unlike the economists of the nineteenth century.

It is difficult to support this account of Heckscher's position by direct quotation from his text, since he presents it more by implication and inference from mercantilist statements than by clear-cut and explicit formulation in his own words. That mercantilists according to Heckscher tended to regard power as the *sole* end is to be inferred by the contrasts he draws between the position he attributes to Adam Smith—wrongly, I am sure—that "power was certainly only a means to the end . . . of opulence," and the "reverse" position of the mercantilists, the "reverse," I take it, being the proposition that wealth was only a means to power. That there is something special and peculiar to mercantilism in conceiving power as an end in itself underlies all of Heckscher's exposition, but the following passages come nearest to being explicit. "The most vital aspect of the problem is whether power is conceived as an end in itself, or only as a means for gaining something else, such as the well-being of the nation in this world or its everlasting salvation in the next." This leaves out of account, as an alternative, Heckscher's "eclectic" version, where both power and plenty are ends in themselves. On John Locke's emphasis on the significance for power of monetary policy, Heckscher comments, with the clear implication that the injection into economic analysis of considerations of power is not "rational," that it is "interesting as a proof of how important considerations of power in money policy appeared even to so advanced a rationalist as Locke.

Heckscher later restated his position in response to

criticisms, but it seems to me that he made no important concession and indeed ended up wtih a more extreme position than at times he had taken in his original exposition.

The second of the aims of mercantilist policy . . . —that of power—has met with a great deal of criticism from reviewers of my book . . . I agree with my critics on that point to the extent of admitting that both "power" and "opulence" . . . have been, and must be, of importance to economic policy of every description. But I do not think there can be any doubt that these two aims changed places in the transition from mercantilism to *laissez-faire*. All countries in the nineteenth century made the creation of wealth their lode-star, with small regard to its effects upon the power of the State, while the opposite had been the case previously.[1]

The evidence which Heckscher presents that the mercantilists considered power as an end in itself and as an important end, and that they considered wealth to be a means of power need not be examined here, since there is no ground for disputing these propositions and, as far as I know, no one has ever disputed them. That the mercantilists overemphasized these propositions I would also not question. Nor will I enter here into extended discussion of the rationality of these concepts beyond stating a few points. In the seventeenth and eighteenth centuries, colonial and other overseas markets, the fisheries, the carrying trade, the slave trade, and open trade routes over the high seas, were all regarded, and rightly, as important sources of national wealth, but were available, or at least assuredly available, only to countries with the ability to acquire or retain them by means of the possession and readiness to use military strength.

In the seventeenth and eighteenth centuries also, "power" meant not only power to conquer and attack, and the prestige and influence which its possession gave, but also power to maintain national security against external attack. "Power as an end in itself" must, therefore, be interpreted to include considerations of national security against external aggression on the nation's territory and its political and religious freedom. Given the nature of human nature, recognition of power as an end in itself was therefore then neither peculiar nor obviously irrational unless there is rational ground for holding that the promotion of economic welfare is the sole sensible objective of national policy to which

[1] From Economic History Review, VII (1936), 48; reprinted above. [Editor's note.]

every other consideration must be completely subordinated.

There remains, therefore, to be examined only whether Heckscher has demonstrated that mercantilists *ever* regarded power as the *sole* end of foreign policy, or ever held that considerations of plenty were *wholly* to be subordinated to considerations of power, or even whether they ever held that a choice has to be made in long-run national policy between power and plenty.

Despite his wide knowledge of the mercantilist literature, Heckscher fails to cite a single passage in which it is asserted that power is or should be the *sole* end of national policy, or that wealth matters *only* as it serves power. I doubt whether any such passage can be cited, or that anyone ever held such views. The nearest thing to such statements which Heckscher does cite are statements maintaining that wealth is also important for its own sake. In almost every case he cites, it is possible to cite from the same writer passages which show that wealth was regarded as valuable also for its own sake. The passage of this type which Heckscher most emphasizes is a "passing remark" of Colbert in a letter: "Trade is the source of finance and finance is the vital nerve of war." Heckscher comments that Colbert here "indicates clearly the relationship between means and ends." But argument from silence is notoriously precarious, and if it were to be pressed would work more against than for Heckscher's thesis, since there is a great mass of mercantilist literature in which there is no mention whatsoever, and no overt implication, of considerations of power. Colbert does not here indicate that the relationship was a one-way one. To make a significant point Heckscher would have to show that Colbert would not also have subscribed to the obverse proposition that strength is the vital nerve of trade and trade the source of finance.

Of all the mercantilists Colbert is the most vulnerable, since he carried all the major errors of economic analysis of which they were guilty to their most absurd extremes both in verbal exposition and in practical execution, and since, either as expressing his own sentiments or catering to those of his master, Louis XIV, he developed more elaborately than any other author the serviceability to power of economic warfare, the possibilities of using military power to achieve immediate economic ends, and the possibilities of substituting economic warfare for

military warfare to attain national ends. Even in his case, however, it is not possible to demonstrate that he ever rejected or regarded as unimportant the desirability for its own sake of a prosperous French people or the desirability of guiding French foreign policy, military and economic, so as to augment this prosperity. In many of his official papers he is obviously catering to Louis XIV's obsession with power and prestige, or perhaps to a conventional fashion of *pretending* that a great monarch would be so obsessed. . . .

Certain peculiar features of mercantilist economic analysis—features incidentally which modern apologists for mercantilist economics such as Lipson seem strangely to avoid discussing—do seem to imply a disregard on the part of mercantilists for economic welfare. What was apparently a phase of scholastic economics, that what is one man's gain is necessarily another man's loss, was taken over by the mercantilists and applied to countries as a whole. They incorporated this with their tendency to identify wealth with money, and with their doctrine that, as far as money was concerned, what mattered was not the absolute quantity but the relative quantity as compared with other countries. Since the quantity of money in the world could be taken as constant, the quantity of wealth in the world was also a constant, and a country could gain only at the expense of other countries. By sheer analogy with the logic of military power, which is in truth a relative matter, and with the aid of the assumption of a close relationship between "balance of power" and "balance of trade," which, however, they failed intelligently to analyze, the mercantilists were easily led to the conclusion that wealth, like power, also was only a relative matter, a matter of proportions between countries, so that a loss inflicted on a rival country was as good as an absolute gain for one's own country. At least one mercantilist carried this doctrine to its logical conclusion that plague, war, famine, harvest failure, in a neighboring country was of economic advantage to your own country. On such doctrine, Adam Smith's trenchant comment is deserved, although he exaggerates its role in mercantilist thought and practice:

By such maxims as these, however, nations have been taught that their interest consisted in beggaring all their neighbours. Each nation has been made to look with an invidious eye upon the prosperity of all the nations with which it trades, and to consider their gain as its own loss. Commerce, which ought naturally to be, among nations, as among individuals, a bond of union and friendship, has become the most fertile source of discord and animosity. The capricious ambition of kings and ministers has not, during the present and the preceding century, been more fatal to the repose of Europe, than the impertinent jealousy of merchants and manufacturers. The violence and injustice of the rules of mankind is an ancient evil, for which, I am afraid, the nature of human affairs can scarce admit of a remedy. But the mean rapacity, the monopolizing spirit of merchants and manufacturers, who neither are, nor ought to be, the rulers of mankind, though it cannot perhaps be corrected, may very easily be prevented from disturbing the tranquillity of any body but themselves.

Heckscher cites mercantilist doctrine such as Adam Smith here criticizes as evidence that the mercantilists were not interested in economic welfare for its own sake, but subordinated it to considerations of power. Adam Smith's assumption that the exposition of such doctrine was confined to merchants rather than statesmen (or philosophers) is invalid. But in so far as it was expounded by merchants, it is scarcely conceivable that these were so different from merchants at other times that they were governed more by chauvinist patriotism than by rapacity. The significance of such doctrine is not that those who adhered to it placed power before plenty, but that they grossly misunderstood the true means to and nature of plenty. What they were lacking in was not economic motivation but economic understanding.

What then is the correct interpretation of mercantilist doctrine and practice with respect to the roles of power and plenty as ends of national policy? I believe that practically all mercantilists, whatever the period, country, or status of the particular individual, would have subscribed to all of the following propositions: (1) wealth is an absolutely essential means to power, whether for security or for aggression; (2) power is essential or valuable as a means to the acquisition or retention of wealth; (3) wealth and power are each proper ultimate ends of national policy; (4) there is a long-run harmony between these ends, although in particular circumstances it may be necessary for a time to make economic sacrifices in the interest of military security and therefore also of long-run prosperity.

The omission of any one of these four propositions results in an incorrect interpretation of mercantilist thought, while additions of other propositions would probably involve internal dispute among mercantilists. It is to be noted that no proposition is included as to the relative weight which the mercantilists attached to power and to plenty, respectively. Given the general acceptance of the existence of harmony and mutual support between the pursuit of power and the pursuit of plenty, there appears to have been little interest in what must have appeared to them to be an unreal issue. When apparent conflict between these ends did arise, however, differences in attitudes, as between persons and countries, did arise and something will be said on this matter later.

D. C. COLEMAN

HECKSCHER'S MERCANTILISM: DID IT EXIST?

In an able review of the revised edition of *Mercantilism* (London, 1955) that might better be titled "Heckscher Revisited or Heckscher Twenty Years Later," D. C. Coleman of the London School of Economics reiterates the point made by Viner that Heckscher as a follower of Adam Smith accepts the Smithian notion that mercantilism was a coherent system. Once the notion of coherence is established, Coleman notes, Heckscher insists—and this assumption is a key to his whole approach—that economic policy is not to be seen as "the outcome and result of the actual economic situation," but a part of the continuity of economic ideas.

It would be impossible to summarize all of Coleman's arguments; but in reading this review, the student might well keep in mind these recurring questions: What is the relationship between mercantile ideas and practice? How does the Dutch position in the mercantile system differ from that of the English and French? What is the connection between the Mercantile Era and the Middle Ages? Was there, as Heckscher suggests, a coherence in mercantile thought? And lastly, a question that runs throughout the essay: Was there such a thing as mercantilism? Or, more to the point, was there ever such a thing as Heckscher's mercantilism?

It is more than a quarter of a century since the late Professor Eli Heckscher's *Mercantilism* first appeared, in Swedish (1931), and nearly as long since it became available in German (1932) and in English (1935). The recent publication of a revised English edition[1] offers an opportunity for a re-appraisal both of the work and of the concept with which it is concerned. The latter has loomed large in the writing of economic history and in the study of economic thought. What is its value? What did it become in Heckscher's hands?

I

Adam Smith saw political economy as having two distinct objects: to provide revenue or subsistence for the people or to enable them to provide these for themselves; and to supply the state with revenue for the public services. There were two different systems by which these ends were achieved: the commercial or mercantile system and the system of agriculture. The former was "the modern system." He spent the whole of Book IV of the *Wealth of Nations* constructing it, examining it and denouncing it. In reality, the "system" was the reverse of systematic: a jumble of devices, assembled over the course of a century or more to meet the demands of state finance, sectional interests and power politics. But there was enough theoretical similarity in its constituent parts for Smith, superb systematizer that he was, to be able to present it as a systematic absurdity.

But Smith's presentation of the mercantile system was limited in scope. It assumed, he said, that wealth consisted in gold and silver; and that, for a country not possessing gold and silver mines, the favourable balance of trade was the only way of securing this wealth. Therefore, it became the object of political economy to discourage imports and encourage exports. And this was done by the following

means: two sorts of restraints upon imports — high duties and prohibitions; and four sorts of encouragement for exports — bounties, drawbacks, treaties and colonies. Smith saw the system thus defined as prevailing from the end of the seventeenth century, presumably supposing that economic life was previously unencumbered by it, for he admitted that he thought it improbable that "freedom of trade should ever be entirely *restored* in Great Britain" (my italics). Though exempting from his condemnation the Navigation Act of Charles II, on the grounds of political expediency, he damned this apparatus of government action comprehensively and vigorously. He damned it in order to construct, on the wreckage of its absurdities, his own theoretical structure of economic *laissez-faire*. Though he wrote the following words in particular relation to English colonial rule, they summarise adequately his particular blend of economic and moral fervour:

To prohibit a great people . . . from making all that they can of every part of their own produce or from employing their stock and industry in the way that they judge most advantageous to themselves is a manifest violation of the most sacred rights of mankind.

The Wealth of Nations preached doctrines allegedly of universal validity and in practice peculiarly apt for the expanding, industrializing Britain of the time. It became the Bible of a new politico-economic era. For nearly a century after its publication little was heard in Britain of the out-dated "mercantile system," save for occasional shouts by some of the popularisers of classical economics, deriding the evident fatuity of its supposed principles. In the later decades of the nineteenth century, however, it reappeared on the stage, refurbished by the opponents of *laissez-faire*, and inflated by them into a gigantic theoretical balloon. Its re-appearance was a reflection of the changing economic relationships of the time; the rising power and wealth of Germany was being developed with substantial government protection; and the challenge to British economic supremacy, both from Europe and from across the

[1] E. F. Heckscher, *Mercantilism* (Revised Edition, Ed. E. F. Söderlund, London, 1955). All page references given in the present article are to this edition.

From D. C. Coleman, "Eli Heckscher and the Idea of Mercantilism," *The Scandinavian Economic History Review*, V (1957), 3–25. Reprinted by permission of *The Scandinavian Economic History Review* and the author.

Atlantic, brought a challenge to the creed of *laissez-faire*—a notion taken over from a Frenchman, developed by a Scotsman and put into practice by the English. . . .

III

With the exception of Viner's point about Heckscher's treatment of the question of power, this general body of criticism is not significantly reflected in the new edition. Had serious heed been taken of the more searching criticisms, then as Heckscher himself wrote, in the preface to the second edition, "this would have meant an entirely new book. . . . So basic is this criticism that it might be said of the book as it has been said of the Jesuits: they must be as they are or not be at all." Apart from a number of modifications to the earlier text, particularly to meet Viner's criticisms, the main difference between the two editions is the presence of an additional chapter, in Vol. II, on "Keynes and Mercantilism." The content of this first appeared as an article in Swedish, in 1946; it does not suggest any significant change in Heckscher's approach to the subject. . . . What, then, of mercantilism and *Mercantilism* today?

A question which readily comes to mind when examining the idea of mercantilism is simply: Is this about economic thought in the past or is it about economic policy?

The curiously hybrid parentage of the notion provides an important source of this confusion. It was, as Judges put it, "conceived by economists for purposes of theoretical exposition and mishandled by historians in the service of their political ideals." One might add, moreover, that it was first mishandled by historians who were primarily *political* historians and then developed by an economist-cum-economic historian whose *economic ideals* had much in common with those of Adam Smith himself. This is one reason, perhaps, not only for the seeming unreality of the idea to the economic historian of today but also for its meaninglessness or irrelevance to the political historian. So the notion of mercantilism, as developed, is yet another of the wedges helping to keep open the gap between political and economic history. The gap is still wide today. It is not simply the product of an argument about the economic interpretation of history, though it has often been made to seem as though it were. Adam Smith had a low opinion of the wisdom of

political action, but a great belief in the efficacy of certain economic principles. In speaking, for instance, about whether retaliation in a tariff dispute should be allowed, he described this as a difficult question of judgment belonging not so much to the science of the legislator whose deliberations should be governed by general principles which remain constant but "to the skill of that insidious and crafty animal, vulgarly called a statesman or politician, whose councils are directed by the momentary fluctuations of affairs." Cunningham's emphasis fell upon the pre-eminence of politics; he believed in protectionism in his own time and in the merits of political action in other times: "our national policy is *not* the direct outcome of our economic conditions . . . politics are more important than economics in English history." Schmoller's political orientation was even more striking. So engrossed was he with the idea of political achievement that he believed that the conception of national economic life, of national agriculture, industry, shipping, fisheries, of national currency and banking systems, of national division of labour and trade must have arisen before "the need was felt of transforming old municipal and territorial institutions into national and state ones." To English history, this is largely irrelevant. Whatever its relevance elsewhere, it was in truth all part of the distasteful business by which history is pressed into the service of aggressive nationalism. His words in the 1880's found a sinister echo in the 1930's:

The ideals of Mercantilism . . . meant, practically, nothing but the energetic struggle for the creation of a sound state and a sound national economy . . . they meant the belief of Germany in its own future, the shaking off of a commercial dependence on foreigners which was continually becoming more oppressive, and the education of the country in the direction of economic autarchy.

Heckscher's approach resuscitated the Smithian ideas, though without Smith's concession to political realities, but also took over Cunningham's insistence on the secondary importance of economic conditions and Schmoller's interest in state-building. Consequently mercantilism in Heckscher's hands, is not, as he claims, "a phase in the history of economic policy" but is rather an explanatory term for the phase in economic thought which was roughly coincident with the early growth of state power in Europe. The price paid for the extension in range of the term and for the brilliant explanatory synthesis achieved was the severe damage done to its relationship with historical reality.

One of the bases of this divorce between ideas and reality was Heckscher's use of sources. Though he spoke of policy, in fact as already noted, he pressed into service all forms of economic pronouncement: statutes, edicts, pamphlets, tracts for the times. All sources thus become equal. Time and time again, Heckscher notes the possibility that a particular piece of economic writing may have born some relation to the circumstances of the time, only then to insist on the relative unimportance of this factor. Although, for instance, he admits that Thomas Mun[2] and Sir Josiah Child[3] had good practical reasons as East India merchants to hold the views on money that they expounded so skilfully, the events of the time "played no essential motivating part in mercantilism as a monetary system though their influence was not altogether absent."

And this leads to the key assumption of Heckscher's whole approach—the insistence that economic policy is not to be seen as "the outcome and result of the actual economic situation," but what matters is the power and continuity of economic ideas. This is not simply a viewpoint set out in the course of introductory remarks; it is reiterated insistently, hammered home in regard to all aspects of the subject. It will suffice to quote a few examples:

if economic realities sometimes made themselves felt, this did not divert the general tendency of economic policy. (i, 268)
As used in this book [protectionism] does not refer to the presence or absence of governmental measures as such. . . . Protectionism is taken to be the outcome of a definite attitude towards goods. . . . (ii, 58)
Our concern here is not with economic realities but with the world of economic ideas. (ii, 151)
We need no longer suppose that some peculiar state of affairs existed, corresponding to the mercantilists' theoretical outlook. (ii, 199)

This attitude secures its most extreme expression in the new chapter on "Keynes and Mercantilism":

There are no grounds whatsoever for supposing that the mercantilist writers constructed their system—with its frequent and marked theoretical orientation—out of any knowledge of reality however derived. (ii, 347)

In practice, it was impossible for Heckscher consistently to maintain this position. Sporadically he makes concessions to that real world in which meditation upon the complexity of economic forces is sometimes distressingly absent or often pursued in an atmosphere polluted by the baneful winds of interest and expediency. The result is a curiously capricious appeal to reality. Governmental need for revenue is the practical problem to which Heckscher is most willing to make concessions. It is hardly possible to avoid it. But Heckscher's approach means that his treatment of financial policy sits most awkwardly within the general framework which he constructed. Thus, as Heaton pointed out, he goes through 42 pages of description and discussion of French guild monopolies before admitting that financial needs were of paramount importance. Though Colbert's efforts to create national trading companies in France may perhaps be made to fit into mercantilism under "unification," the formation of similar English companies in the late sixteenth century fits very oddly into that category; and the rider that in fact these companies "served as milch cows to the Government in its perpetual financial straits," whatever its degree of truth, hardly makes their situation in Heckscher's work more convincing. And the treatment of English protectionism from the late seventeenth century onwards largely in terms of theoretical ideas and without significant reference to war finance and Anglo-French politico-economic relations further emphasises the fact that this is really a work about economic thought and not about policy.

Again, whatever the truth of Heckscher's assertion that the Netherlands "did not really follow mercantilist practice" and were "less affected by mercantilist tendencies than most other countries," it is arbitrary largely to ignore Dutch economic policy, save for some reference to trading companies. Heckscher indeed belittled the importance of regulation and control in Dutch trade and industry, and ignored changes and conflicts in Dutch policy which were clearly built not simply upon ideas but upon the changing economic circumstances of Holland. Contemporaries had no doubts about the practical realities which underlay Dutch policy and success. Sir William Temple[4] wrote of Holland in 1673:

Thus the trade of this Country is discovered to be no effect of common contrivances, of natural dispositions or situa-

---

[2] Thomas Mun (1571–1641) was an important mercantilist who wrote arguing in favor of a favorable balance of trade against those who sought to stop the flow of money out of England.

[3] Sir Josiah Child (1630–1699) was governor of the East India Company; he too wrote on the importance of a favorable balance of trade. [Editor's note.]

[4] Sir William Temple (1628–1699) was an important diplomatist during the reign of Charles II, serving chiefly in the Spanish and the Dutch Netherlands. [Editor's note.]

tions, or of trivial accidents; But of a great Concurrence of Circumstances, a long course of Time, force of Orders and Method, which never before met in the World to such a degree, or with so prodigious a Success and perhaps never will again.

In this, was he not nearer to reality than Heckscher's appeal to "the national characteristics of the people"?

Heckscher's insistence upon the unimportance of actual circumstances in shaping policy reflected a strong distaste for anything which he regarded as smacking of economic determinism. It found him defending some indefensible positions, as in his dispute with Charles Wilson over the use of bullion in international trade in the seventeenth century. Apparently what fired him to retort as vigorously as he did was that: "Mr. Wilson starts from the attitude of Lord Keynes and Professor G. N. Clark and, like them, he wants to find an explanation of mercantilist tendencies in the actual economic conditions of the times." Similarly, he attacked Bruno Suviranta's effort to show that the balance of trade theory had its roots in the circumstances of the time. Heckscher conceded that Misselden[5] and Mun created "the mercantilist monetary and commercial doctrine in its narrowest sense"; and recent research has shown that in fact much of Mun's formulation of the balance of trade doctrine sprang directly from his enquiries into the depression of 1622–3.

The final irony in Heckscher's determination to stand by his principles, at whatever cost, is reached in his chapter on "Keynes and Mercantilism." Having vigorously denounced Keynes for supposing that the mercantilists, or indeed any other economic writers, ever reached their conclusions by their perceptions of actual experience, he then executed a complete volte-face in regard to Keynes' own work. The *General Theory* "should be read in its historical context . . . its *specific* motivation is to be found in the persistent unemployment in England between the two World Wars."

Of more fundamental importance perhaps than any of these anomalous positions into which Heckscher thus led himself by insistence on this key assumption was that which arose from the problem inherent in the assumption itself. If at any given time, the approach to a problem is to be assessed not in terms

of any contemporary awareness of reality, but in terms of the continuity of ideas, the question immediately arises: how did those ideas themselves arise in the first place? Did they spring fully-armed into the mind of man? Or was there some unregenerate past in which reality and mentality had some more positive relationship? Heckscher votes, though hardly enthusiastically, for the latter. The answer lies in that blurred historical distance where life was somehow different—the Middle Ages:

town policy was also determined by certain ethical considerations . . . [which] arose from the general social ethic of the Middle Ages . . . these considerations also finding some support in the economic circumstances of the time. (i, 129)
In the Middle Ages, the economic life and political outlook of the town had been largely a product of the conditions of the time. . . . (i, 135)

This enables Heckscher, in dealing w■■the regulation of economic life, consistently to appeal to the "medieval heritage" as a determinant of action. But it raises a pretty problem in the transition from the "policy of provision" which he associates peculiarly with medieval towns, to the "policy of protection" of the "mercantilist" era. And here the *deus ex machina* which is invoked to explain the change is the transition from natural to money economy:

the facts were seen much more clearly by medieval observers than by those of later times, because the conditions in precisely this connection were so much simpler.
  It was the condition of *natural economy* which brought out these facts. . . . (ii, 103)

The doubts which Heaton threw upon Heckscher's assumption of the prevalence of "natural economy" in medieval Europe have been fully supported in the twenty years since Heaton wrote; indeed the twin notions of "natural economy" and "money economy" now seem to be of rather dubious validity and limited application. In his concern with "natural economy," Heckscher was heavily influenced by his work on sixteenth century Sweden, and it would seem in retrospect that, valuable as that work is, it does not in all aspects provide a safe basis for generalizations about European economic life as a whole.

But if Heckscher wished to invoke this transition in order to explain one sort of change in economic policy, he was unwilling to use it to explain the "mercantilist's" desire for bullion. This led him to further contradictions of his own position. Having

---

[5] Edward Misselden (ca. 1654) was a merchant active in the affairs of the East India Company and a writer on economic matters, especially free trade. [Editor's note.]

correlated the rise of a money economy with protectionism and dated it from thirteenth-century Italy, extending to France and England in the fifteenth century, when he comes to deal with monetary questions, he asserts that it was the sixteenth and seventeenth centuries which formed, "at least in many countries . . . the period of transition from a predominantly natural to a predominantly money economy and at the same time from an insignificant to an extremely abundant silver production." It is perhaps scarcely surprising that he was later moved to observe that "the transition to a money economy never occurs at once and can hardly be assigned to any definite period whatsoever." He demonstrated instead that the "mercantilists" wanted bullion for a set of theoretical reasons, the exposition of which by contemporary writers was substantially later than the supposed transition from natural to money economy and the influx of precious metals from the West. And so, again, "the circumstances of the time were not decisive."

If the continued concern with natural economy makes the new edition of *Mercantilism* seem rather old-fashioned, so also does its invocation of "medieval universalism." The latter still has a tight hold on history, but its grip is slowly being loosened. To Heckscher, however, it was real enough:

the medieval combination of universalism and particularism. . . . (i, 22)

the fundamental unity of medieval culture. . . . (i, 327)

those universalist factors such as the Church and the empire which had fashioned medieval society. . . . (ii, 13)

the Middle Ages which their universal static ideal. . . . (ii, 26)

As for the general conception of society, a sharp division obtains between the Middle Ages and the following period. . . . (ii, 271)

Once again, because of his unwillingness to take into account the differing elements of continuity or of change in economic circumstances, he was led to adopt mutually confusing positions. Though he attributes to the medieval world and "the medieval mind" these especial and temporally limited qualities, he also endows them with remarkable staying powers in themselves and irrespective of that transition from natural to money economy which is otherwise supposed to have transformed medieval conceptions. Thus if middlemen in the trade in foodstuffs were attacked in Tudor and Stuart England, it was not because of special circumstances but because of a "medieval conception"; and the general reason for the persistence or recurrence of elements of the "policy of provision" was to be found not in any external conditions but because "municipal economic principles stood out as almost the only clear principles of economic policy, and remained so for centuries, even after the political influence of the cities had ceased."

Heckscher emphasised the need to distinguish between economic conditions or economic reality and the attempts made by governments to influence or alter those conditions. This distinction is made briefly in *Mercantilism* and more clearly in the *Sveriges ekonomiska historia*[6] where he further stresses the dangers of using information about policy as a means of getting to know about economic reality. Acts of economic policy are statements of intention and not descriptions of reality. They will be a reflection of what is not to be found in the economy rather than what is. This is important and salutary advice when considering the development or structure of a country's economy, but it does leave policy as an entity in itself, exogenous, a determinant rather than in any way determinate. Heckscher admitted that the policy and conditions were "inextricably bound up," but his approach is most clearly stated thus: "economic policy is determined not so much by the economic facts as by people's conception of those facts." Now Heckscher had a low opinion of the economic perception of those who lived in the "mercantilist" era. Consequently, because of his reluctance to concede that the ideas and policies of the time might owe something to contemporary awareness of economic reality, however crude or empirical, Heckscher did not bring out at all clearly certain fundamental distinctions both in ideas and in circumstances in the so-called "mercantilist" period. He stressed the importance, for example, of the static conception of economic life, of economic resources and activity so evident at that time; he emphasised that this provided one reason for the many commercial wars; implicit in the "tragedy of mercantilism" was the belief that what was one man's or country's gain was another's loss. Yet, vital as this is, as he himself says, to an understanding of the attitudes of the time, he nowhere asks why men should have believed it to be true.

[6] *An Economic History of Sweden*, tr. Göran Ohlin (Cambridge, Mass.: Harvard University Press, 1954).

But is it in fact a surprising notion in the pre-industrialized economy? It was, after all, a world in which population remained remarkably static; in which trade and production usually grew only very gradually; in which the limits of the known world were expanded slowly and with great difficulty; in which economic horizons were narrowly limited; and in which man approximated more closely than today to Hobbes' vision of his natural state: for most men most of the time, life *was* "poor, nasty, brutish and short." The pervasive conception of a prevailingly inelastic demand, not readily capable of expansion, changeable not so much by economic forces as by the dictates of authority, is not unreasonable in a political world of absolute monarchs and an economic world in which population and trade did not move rapidly and in which the purchasing power of the overwhelming majority of men and women remained very low and changed very little. Nor were informed contemporaries unaware of such matters. When Botero[7] commented on static population, when Gustav Vasa or John Wheeler defended the merits of "passive trade," or when Colbert observed that the trade and shipping of Europe could not be increased "since the number of people in all the States remains the same and consumption likewise remains the same"—is it not reasonable to suppose that their conceptions of economic reality may have approximately coincided with the facts? Conversely, when Heckscher simply assumed that the demand for English cloth was necessarily elastic and chided the mercantilists for not being "alive to the consequences of this elementary facts of everyday life"—does this suggest a necessarily appropriate conception of economic reality?

These characteristics of the pre-industrialized economy, as well as others too numerous and complex to be considered here, were true not simply of the "mercantilist" times but of earlier centuries. The continuity of ideas which Heckscher was eager to stress was paralleled by a continuity of basic conditions which he ignored. It is upon these substrata of economic life that are built the general conceptions of economic life which men hold. These concep-

tions are not necessarily the same as what is commonly distinguished as the "economic thought" of the age. They are the latent assumptions of belief and action, counterparts in the economic sphere to those which underlie philosophy or religion or art. Contemporaries often did not bother to note them because they were too obvious to need noting. The historian has to dig for them. Sometimes, on the other hand, contemporaries did write down such things, and then the problem is to distinguish this from attempts at systematic, rational analysis of economic phenomena. Colbert was an administrator of genius but he had the ordinary man's view of economic life. Is his vision of reality the same as that of Petty or North or Davenant?[8] This was a distinction which Heckscher did not make. And it is an important one, for he viewed the economic thought and policy of an age in which no systematized body of economic analysis existed, through the spectacles of an age in which it does. Consequently, apart from his unwillingness to take into account the special circumstances in which tracts were written or enactments made, he also failed to distinguish between: (a) limited descriptions of observed phenomena, (e.g. descriptions by contemporaries of exchange movements); (b) accounts or explanations drawing upon the long-held, deeply embedded economic pre-conceptions of the day (e.g. notions embodying the static view of economic activity, or the labour theory of value); and (c) attempts at rationalized analysis or calculation (e.g. some of the work of the "Political Arithmetic" writers). By his methods, all were implicitly given the same weight and influence. Implicitly he identified a "conception of economic reality" with the classical or neo-classical economists' conception. And he did not consider why they might be different.

At the same time as certain basic characteristics of economic life remained the same during these centuries, so also were forces of change gradually making themselves felt. Two main channels through which they made themselves felt were the great expansion of trade, to the East, to Africa and above all to the New World; and the growth of industry in

---

[7] Giovanni Botero (1543–1617) was an Italian who wrote on politics and economics; among his concerns was the problem of population and the forces which limited its growth. Gustav Vasa was king of Sweden from 1523–1560; his chief economic concern was exploiting lands taken from the church as the major prop of a strong monarchy; he was extremely cautious in matters of foreign trade. John Wheeler was an early seventeenth century merchant and economist in England who wrote in defense of regulated trade. [Editor's note.]

[8] Sir William Petty (1632–1687) was an English political economist whose writings challenged some of the precepts of mercantilist doctrines and advanced highly sophisticated economic concepts. Sir Dudley North (1641–1691) was a statesman and economist who argued for free trade and propounded ideas about the real wealth of a nation which challenged mercantilist views. Charles Davenant (1656–1714) was still another economist who wrote extensively on economic matters, especially trade. [Editor's note.]

The Early Modern Era

many nations of Europe. As the economic implications of these new developments gradually became apparent, the old ideas of fixity and limited horizons became intolerable. In the course of the seventeenth century, for instance, imports from American sugar and tobacco plantations grew at rates unprecedented in the economic development of the era; by the end of the century imports of Indian textiles were creating severe problems for existing European textile industries. Is it unreasonable to suppose that such developments left a mark on thought and policy? Much of the policy of the later seventeenth century is an attempt to deal with the new developments in terms of old conceptions: the so-called "Old Colonial System" is one example. And the anticipation of "Free Trade" ideas in late seventeenth-century England was partly a product of Indian textile imports. But just as the old lingered with the new in economic circumstances, so it did in ideas. Faced with the decay of Dutch trade, the Amsterdam merchants who in 1751 drew up proposals for its rejuvenation still built on old and familiar conceptions: "by these general amendments, we shall put ourselves in a condition to *reduce* the trade of Hamburgh, Bremen, Lubeck, Denmark, and other places; at least to prevent them doing us a further prejudice" (my italics). Though they put forward the idea of a free port, the idea of mutual benefit from general expansion was not present; one port's loss was another's gain. And this in the country "less affected by mercantilist ideas."

Here, then, is another sort of distinction which Heckscher's treatment tends to obsure: the counterpoint of old and new conceptions. It developed particularly in the century from approximately 1650 to 1750, as the implications of European expansion made themselves felt. To compare the prolific "mercantilist" writings of this period with their far fewer counterparts a century or more earlier, can be dangerous if it leads one to believe that because men in the earlier period were not attempting formal analysis of economic life, they did not know what was going on in the economic world. Colbert thought it "in the natural order of things" that each nation should have its share of ships and commerce in proportion to its power, population and sea-coasts. But the course of economic change was to show that this was an untenable concept, just as the birth of modern scientific ideas was to put an end to that other "natural order" which was the inheritance of the natural philosophy of Aristotle.

The converse of Heckscher's unwillingness to grant much weight to current economic conditions in the formulation of policy was his insistence upon the importance of economic ideas, and their continuity in informing the actions of policy. How realistic is this for "mercantilist" Europe? Today, faced with particular economic problems the governments of advanced societies draw upon the advice not only of businessmen or trade unionists, but also upon that of professional economists. Moreover, governments are increasingly coming to include men who have either had some formal training in economics or at least are acquainted with its teachings. Until comparatively recent times those teachings have been primarily those of classical economics, extended, modified, refined, but in essence the political economy of *laissez-faire* England. Eli Heckscher was peculiarly a product of this situation. An admirer of England and English economic institutions, an eminent theoretical economist, accustomed to handling problems of government economic policy, he had grown up in a rapidly industrializing Sweden in which various economic questions came more or less quickly to the forefront of discussion, and which threw up a number of economists of outstanding ability. It is perhaps hardly surprising that he should have exaggerated the role of economic thought in the formulation of policy.

It would be absurd to suggest that the ideas which men held about economic life had no influence on policy. But they are only one element in policy formulation, and their relative importance varies from place to place and time to time. The great value of Heckscher's work lies in its broad and searching presentation of the nature and complexity of those ideas, in spite of the fact that it is less successful in fitting them into the historical context of practical policy. George Unwin's dictum on policy in action, although going too far in the opposite direction, offers a useful antidote:

Policy, as actually found in history, is a set of devices into which a government drifts under the pressure of practical problems, and which gradually acquire the conscious uniformity of a type, and begin, at last, to defend themselves as such.

Heckscher's broad and synthesising approach to mercantilism left virtually no element of economic and social policy "between the Middle Ages and the end of laissez faire" that could not somehow be brought within its comprehensive embrace. Many acts of policy considered by him under the heading of "unification" had little in common with each other and sometimes still less to do in practice with "unification." It is, for example, only by dint of this vast concept that Heckscher is enabled to write as he does, that "The French tariff of 1664 ranks with Elizabeth's Statute of Artificers as one of the two unquestionable triumphs of mercantilism in the sphere of economic unification." But is this true in historical reality? Did the English Statute aim at or achieve unification in the same way as Colbert's enactment was concerned to unify and co-ordinate in matters peculiarly requiring unification and coordination? And what are the real links between these two, with a century separating them, and all the other edicts, be they about bullion, gilds, patents, cloth inspection, trading companies or catching herrings, which can, by Heckschers' definitions, be labelled as "mercantilistic"?

Using a shorter historical focus, the Statute of Artificers can be seen as "a classic example of the restrictive legislation which great depressions tend to produce." In this context, it was one of various measures taken after the collapse in the English boom in woollen cloth exports during the first half of the sixteenth century. It was part of the reaction to falling trade, increased unemployment and anxiety about home food supplies following upon much conversion of arable land to sheep pasturage; it was at once a naturally conservative reaction to the problem of public order and poverty as well as a move in the sharpening politico-economic conflict between Burleigh and Granvelle. Using a still shorter focus to examine the details of its enforcement, we find that in practice one of its important clauses—that demanding a seven-year apprenticeship—was enforced more by the pressure of private interests than by the force of public policy. The trading jealousy of competition during periods of declining trade and the greed of the professional informer during the booms were the effective agents of such enforcement as there was of this particular item of "mercantilism." The government—central and local—showed itself to be more concerned with the pressing realities of an economy of widespread underemployment and periodic unemployment, with its poverty, vagrancy and inherent threats to public order. The "really efficient central administration" of the years of Charles I's personal government meant in practice, so far as the enforcement of apprenticeship was concerned, prosecutions by professional informers and trade rivals, most of which were inconclusive or ineffective in their results.

This was the reality of "mercantilism." It is a long way from simple *Staatsbildung*. And does it suggest the intention or achievement of unification in the Statute of Artificers?

It was by dint of his synthesising treatment that "mercantilism" in Heckscher's hands became, as Professor C. W. Cole observed, "a real entity . . . which manifested itself through the centuries in various countries." Heckscher noted this criticism in the new edition, denied knowledge of what was meant by it, and observed that no specific quotation had been given. It is not difficult to find such quotations:

mercantilism in its struggle against the disintegration within the state . . . (i, 137)

the incapacity of French mercantilism to master even the particularisation of municipal policy . . . (ii, 209)

mercantilism had to leave much of its work of unification for its successors to complete. (i, 456)

mercantilism would . . . have had all economic activity subservient to the state's interest in power. (ii, 15)

mercantilism often arrived at more erroneous conclusions on economic questions than the medieval mind had ever done. (ii, 112)

we are concerned with the tasks which mercantilism imposed on itself . . . (ii, 272)

mercantilism was indeed a new religion. (ii, 155)

In the preface to the first edition, Heckscher voiced his disapproval of "the method of treating all sorts of disconnected tendencies . . . under the name of 'modern capitalism'": he tended to put "capitalism" in quotation marks; he spoke of it as a "Protean conception." However true these strictures may be, they are equally applicable to his own treatment of mercantilism, though in truth there is little meaning in any comparison between "mercantilism" and "capitalism." Capitalism has been written of and fought about in its own time, rightly or wrongly. It has come near to being a religion; Communism has come far nearer. But no man recognised and defended the cause of mercantilism during its supposed reign; no war was fought under its banner. Mercantilism was *not* "a new religion." So again we come back to asking what was this "mercantilism." Did it exist? As a description of a trend of economic thought, the term may well be useful, and worth retaining. As a label for economic policy, it is not simply misleading but actively confusing, a red-herring of historiography. It serves to give a false unity to disparate events, to conceal the close-up reality of particular times and particular circumstances, to blot out the vital intermixture of ideas and preconceptions, of interests and influences, political and economic, and of the personalities of men, which it is the historian's job to examine. It was in 1923 that G. N. Clark (Sir George Clark as he has since become) stressed the dangers of using the concept of the "mercantile system" in dealing with the protagonists in international politico-economic conflict in the seventeenth century. Heckscher's further inflation of the balloon of "mercantilism" did much to obscure that admirable advice.

As a contribution to the history of. economic thought, there can be no doubt whatsoever that Heckscher's work remains outstanding, still invaluable to the student of the period. Nor can the economic historian afford to ignore it. Nevertheless, for the economic historian, although packed with valuable information, it is curiously unrealistic. Taken as a whole, it is unquestionably a brilliant and stimulating study, a product of scholarship, immensely wide reading in several languages and intellectual ingenuity of a very high order. Yet at one and the same time as its range, subtlety and learning are formidable and impressive, so also is it misleading, a signpost built upon strangely unreal assumptions, pointing to an historical no-man's-land. In real life, policy is carried out by governments and governments are composed of men who, whatever their preconceived ideas and whatever their ultimate aims, deal in particular contexts with particular problems. In *Mercantilism*, Heckscher shunned particular contexts and particular problems: he ignored the composition of governments; and with the significant exception of Colbert, most of those mentioned in his pages were concerned less with governing than with writing economic tracts or with trading.

4

ENLIGHTENED DESPOTISM: DID IT EXIST?

The term "Enlightened Despotism" was seldom used by writers in the eighteenth century. Instead, borrowing from the works of the French Physiocrats, they spoke of "legal despotism," by which they meant a state ruled by a prince or minister who conceived of himself as the "first servant of his people" and as the initiator—or fountainhead—of enlightened reforms. These reforms, often nominally borrowed from the writings of the great legalists of the eighteenth century, Montesquieu (1689–1755), Marchese di Beccaria (1738–1794), William Blackstone (1723–1780), and Jeremy Bentham (1748–1832), included the amelioration of the tax burden, the codification of the laws, the abolition of harsh and unusual punishments, the destruction of the institution of serfdom, the rationalization of the rules governing industry and commerce, and the separation of church and state. Among the rulers and statesmen who may be termed legal or enlightened despots were Joseph II of Austria (1741–1790); Frederick II, the Great, of Prussia (1712–1786); Catherine II, the Great, of Russia (1729–1796); Leopold of Habsburg, Grand Duke of Tuscany and later emperor of Austria (1747–1792); Carlos III of Spain (1716–1788); Sebastian Carvalho e Mello, marquis of Pombal in Portugal (1699–1782); and Johan, count Struensee of Denmark (1731–1772).

Of these so-called enlightened or legal despots the three most renowned were Joseph II, Catherine the Great, and Frederick the Great. Frederick II of Prussia, who ruled his country from 1740 to 1786, was in his early years an enthusiastic disciple of the great French *philosophe* Voltaire. As king he continued the administrative reforms begun by his father, Frederick William I (1713–to 1740), and instituted his own program for the advancement of the arts and sciences. His reputation as an enlightened ruler was, however, marred by his love of war. Twice his ambitions were in part responsible for plunging his nation and Europe into costly, bloody conflicts: first in the War of the Austrian Succession, 1740–1748, and again in the Seven Years' War, 1756–1763. As his reign wore on, his actions seemed to be governed less by the altruistic spirit of Voltaire and more by considerations of reason of state or what the Germans later termed *Realpolitick*.

Frederick's fellow monarch Catherine II of Russia was likewise guided by circumstances rather than by principle. Catherine, a most remarkable woman, possessed of impressive intellectual and physical prowess, ruled Russia with a determination worthy of the strongest man, professed herself like Frederick II to be a follower of the *philosophes:* yet her program of Westernization was largely a mockery of the Enlightenment. In fact it was during her reign that many of the peasants were reduced to serfdom and the power of the landholders greatly increased. As one critic put it, her reforms were "mere dust in the eye."

Thus of all the major enlightened reformers, Joseph II of Austria was perhaps the most honest and the most dedicated. After the death of his mother, Empress Maria Theresa, in 1780, Joseph, long constrained by her cautious policies, undertook revolutionary changes in his far-flung lands. Unlike Catherine of Russia, he freed the serfs. He increased the power of the bureaucrats in Vienna, instituted tax reforms, and attacked clerical privilege, at once confiscating monastic properties and reducing the number of clerical offices. He also instituted a new legal system and called for freedom of internal trade. Such salutary reforms met with bitter opposition both from the peasants, frightened by Joseph's attacks on established religion, and by the nobles, incensed by his attacks on their feudal privileges. So strong was their combined resistance that by the end of Joseph's reign the Austrian Empire was in a state of revolution—a conservative revolution. When Joseph's brother, Leopold II (emperor from 1790–1792), himself no enemy to the Enlightenment, ascended the throne he was forced to rescind most of Joseph's decrees. More successful than Emperor Joseph in their quest for enlightened reformation— perhaps because they were more cautious—were Carlos III of Spain, the Marquis Pombal of Portugal, and certain of the French intendants (royal representatives in the provinces), particularly Anne Robert Jacques Turgot (1727–1781). Yet even these wise and moderate princes and ministers were not able to stem the great revolutionary tide that was to engulf the Atlantic world by the early 1790's.

The question that the student must ask himself about the so-called Enlightened Despots are these: Why are historians at odds as to when and where the Enlightened Despots first appeared—if they did—in Europe? What exactly were the programs espoused by these despots? And in fact just how "enlightened" were these despots?

PAUL VAUCHER

LEGAL DESPOTISM

Emeritus professor of the University of Paris, Paul Vaucher postulates in his Sorbonne lectures of 1954 a classic interpretation of Enlightened Despotism by asserting that in the later eighteenth century a group of princes and statesmen, who held so-called enlightened views of society, inaugurated similar programs of reform. Professor Vaucher, however, introduces interesting variations on the theme of Enlightened Despotism. First, he insists that the word "legal" rather than "enlightened" was used by the writers of the eighteenth century and that this term was borrowed from the French Physiocrats. Second, in studying France, Vaucher finds evidence of the practice of legal despotism not only by Louis XV's Maupeou *parlements* but in the work of the provincial intendants and the ministers of state, men like Sénac Meilhan, Bertier de Sauvigny, Turgot, and Machault. He doubts, however, that they transformed France into an Enlightened Despotism. Third, Vaucher gives a prominent role in the advancement of enlightened ideas to the writings of the Physiocrats, those French economic thinkers who made popular the phrase "laisser-faire, laisser-passer." And lastly, Vaucher urges his students to ask the pertinent question: what is the connection between eighteenth-century enlightened ideals and eighteenth-century practical politics?

The words "Enlightened Despotism" did not exist in the eighteenth century. We do not exactly know their origin, but they probably date from the nineteenth century. How may "Enlightened Despotism" be defined? Historians are far from agreed. The most convenient definition, although rather vague, is given by the great Belgian historian, Pirenne. He calls it "the rationalization of government."

This investigation will show that historians are not agreed either as to the meaning of the words "Enlightened Despotism" or, what is more serious, as to the origins of the movement. There are two points of view, consequently there are two ways of studying the subject.

1. The first, which is consistent with French thought, would indicate that Enlightened Despotism was a movement born of ideas French in origin. If we adopt this view, we must certainly analyze . . . the movement of political ideas and then the system that resulted from them. But we must be careful not to omit two other aspects of the intellectual movement which are also characteristic of Enlightened Despotism. The first is the crusade led by the *philosophes* against the Church and against religion itself. This crusade was inspired by the idea of tolerance, one of the most important facets of Enlightened Despotism. The second is the economic aspect. Enlightened Despotism was in many ways a reflection of the Physiocratic movement. The Enlightened Despots often followed the economic concepts of the Physiocrats while at the same time remaining faithful to the ideas of mercantilism.

If the men of the eighteenth century did not speak of "Enlightened Despotism," they talked about "legal despotism." One of the leaders of the Physiocratic school, Mercier de la Riviere, casually mentioned this expression in an important work entitled the *Natural and Material Order of Political Societies* (1767). The reader will find the theory of legal des-

From Paul Vaucher, *Le despotisme éclaire, 1740 à 1789*, (1954), Centre de Documentation Universitaire. pp. 3–5, 86–98, 104–106. Reprinted by permission. [Translated by the editor.]

potism outlined in this book. Legal despotism is not precisely the same thing as "Enlightened Despotism," but it does admit that despotism is a suitable system of government so long as it is based on reason, which means that it must be compatible with a system of laws; if it is, it will win public support, and the very weight of its "right reason" will carry it along on the force of circumstance; right reason will thus become the driving force within despotism.

. . . Enlightened Despotism may thus be considered as a part of a great movement of ideas which were not exclusively French—because many of the ideas were English in origin—but were carried along principally on a wave of French culture.

2. There is yet another way of looking at the subject of Enlightened Despotism and that is from the viewpoint of the German historians. For them, Enlightened Despotism is tied to its historical development. Frederick II [the Great] is the prototype of the Enlightened Despot. Consequently, for the German historians, Enlightened Despotism should be studied from its Prussian origins. Frederick II was inspired by French ideas but his system of government had its roots deep in Prussian traditions and particularly in Prussian institutions. Enlightened Despotism became thus not only part of the German Enlightenment but expressed its political tendancies. The only other great Enlightened German Despot who may be compared to Frederick II is Joseph II [of Austria].

3. As for the Italian historians writing in the years that preceded the Second World War, they claimed that Italy had suffered an intrusion of alien French thought during the Enlightenment. Enlightened Despotism, in their opinion, stemmed from the [Italian] Renaissance and [in time] formed the first chapter of the movement for independence known as the "risorgimento." It was truly a national movement.

Enlightened Despotism was in time extended to the great part of the Russia of Catherine the Great, to Scandinavia, to the Spain of Carlos III, and to Portugal where the minister Pombal was one of the truly important Enlightened Despots of his day. [However] was Enlightened Despotism also achieved in France? It is debatable. Pierre Gaxotte [the French historian and member of the French Academy] views the last years of Louis XV's reign, the years of the Triumvirate [the rule of three ministers: Chancellor Maupeou; Abbé Terray as head of finances; and the Duke d'Aiguillon, 1770–1774] as a period

of Enlightened Despotism. Many of our great intendants of the eighteenth century were likewise pictured as Enlightened Despots. One must ask oneself how close Machault, the great controller general [from 1745–1754] and also Turgot [controller general from 1774–1776] came to being Enlightened Despots. . . .

As we have said before, it is from France that many of the ideas spring that made up the basic program of Enlightened Despotism. But what can be said were the accomplishments of Enlightened Despotism in France itself? After all, there was not one French king in the eighteenth century who considered himself an Enlightened Despot. It is true that Pierre Gaxotte in his book on Louis XV shows us that the king created at the end of his reign a type of Enlightened Despotism. The suppression of the *parlements* in January, 1771 by Maupeou was an attempt to break the resistance of the magistrates who were opposing reforms. . . . The [new] *parlements* Maupeou formed of civil servants . . . were to become the instruments of a despotism which, according to Gaxotte, strived to be enlightened. The Maupeou reforms also laid the foundations for indispensable financial reforms that Abbé Terray had in mind. Moreover, Maupeou wanted to cap his work by a thorough-going reform of judicial procedure generally. His secretary Lebrun was in fact to transmit Maupeou's ideas to Napoleon.

Gaxotte's thesis, however, does not seem to be justified. He forgot that the fall of the *parlements* was in part due to the vengeance of the Jesuits. [Who hated the *parlements* for supporting their enemies, the strict religious order of the Jansenists.] His thesis also neglects the fact that the crown, forced into action by the exigencies of the financial situation, seemed to have as its real goal the securing of [temporary] financial relief [rather than long-range planning]. Gaxotte also obviously ignores the unpopularity of the entire Maupeou enterprise. In fact the "coup d' état" of Maupeou, far from making Enlightened Despotism possible made it extremely unpopular in France.

If there was not, then, a sovereign to become an Enlightened Despot there were enlightened despots on a small scale: these were the intendants. During the reign of Louis XVI these intendants remained in office a long time: in fact, twenty-four of them for twenty years, and thirty-nine for over ten years. These intendants had plenty of time to act—they were full of initiative and of enlightened ideas. A great deal was accomplished during their tenure in the field of charities; efforts were also made to reform the *taille* [the principal royal tax in France] and to suppress the *corvée* [forced labor, usually on roads]. They also helped create bureaus for the supervision of charities [alms houses] and workhouses. The intendants also made efforts to develop agriculture and commerce and to improve navigable waterways. They became patrons of arts and letters and aided in city planning.

Among the most famous of these intendants we can point out Sénac de Meilhan, intendant for Valenciennes, a highly cultured man who emigrated during the French Revolution and [writing in exile] left us a picture of French society at the end of the Old Regime. Also Montyon of La Rochelle, a celebrated philanthropist and initiator of the Montyon prizes which are awarded by the Academy. Often these intendancies were handed down from father to son such as in the case of the La Galairière of Strasbourg and the Bertier de Sauvigny (1744–1789) in Paris. But these random and dispersed efforts of the intendants do not allow us to conclude that there really existed an Enlightened Despotism in France [as represented by the intendants]. However, in turning [from the provinces] to the central government, we can distinguish a [more concerted] effort for reform. We can point out the role of the council of state (*Conseil d' état*) which recruited most of the intendants who worked as masters of request [legal advisers to the Council] and who often later became intendants. . . . But we must not forget that the members of the Council of State and the intendants recruited from among them were and remainded Parlementarians and magistrates at heart, and it is difficult to conceive of an Enlightened Despotism exercised by Parlementarians who by their very nature were a privileged body pledged to defend the interests of their caste.

We must then ask ourselves if Enlightened Despotism existed in the work of some ministers of the crown in the eighteenth century, for example, Machault d'Arnouville (and his financial reforms), Bertin, who was controller-general of finance in 1763, and lastly Turgot. We can separate the case of Machault from the other two. Bertin and Turgot both had close connections with the *philosophes* (especially Turgot) and their ministerial activity was closely associated with the Physiocratic movement. In fact their work appears as a study in the applica-

tion of Physiocratic doctrines. If then the Physiocratic movement is the closest link to Enlightened Despotism we should discuss it, [before looking back to Machault].

The Physiocratic movement had its flowering between 1763 and 1770. Its leader, Dr. Quesnay, was physician to King Louis XV, thus insuring the movement royal protection. Quesnay and the Marquis de Mirabeau, father of the great (French Revolutionary leader) Mirabeau, both espoused Physiocratic doctrines. Quesnay published his ideas in 1758 in his *Tableau Économique* (Economic Picture) and the elder Mirabeau published his ideas in 1759 in *La Philosophie rurale* (Rural philosophy). The propagandist activity of the Physiocratic party became very active after 1763 . . . [when] the movement obtained the support of Bertin, the controller general until the end of 1763, of his successor Laverdy, and of Trudaine, one of the great civil servants of the era. Their support is mirrored in the edicts of 1763 concerning the free internal circulation of produce and in the edict of 1764 for the free exportation of grains.

In 1767 the political ideas of the Physiocrats were expounded in a work, *The Natural and Material Order of Societies*, whose author Mercier de la Rivière was a great Parlementarian and civil servant, who after the Seven Years' War was twice sent on mission to the Antilles (West Indies). After his conversion to Physiocracy, Mercier developed the political aspects of the movement. The spread of Physiocratic ideas proceeded apace during the years 1767 and 1768 but at the same time resistance forces gathered. Their ideas can be seen in Voltaire's tract "Man of Forty Écus [Crowns]" and in Rousseau's protests against the political ideas of the Physiocrats and against the concept of the despot, which he finds anti-democratic. Others, merchants and industrialists, disliked the emphasis that the Physiocrats attached to land. The *parlements* also seized on some of the same questions, but they are divided—those in the south favored the freedom of grain trade while those in the north (Paris and Rouen) were hostile to it. The Physiocrats really tended to lose out when Abbé Terray, who was hostile to them, became controller general in 1770. At the same time Physiocratic ideas were attacked by other *philosophes*, the most vocal being [Baron von] Grimm and Abbé Galiani.

In the economic sphere the essential idea for the

Physiocrats was the productivity of the land, which they believed was the only source of wealth and of revenue. They were opposed to commerce and industry which they considered to be sterile pursuits. Indeed they favored the development of farming at the expense of the development of capitalism.

The political ideas of Mercier de la Rivière had as a goal the establishment of a social order based on individual private property and economic liberty. The Physiocrats also admitted that inequality among men is a natural phenomena. In matters that concerned the government they thought that the role of the sovereign was to maintain private property and economic liberty. It represented a great reduction of the function of the State. . . . Of course sovereign power had the right to collect taxes; but the government whose sphere of activity was thus limited [as it was in France] must of necessity become despotic. . . . Thus despotism, as such, seemed necessary to the Physiocrats. But it had to be legal despotism. What did they mean by that term? First, the right of taxation was tied to the needs of the state; secondly, the independence of the magistrates must be respected because it was the magistracy that saw to it that the Despot conformed to the laws of the land. Lastly, the Physiocrats attached great importance to public opinion which must be guaranteed the right of petition. The Physiocrats were thus supporters of a legal despotism that conformed to the laws. They believed that a despotic regime will not be tyrannical because its actions must rest on "right reason" which is the essential driving force within despotism. This political theory, developed by Mercier de la Rivière in 1767, calls for two comments:

1. First, do the ideas of the Physiocrats conform with the interests of the people?

On the one hand their political concepts are contrary to those of democracy; and on the other, they do not respond to the advances made in industry and commerce. By the opposition they aroused among many people and by the influence their ideas had in encouraging a type of feudal reaction among the nobility, the Physiocrats contributed [in the negative sense] in bringing about the French Revolution.

2. Second, Is legal despotism the source of Enlightened Despotism? Enlightened Despotism appeared as early as 1740 and well before the ideas of legal despotism, which were not clearly stated [in their political form] until 1767. Besides that there is an obvious difference in the conception between legal and Enlightened Despotism.

[Now that we have looked at the work of the intendants, the ministers, and the Physiocrats] we must return to the [special] case of Machault, controller general of finances, who in 1749 tried to instigate vast social and financial reforms. We must remember that he wanted to establish a tax of a "twentieth" which was to be paid by everyone within the state [regardless of rank]; he wished also to destroy certain (feudal) rights. . . ."

[It is an interesting coincidence that during Machault's tenure in office a great flood tide of works by the *philosophes* began to appear in print]:

1748: *The Spirit of the Laws* [Montesquieu]
1749: *The Natural History* of Buffon
1750: *The First Discourse* of Rousseau
1751: The first volume of the *Encyclopédie*
1751: *The Age of Louis XIV* [Voltaire]
1755: The *Second Discourse* of Rousseau
1755: Morelly's *Code of Nature*
1756: *The Essay on the Mind and Manners of Nations*
1758: *On the Mind* by Helvétius
1760: *The New Heloise* [Rousseau]
1762: *The Social Contract* of Rousseau

["Why this great outburst?] First, we should note that Mme. de Pompadour, in her role as King [Louis XV's] great favorite, was a perennial target of abuse on the part of the clergy. Thus, quite naturally, she became the champion of the *philosophes*, particularly of Voltaire and of the *Encyclopedia*. Secondly, at this time censorship was relaxed because Malesherbes, who had become the "Director of Publications," favored the appearance of all the works listed above. He put them under the category of "works published abroad"; he too was the patron of the *Encyclopedia*. The circumstances were thus favorable to the *philosophes*. But it was evident that the decisive battle fought by Machault against the *parlements* and the clergy exercised a strong influence on the intellectual movement of the time. The *philosophes* took Machault's part. In the year 1749 Voltaire wrote his *Letter on the Twentieth;* and though the Papacy condemned his pamphlets which were hostile to the fiscal immunities of the clergy Voltaire continued his campaign in a serious tone, writing *The Voice of the Prudent Man and of the People* in which he demands the seizure of property held under the dead hand [of the Church]; then in a tone of irony he wrote his *Decrees of the Sacred Clergy* in which he defends the work of Machault whom he represents as Antichrist. In 1755 Rousseau likewise intervenes [on Machault's side]; but his efforts were in the field of social planning where he undertook an attack on the privileged orders and on social inequality. Thus did many of the *philosophes* take Machault's side. Yet can we conclude that Machault's attempts at reform were the undertakings of Enlightened Despotism? That is open to question.

Let us look at certain conclusions [concerning Enlightened Despotism in France]:

The *philosophes* held quite varied interpretations concerning government. Montesquieu's concept of government shared with "Intermediate Powers" (the *Parlements,* Estates, municipalities, *et cetera*) was quite contrary to the idea of Enlightened Despotism. In fact Montesquieu's notions were opposed by Voltaire himself and by most of the other *philosophes,* all of whom wanted a strong government, especially one that would destroy the power of the *parlements*. It would, however, be an exaggeration to say that Voltaire was a wholehearted advocate of Enlightened Despotism. As for Rousseau, his conception of popular sovereignty was quite opposed to the idea of Enlightened Despotism. We have only to observe his espousal of a type of [popular] dictatorship as exercised by the general will to realize this. How can one say that Rousseau's idea of the general will takes the place of the Despot? This would force the truth a bit. Voltaire, however, defends aspects of Enlightened Despotism both in his campaign for religious tolerance and in his support of Beccaria's penal reforms as elaborated in the latter's *Treatise on Crimes and Punishments.*

We must also conclude that legal despotism of the Physiocrats differs from the ideas of Enlightened Despotism and from the ideas of most of the *philosophes,* . . . Therefore we must further conclude that although there were attempts made to effect an Enlightened Despotism in France they never came close to fruition.

In completing these lectures I would like to take up again the two questions I posed earlier.

1. The question of definition—What is Enlightened Despotism?

2. The question of origin: Where did this movement come from?

For both of these questions let us take a look at an article by M. Morazé which appeared in the January 1948 issue of the *Annales: Economies sociétés, civilisations.* Let's say first of all that his article, "Finance and Despotism," [see the following selection for the text of Morazé's article] does not treat all aspects of Enlightened Despotism. It does, however, offer some general conclusions.

The problem that interests Morazé is the investigation of the financial resources of the Enlightened Despots. He feels that their main objective was to increase their own revenues.

In analyzing the politics of Frederick II of Prussia Morazé makes two observations (to back up his point):

1. Frederick II takes the economic machinery of government into his own hands in order to merge it with the military establishment. Thus the financial resources of the state were at first meant to reinforce this military establishment, but in time the military became useful to the state—even economically important, because the soldiers who were not on military duty were set to working the land and in businesses, such as the textile industry, which produced goods for the army.

2. Frederick could effectively take economic matters into his own hands because in Prussia the king had by right control over 1/3 of the produce of the land and by royal authority right to preempt the rest.

In Austria [M. Morazé continues], the goal is the same as in Prussia: but Maria-Theresa followed a compromise course in extending her control over the local authorities, especially the provincial Estates. Her control never became complete, however, because the individual Estates [or States] retained the right to collect their own taxes. This delicate balance of governmental interests could easily be ruined if the central power and the power of the Estates came into conflict and such was the case when Joseph II came to power [in 1780].

M. Morazé also takes note of the creation of a Bank in Vienna. But it was an enterprise managed by the municipality of Vienna. The State deposited funds there and the Bank then advanced money to the

State; but the State was required to render account of its disbursements thus limiting its authority; indeed, the government remained dependent on the Viennese bank.

In Russia [as M. Morazé notes] it was very difficult to determine just where the government secured its revenues. . . . Russia by comparison with other countries was rich in men which gave her an advantage in agriculture and as well [potentially] in industry. But the crux of the problem was [everywhere, but particularly in Russia] the relationship between the government and its nobility.

Here we must look at different aspects of this problem about which M. Morazé says very little.

1. *Political aspect:* the nobility was opposed to services they were required to give to the State and wanted to be totally exempt from these obligations. In the first half of the eighteenth century they succeeded in this aim little by little. They finally obtained satisfaction from Tsar Peter III, who, by edict, suppressed the obligatory services the nobility owed the State. Catherine II [the Great] had to confirm this edict.

2. *Social Aspect:* Russia [unlike Western Europe] did not move toward the abolition of serfdom; on the contrary, the control of the nobility over the peasants became greater [during Catherine's reign]. . . .

3. *Administrative Aspects:* By the Reform of 1775 (The Charter of Nobility) Catherine tried to reconcile herself with her nobility by assuring them the election of their own administrative heads (marshals). However, the strong political power of the central government tended to prevent the division of administrative power between the government and the nobility.

a. In the field of central administration the nobles tried to wrest from the government constitutional reforms that would place a Council of Nobles (or a Senate or Assembly) in power next to the great bureaus of the central government. But the Tsars refused them; Catherine, in fact, ceded nothing [substantial] to them and maintained her own autocracy.

b. In the field of local administration, the Reform of 1775 placed the nobility under an "imperial lieutenant" who administered vast areas in the name of the Tsar. There was thus worked out [in Catherine's reign] an alliance between the central government and the nobility, with the nobility subservient to the power of the central bureaucracy. According to Morazé the central power got its support from the petty nobility and at the same time effected a reconstitution of the greater nobility by granting lands to Catherine's favorites. In the nineteenth century many of the great landholders were direct descendants of the favorites to whom Catherine had granted vast lands. This nobility of favorites proved wonderfully docile to the central administration.

* * *

M. Morazé's conclusions are draconic. He does not want to acknowledge the role of the philosophical movement in the work of the Enlightened Despots. He writes: "No reform in Europe was due to philosophical thought." He thinks that the relationship of the Enlightened Despots to French thought and ideas was simply the effect of personal predilection of sovereigns who misled their subjects. It is only a "varnished" deception.

Such a conclusion goes beyond the premises of the article. We have seen that the *philosophes* desired above all else philosopher kings who would be guided by Reason. The same *philosophes* believed they had found such a philosopher king in Frederick [the Great]. They also wanted a powerful ruler in France—one capable of destroying noble privileges and religious superstitions. . . .

[True, neither Montesquieu or Rousseau supported Enlightened Despotism as such: Montesquieu desired instead a division of powers between the responsible nobility—the intermediate bodies—and the ruler; Rousseau desired a type of social democracy governed by a "general will" of all.]

But in contrast, Voltaire was very much in favor of Enlightened Despotism. He wanted, above all, strong rulers, governed by reason, who would practice religious toleration, suppress censorship, and liberate the mind.

The Physiocrats, as we have seen, advocated "legal despotism," founded upon reason and regulated by public law. However, their conception of economic liberty most definitely reduced the power and the functions of the State.

We cannot therefore say that the philosophical

The Early Modern Era

movement as a body of thought evolved a coherent theory of Enlightened Despotism. But it is going too far to deny it, as M. Morazé has done, all influence.

As for the attitude of the Enlightened Despots toward the *philosophes*, Morazé says that only Catherine showed open admiration for them, largely because in Russia the ignorance of the population rendered their teachings far less dangerous than in Prussia, where Frederick II had to display some caution.

This brings up the historical problem of the sincerity in attitude of the Enlightened Despots toward the *philosophes*. The most sincere in his adherence to their ideas was Joseph II [of Austria]; but he understood them the least; it is even doubtful whether or not he had read their works. The least sincere was perhaps Frederick, with Catherine hovering somewhere in between the two. But if one reads her *Notebook* prepared for the Commission of 1767, in which she translates the ideas of Montesquieu and Beccaria, it is difficult to doubt her personal sincerity. Certainly, she was preoccupied with her public image; but nonetheless she made attempts to reconcile the ideas of the *philosophes* with the concept of aristocracy to which she was entirely committed.

On the other hand, it has often been said that Catherine had brought together the Commission [of 1767] with the intention of instituting reforms but that during the sessions she decided to follow a more autocratic course. This description is inexact. One must distinguish two conflicting tendencies within Catherine's political thought: she was always an autocrat, but she did wish to institute certain reforms. There is also something very revealing in her career as a woman of letters. Catherine was a born journalist who believed that by the power of her pen she could spread her ideas of reform. When she saw publicists contradicting her and even ridiculing the works of "Grandmother," she ceased her literary efforts. One sees in this a certain naivete; but it is difficult to deny her sincerity.

Let's now examine Morazé's positive conclusions. He reckons that the Enlightened Despots . . . followed two examples: England and Louis XIV.

The example of England is noted in the attempts made to establish banks. [The Bank of England was founded in 1696]. This is possible, but one must distinguish between the banks of the Enlightened Despots, which were state enterprises, and the Bank of England and the great English trading companies, which were shareholding enterprises supported by the public.

The prestige of Louis XIV is still great in the eighteenth century. Voltaire exalts him in his *Age of Louis XIV*. This prestige had its great impact upon the small German courts where many of the German princes were playing at being Enlightened Despots. Charles-Augustus of Weimar created the most brilliant intellectual center in Germany. Charles-Frederick of Baden suppressed serfdom. Karl-Theodore Dalberg, who was the co-adjuter of the archbishop of Mainz and later archbishop in his own right, was a supporter of Enlightened Despotism who in 1793 published a defence of it.

After the death of Frederick II (1786) it was the task of Joseph II to continue the tradition of Enlightened Despotism in Germany among the smaller states, especially because King Frederick-William II of Prussia, contrary to Frederick II's reforms, abolished religious toleration and reëstablished censorship. Yet it is quite clear that what attracted the smaller German princes to Louis XIV, and what they imitated, was the decor of Versailles and the magnificence of his Court. Certainly it is evident that Louis XIV was not himself an Enlightened Despot nor even a precursor. He was a king by divine right who did not conceive of his "métier de Roi" [profession of being king] as service to the State. Lavisse [a French historian] has said that Louis XIV was basically a man who organized his life exactly as he pleased. It was not "Reason" that guided Louis XIV. On the other hand, Reason *was* an essential link between Enlightened Despotism and the philosophical movement—this cannot be ignored.

Thus the definition of Enlightened Despotism given by Pirenne ("the rationalization of the State") is correct as far as it goes. I think, however, we can formulate a more precise definition of Enlightened Despotism, one which brings into focus the ideas of reform which all the Enlightened Despots wished to institute. One must show above all that Enlightened Despotism was involved *in strengthening the State* [enhancing its powers at the expense of the Estates]. Finally we must underscore the fact that Enlightened Despotism developed mainly in Central and Eastern Europe, not in the West. In this regard Frederick [the Great] may be regarded as the prototype of the Enlightened Despot.

CHARLES MORAZÉ

A QUEST FOR MATERIAL PROGRESS AND ITS CONTROL

Charles Morazé, formerly a professor at the Institute of Political Science, teaches modern history at the *École polytechnique* in Paris. In his best known works he studies the rise and the triumph of the bourgeoisie in the eighteenth and nineteenth century. The article printed here first appeared in the *Annales: Économies—Sociétés—Civilisations* in 1948. Morazé believes that the key to understanding Enlightened Despotism lies in the financial reforms effected by the Despots and their ministers. These reforms included a revitalized system of tax collection, a massive program of public works, and the establishment of great State banks. Morazé tends to denigrate the role of ideas in history; in fact, he states quite clearly that the influence of the *philosophes* on Enlightened Despotism was negligible. His ideas have been challenged in the previous selection by Paul Vaucher, who believes that Morazé has been too harsh in his judgment of the philosophical movement in France and in Europe.

The work of the Enlightened Despots is generally represented as being the application to government of the philosophic doctrines developed in the West and more specifically in France. The writings of the French thinkers are supposed to have been the basis of the considerations which led the rulers of Prussia, Austria, and Russia to transform the regimes which they had inherited, and to have been the force which guided Middle Europe toward a new destiny.

There can be no doubt of the capital importance of the philosophic ideas which enriched eighteenth-century France. Under the circumstances, however, there is reason to doubt that they played the role generally ascribed to them in the development of Enlightened Despotism in Central and Eastern Europe.

The rulers of Prussia, Austria, and Russia, in effect, were concerned first of all with their craft. From the outset they were involved with the general preoccupations that arose out of the very conditions of their life and work. They were submerged by the general questions which, day after day, were posed within the framework of the great economic and political movements of the eighteenth century. A poet admired a poet, a philosopher a philosopher, but, by the very conditions of his life, a sovereign's admiration went first to a sovereign. Louis XIV offered by far and away the best example to be gained from France, and it was on the reasons for his success that these sovereigns meditated, and it was from England that they learned to create wealth.

To be sure, the Enlightened Despots displayed a keen taste for things of the mind, but this was a matter of personal inclination and in general they were little concerned with spreading this taste among their subjects. Joseph II would pay with his good faith for his premature hopes in the enlightenment of the masses. The others rather easily rationalized away the limitations which they would not permit to be imposed on themselves.

So, on the material level, the work of the Enlightened Despots had a surprising result. They benefited from the experiments which France and England had already made. They had only to copy the atti-

From Charles Morazé, "Finance et despotisme: essai sur les despotes élcairés," *Annales: Économies—Sociétés—Civilisations*, Vol. 3 (1948) pp. 279–296. Translation by James Friguglietti. Reprinted by permission of

tudes which brought the former to the summit of political power and the latter to the height of wealth. This imitation of a past which had proved itself preoccupied them much more than the creation of the perfect world imagined by the French *philosophes* of the eighteenth century.

I

Let us examine the case of Prussia. Frederick the Great intended to give substance to the idea that it was his duty as a prince to strengthen his State. Thus his first concern was to provide himself with important financial resources, then to assemble under his authority all those forces which might be useful to him.

The revenues of the King of Prussia were drawn primarily from his own domains. In each corner of his kingdom, these domains were farmed out to a bailiff who was supposed to keep records of all that he produced and spent. These accounts were submitted to a provincial "college"—the Chamber for War, Domains and Finances. The presidents of these colleges corresponded directly with the king. They were, however, responsible to a General Directory in Berlin, on which, moreover, sat the privy councilors and ministers. This Directory thus held valuable cards—an entire documentation on the economy of the royal domains. It could provoke an increase in the price of the "farms" or a decline if the recruiting of bailiffs became difficult. This extreme suppleness allowed the royal possessions to be given maximum service. This important source of income to the Treasury—perhaps an eighth of royal revenues—was so well managed, it must be noted, only because the king was all-powerful in his domains.

In the towns the king collected in addition a service tax proportional to income from both property and wages. This tax produced little, while the excise taxes which bore upon the traffic in goods—a fifth of royal revenues—produced a great deal. These taxes seem to have been levied chiefly on beverages. It also appears that they were reimbursed when the merchandise merely crossed the towns in transit. This flexibility, so useful to commerce, was undoubtedly due to the vigor of the towns in protecting their economic privileges. Finally, tolls and customs provided significant revenue, equal to about a third of the foregoing, a figure which was the result of a bargain between tax collector and merchant, who

might otherwise have succumbed to the burden of real taxes, which were very heavy, notably on the Rhine.

Lastly, in the open plains a tax (the French *taille*) was levied on the basis of a system perfected reign by reign, then codified by Grumbkow.[1] This revenue was important—a third of the total—and the administration regulated it very wisely. These lands were registered in a cadastre which divided them into three categories, each broken down into classes: good, inferior and bad farm land; good and bad meadow land; and good, inferior and bad wood land. Changes in, category, extremely favorable for the Treasury, were effected through land-clearing which, as is known, was encouraged through exemptions.

Only the poll tax was subject to exceptions for those who served their king. Others paid it proportionally to their status. This, however, was a tax with small returns.

To these old or reorganized taxes were added new resources like the salt tax. This was all the easier for Frederick William to establish because all the salt in Prussia was drawn from the saltworks of Westphalia at Hall and Unna. A minister of state had special charge of it. There were privileged saltworks in Pomerania which were only forbidden to sell salt below the royal rate. Frederick the Great took control of the entire organization and had it administered by Frenchmen. Other Frenchmen likewise perfected the production and sale of tobacco, which Frederick reserved to himself in 1765.

Thus the greater part of the king's resources was of agricultural origin, just as in the France of the *ancien régime*, but the enormous advantage of this central European ruler was that he held agriculture firmly in his grasp. He was the absolute ruler of a large portion of his land and subjects; moreover, he was its landlord. If he encouraged progress, the Treasury benefited from it at once. If individual property was relatively less developed, the State was that much stronger. The doctrines favorable to individual property which were developing in France and of which Voltaire in particular became the champion, could only be disagreeable to Frederick. On the other hand, both the technical discoveries which favored

[1] Joachim Ernst von Grumbkow (1637–1690), Prussian administrator. [Editor's note.]

the productivity of the soil and the work of the agron-omists interested him enormously because they con-tributed to the increase of his wealth. Thus Frederick occupied himself with an Academy of Sciences, while dealing contemptuously with the *philosophes,* because the Academy, which at that period was an Academy of Technology, enriched him.

At the same time he saw to it that the villages and sharecroppers' farms which had disappeared were rebuilt. He constructed new ones alongside rivers which he had dammed, for their floods, reinvig-orating to the soil as they may have been, had hith-erto driven men from the land. He aided the new settlers by giving them the wood needed to build their houses, by facilitating their acquisition of cat-tle, and by freeing them (for a time) from taxes and military service. Thus thousands of families estab-lished themselves on the Netze and Warthe rivers. Soon the Oder, the Elbe and the Havel, and even-tually the swamps of Magdeburg, Potsdam and Drömling were objects of the same concern. It is estimated that this intense activity promoted by Frederick since the Peace of Hubertusburg (1763), and in which he had to invest millions of *écus* each year without any immediate reward, permitted the settlement of tens of thousands of families. What he did himself, Frederick pledged certain seigneurs to do, especially in Pomerania and Silesia. He now lent them money at low interest.

All this activity is explained by the fact that the king was the greatest landlord in the country—he owned a third of it. A landowner he intended to remain, and personally draw all the advantages from the agricultural progress that he was striving to promote. This explains his attitude. He was like the owner of a gigantic farm worked by sharecroppers. At little or no expense he secured the planting of alfalfa, clo-ver, and lupine. He reimbursed those who planted useful trees, notably the mulberry. He instituted massive purchases of livestock.

It was also as a landlord that he established im-mense storehouses for grain everywhere. These he filled in the good years and emptied in case of scar-city or war, thus constituting managed reserves.

Of course, the good French *philosophes* began to look askance at this policy. These storehouses greatly resembled monopoly and they were contrary to the principle of the free movement of grain. The king, praised for other endeavors, came under some criticism on this point. Besides, did these reserves not also conceal disturbing military ambitions? This line of criticism often went further. The *philosophes* reproached the king for failing to take advantage of the fact that as the proprietor of the kingdom he could effect a vast redistribution of land that would encourage small or middle-sized peasant property. All the followers of Voltaire, for whom individual property was the source of wealth, be-gan to grow indignant.

On the other hand, the more realistic Arthur Young[2] had a better appreciation of Prussian policy. It was not the king's aim to create a better society, but rather a strong State. This strong State presumed stocks of food supplies. This strong State had need of a full treasury, and the king earned far more with his farms and bailiffs than he would by developing small property. Young added further that the indi-vidual peasant would work the land less rationally. The profits of enclosure went to the bailiffs and thus to the king, so that Frederick the Great encouraged this development along Western lines, but as one that served the State and not the individual.

In this way enormous advantages were secured for the Prussian monarchy. It legislated like Louis XIV, but had better possession over land and subjects. Property rights, which had developed in France and England to the detriment of the sovereign, were here developed to the profit of the State. The backward character of the Eastern economy was of great ben-efit to Frederick, for its progress served his power and not the development of a new society.

This prime consideration explains the strength of the Prussian army. The king had an army of 200,000 soldiers who were always ready to march. Half of them were the sons of peasants and daylaborers, who in the spring underwent intensive drill, then returned to work on the land. It was commanded by an ancient but poor nobility, which for this reason was the more patriotic. The other half was com-posed of foreigners whose regiments were quartered in the towns. These troops exercised military func-tions only twice a week. The other days they sought work and found it easily. The foreign soldiers could marry and were encouraged to do so, since this way they soon became nationals and settled in the coun-

[2] Arthur Young (1741–1820) was an English specialist on agriculture who travelled extensively and wrote descriptions of agricultural conditions in the lands where he travelled. [Editor's note.]

The Early Modern Era

try. The 24,000-man Berlin garrison had so many women and children that the "total rose to 60,000 persons," as a contemporary traveler said. At Potsdam a home for 5,000 children of soldiers was maintained. A large number were destined to help the peasants, to whom 13 *écus* were given to raise them, and these children became the best workers in the Prussian countryside.

When he was not working the land, a soldier, especially the foreigner, worked in industry in the towns. He thus gave the appearance of being engaged in useful activity. But the king, by his own initiative, could militarize this activity. As master of the factories, he was able to direct the latter toward equipping the army.

The king was therefore led to take industry into his hands just as he had done with agriculture. Everywhere—notably at Berlin and Potsdam—Frederick created factories that soon began to export. He granted them monetary advances and privileges. He established storehouses for raw materials and concluded trade agreements to assure foreign markets. His factories were rarely devoted to the production of luxury goods, despite some efforts on his part to develop silk and porcelain, the manufacture of which had been nonexistent before his reign.

After the Seven Years' War, Frederick developed mining and ironworks. He was particularly interested in the Mark and Silesia, despite the initial low output of their mines and furnaces. But he most desired to see wool and cotton goods produced since they were useful for uniforms. Textile exports, moreover, compensated for the king's need to have iron ore brought in from other countries.

Thus, because he was the landlord of his kingdom, the King of Prussia had available an economy that was entirely at the service of the great idea of his reign—victorious wars.

Hertzberg's[3] eulogies are certainly excessive: "The Prussian army, however numerous it may be, is not disproportionate to the population of the State . . . ; it increases rather than decreases the population . . . ; moreover, it has a great economic value . . . for it is so well distributed in each province and each village that the money it receives in pay and which constitutes two-thirds of the revenues of the State, goes back into circulation in each province and in this way enables tax payers to meet their responsibility fully. . . . I add the further reflection that the king is now accused of having inspired other rulers with the idea of maintaining larger standing armies. When an army is composed and employed like ours, it is not burdensome, but useful rather to the State. . . ."

There is much to think about in this declaration. As has been seen, the strength of the Prussian State lay in the ability of the king, because of the backwardness of his people and the mediocrity of his nobility, to put everything in the service of his own plans. Thus one conquest promoted another and nourished the economy. At the center of everything, the army benefited from everything. Large-scale trade, the wealth of the older parts of the kingdom, was virtually enveloped in this gigantic centralizing effort which left its mark on the economy. Trade served the king by sustaining his ventures and in the negotiation of treaties.

It threatened, however, to escape him in many ways. The old liberal traditions of the German towns might reawaken and ruin all his efforts by their particularism and their liking for freedom of property. This is why Frederick the Great was not at all interested in having doctrines of Voltaire spread within his country. He even despised them enormously and preferred the good, practical English institutions. These he modified, transforming them to his own profit, with Law's[4] experiment behind him, by creating, on January 17, 1765, the Royal Discount Payment Bank, with branches that extended to Königsberg, Magdeburg, Minden, Stettin and Frankfurt on the Oder.

All bills of exchange over 100 *écus* had to be paid into the bank, where they were redeemed by bank *thalers* worth more than the metallic ones. The royal bank practiced discounting at a very low rate (3 per cent) and was nourished by *funds lent by the king*. This institution was completed by a "Great Deposit Bank" that lent on security. Thus in his accounts the king could follow the entire financial activity of his kingdom. If he succeeded in making the State the

---

[3] Ewald Friedrich, Count von Hertzberg (1725–1795) was an important figure in the foreign office of Frederick the Great and Frederick William II. He wrote extensively in defense of the policies of Frederick the Great. [Editor's note.]

[4] John Law (1671–1729) was a Scottish economist and organizer of financial ventures, the most famous of which was the Mississippi scheme, a project which led to vast speculation and then panic in 1720. [Editor's note.]

manager of a Discount Bank, it was not only because he did not expect his bank to serve him financially, but, on the contrary, because thanks to the wealth of his royal treasury he could back its bourgeois clients.

Since two precautions were better than one, Frederick, after his success in establishing this control over monetary values, attempted to control goods as well. In 1772 appeared the forty-three articles which constituted the famous Society of Commerce charged with maritime relations between his ports and those abroad. To it he reserved the important privileges of transporting salt and wax from the Vistula, of which he had just become the master.

In this way the King of Prussia, profiting from the fact that he was the chief landlord of his monarchy, was able to become the great entrepreneur, financier and merchant of his entire kingdom.

II

Compared with Frederick the Great, the other rulers who have been styled Enlightened Despots cut a poor figure, but it is interesting, nevertheless, to evaluate their role in the building of the West.

We do not know much about the Russia of Catherine the Great, undoubtedly because there is little to know. This country had remained in what has been called a "feudal" state. This adjective is still too precisely evocative to suit this "unformed and unordered mass" of which travelers who had spent a little time there spoke. Yet few rulers were praised like Catherine! She was the idol of the French *philosophes*. This was because they judged the person rather than things. Catherine the Great was a very seductive woman who joined a sure knowledge of the uses of her femininity to an astonishing prodigality in gift-giving. What she really gave has been exaggerated still, but not with the intention of denigrating her!

But in considering the estimates that contemporaries made of the budget of Russia, one wonders what Her Majesty drew on for all these flattering gifts. The revenues suggested by Coxe,[5] for example, were hardly enough to pay the army and navy. It is true that even with the figures for the army and navy

themselves, we are not on more solid ground, and that those published by the government (1762–81), however much they may differ from one another, only appear more suspect when considered as a whole.

For all that, we should not call the government of the tsars a monument to hypocrisy and error. It itself must have had great difficulty in knowing the exact amount of its resources. In any case, it seems that an essential source of its power was its men, its manpower. A piece of land, a fortune, was evaluated in men. Men were given away and lent—"souls," as they were called, about whom Gogol would write so fine a novel. This generous abundance in human resources perhaps explains everything. The State was modified with the same ease that the army was recruited, and with the same ease that a flourishing industry might be created, a valet was given to an officer or a factory owner provided with a labor force. This enormous consumption of human beings could spare the Treasury much expense. Thus the chief occupation of the government in Russia before Catherine was parceling out men!

The problem was linked to the collection of taxes which were supposed to be paid primarily in kind, since a portion of the troops' pay was paid in kind. The three bureaus of the Senate concerned with these affairs were alone in sitting in the old capital of Russia, Moscow. The college of the Chamber regulated the collection of taxes, which consisted chiefly of a levy made on landed property. The feudal chancellery regulated the vital questions of the landed property of private citizens. Its duty was to maintain the relations among the nobles, that is, free men who possessed land and workers as their property. Finally, the Chancellery of Confiscations concerned itself with authorized sales and the collection of fines, as well as the tribute from recently annexed governments like the Ukraine. Such would be the essential yet badly understood support of the treasury of the tsars.

In imitation of the West, additional resources were secured through the salt tax, which was farmed out and which (as might be imagined) was extremely variable from one part of the country to the other. An important share of the income of the crown, it is said, was due to its monopoly over alcohol (1764). Lastly, Peter the Great had established a poll tax, and censuses were taken for it periodically in con-

[5]William Coxe (1747–1828), English clergyman and historian. His *Travels into Poland, Russia, Sweden and Denmark* appeared in 1784. [Editors' note.]

The Early Modern Era

ditions which (as Coxe tells us) remain difficult to define.

Russia was, in reality, characterized by the extraordinary attachment of the people to its soil and to the sovereign who represented this Russian soil. This obedience did everything. It can be partly explained by the inorganic state of the social structure and the absence of culture. This vast country, whose economy might have been described as the prehistoric type, provided for a sovereign who was its god. Under these circumstances it was easy for the tsar to assemble his armies—provided, however, that they did not fight too far from Russian soil—to assure the defense of a land which Nature preserved.

To be sure, a noble class existed between the sovereign and the people of the earth. Master of its lands, this class too would fall under the seductive charm of the monarchy which held the door open to the West and illuminated it with a dazzling culture.

All the rest was veneer, but veneer enough to fool the *philosophes*. It must surely be recognized that the famous "Instruction" (*Nakaz*) of Catherine the Great to the commission charged with drawing up a project for a new code was extraordinarily adroit. One is struck in each of its lines by her extensive knowledge of Western thought, by her talent as a *philosophe*, and by the high moral purpose of the new code's intentions. How could the good Diderot not adore the woman who could write: "What is the object of an absolute government? Certainly it is not to deprive men of their natural liberty, but to direct their actions toward the greatest of all goods. Thus the government which more than any other strives toward this goal by least restraining natural liberty, is that which best fulfills the aims which must be supposed in gifted beings and responds best to the purposes that men proposed in creating civil societies." This last phrase, applied to the Russian serfs, is particularly appropriate. She continued: "The intermediate powers"—this is Montesquieu—"constitute the nature of government," and so on.

The tradition of fine phrases was in the style of the old tsarina. Had not Elizabeth also solemnly abolished the death penalty, which (according to Coxe) does not seem to have appreciably diminished executions or the repeated and refined tortures practiced either in the name of the king or of the nobles.

This was because Russia in effect could not read.

Nevertheless, it would be foolish not to sense the extraordinary intelligence of the Russian people. It was all feeling, the feeling of a community tied to the Russian earth. Western philosophy did not move it, but *feeling* it was loved, it was overwhelmed. There is no doubt that Catherine, if she had no illusions about the impact of the philosophy she displayed to please the West, did have affection for her empire. She was the "mother of her country" in 1767.

It was through this expedient that some of her measures would prove durable. She would contribute to the definition of what we would call the autocratic patriotism of old Russia.

The absence of culture among her people, the certainty that they would never read the ideas of the *philosophes* permitted her to proclaim them so boldly. Who in Russia would understand Voltaire's ideas on individual property? Thus Catherine could prove more generous in words than Frederick the Great, who addressed himself to his better-informed subjects. Of how little importance were the phrases Catherine used, her good intentions, and the precise expressions that she employed! Her subjects did not understand them.

But this was not all. The tsars of the eighteenth century had to face specific problems of government. From their mass of men they had to recruit qualified personnel. In this mass of raw wealth they had to discover liquid assets. These two preoccupations were the essence of their concern as administrators. The solution to the former had been indicated by Boris Godunov.[6] As early as the sixteenth century there had been a struggle among the nobles to assemble land in very large estates. In this struggle the lesser nobility was gradually crushed by the great feudal lords who rose alone above the mass of the peasantry. It was this lesser nobility whom the tsar needed to establish his services, his administration, and his army. One of the most useful economic weapons of the rich nobility was to draw men to its lands. This was why Boris decided in 1597 to attach the peasants to the soil. Likewise, he proscribed sharecropping which favored the peasants of the wealthy landlord.

Through these remedies which enabled the monar-

[6]Czar of the Duchy of Muscovy (1598–1605) who played an important role in strengthening royal power in emergent Russia. [Editor's note.]

chy to maintain itself and to preserve the unity of the Russian lands, the freedom of the serfs, the very safety of their lives was placed in jeopardy. But the method in question was necessary and too useful for the preservation of the lesser nobility to be interrupted, and it remained the rule of conduct for the Chambers of Moscow, which not only guaranteed the possession of landed property, but also carried out the confiscation of that of interlopers.

To be sure, this policy would have severe consequences. The lesser nobility that it protected had little culture and was often brutal. It abused its exercise of a justice which remained pitiless and included torture and exile. But the Reformer remained deaf to the pleas for a reform that would be to the disadvantage of the lesser nobles. She told Diderot exactly why: a too rapid westernization of Russia would undoubtedly have had as its consequence the fall of the regime and the dismemberment of the Empire to the profit of the greater nobles.

This fidelity to the old Russia did not prevent the formation at St. Petersburg of Chambers more modern in character. Of course, not all of them worked for the emancipation of the people, and the poll tax, for example, was still only a disguised means to protect the lesser nobility against the peasantry, this time by lumping together both slaves and the free poor in the censuses. In fact the Code itself forbade neither the knout (established in 1713) nor the right of a master to assess dues in taxes and recruits.

Lastly, commerce was encouraged; an attempt was made to man the ports and a fleet, and to train sailors. Encouragement was given to the development of manufactures of the Western type which would give the court some of its brilliance.

Catherine particularly watched over the education of the lesser nobility which had to be the seedbed of the future administration. The social graces were taught amidst ostentatious and frivolous merrymaking. She built schools for the "poor," as they were called, where young girls and boys were separately confined for fifteen years to learn conscientiously the trades they would practice and the work they would perform. The French *philosophes* rejoiced at these schools, for they must have already seen in them honor being taught as the noblest of rewards, a practice that in time would spread into the provinces. These were encouraging aims for the future. For the present, Catherine dreamt of the needs of her

government. This was why she refrained from applying the multitude of programs for education which reached her from Paris, where the idea was to make free and enlightened citizens. Most important to her was the education of a few good technicians. These so-called poor, we must not forget, represented a small and extremely privileged minority in comparison with the mass of serfs.

Catherine's second preoccupation was to create a currency. Russia was dependent on foreigners for gold and silver. Peter the Great had already stipulated that customs duties paid by foreigners be in Dutch money. This time Catherine in her turn utilized an English invention and created a bank and a bank note. Having only copper coins at its disposal, Russia thus had enormous cellars in its Bank of Assignation, where the copper was piled and paper notes were manufactured. The directors of the bank told Coxe that the notes in circulation equalled the copper withdrawn. The traveler believed none of it. He estimated that of the 10 million pounds sterling in circulation, scarcely half of it was guaranteed in either Moscow or St. Petersburg.

There must have been no little anxiety while the results of this first circulation of paper money were awaited in a country that was so far removed from a modern economy. Certainly these notes were at first poorly received, especially in the outlying regions. But they soon came into general use. After having lost 3.5 per cent of their value compared with copper money, they soon gained 1.5 per cent over it, an advance due to their very great convenience. The success of the notes, which was due to technical reasons, soon made them worth almost as much as copper coinage.

Thenceforth, the Russian Empire had the monetary instrument which would permit it to build for modern progress as its human resources became refined. Did the Russian government abuse this process? Many Westerners became disturbed. And in fact was the Bank of Assignation not soon joined by a kind of pawnshop where nobles and towns might secure loans on security? Even serfs could be pledged to the sum of 40 rubles — this was the basis of Gogol's novel. Soon the coining of money depended on two merged establishments, and the whole of Russia's internal and foreign trade was thus controlled by the government, with these monetary institutions (needless to say) being under the immediate protection of

Her Majesty and responsible only to her, although a part of the capital might come from the nobles.

In any case, by the end of the century Russia was almost free of debts despite wars, and if the published balance sheet of the banks is truthful, it may be said that the technical success of Russian money was one of the most remarkable in Europe. Catherine had succeeded where the Regent, Louis XV, and Louis XVI failed!

Thus, building on an enormous mass of people which had scarcely yet entered history, the tsars created great institutions, copied from France of the seventeenth century and England of the eighteenth, which permitted the advance of Russia's material civilization. The State benefited from this progress through the intermediary of the relatively poor segment of the privileged class.

Because the financial system was of the Western, Prussian type, Catherine was able to adopt a certain number of the methods of Frederick the Great. Because her subjects were ignorant, she did not, like him, have to fear the consequences of the diffusion of the philosophic doctrines which reached only the highest classes of the nobility. Moreover, she directed all the efforts of the government and economic life against them.

III

Beside the brilliant successes of Frederick the Great and Catherine, the unhappy Joseph II appears as the unlucky member of the Enlightened Despots. But were his aims really those of his rivals? Were the means he used of equal intelligence? Everything makes it appear that Joseph II lacked sufficient perception to measure accurately the forces in the State he ruled, and it must indeed be said that the conditions of authority were not as easily defined in the hereditary states of the House of Austria as they were in Russia or Prussia.

Burdened with titles—a listing would require a page—the emperor who resided at Vienna had real authority only in the states of his family, an aggregation of varied peoples who made up the Italian and Belgian possessions, the Alpine valleys, the quadrilateral of Bohemia, the immense plains and all the rest. Maria Theresa was strong because she had not disturbed anything or anybody. She ruled through charm and lived long. How impatient her son must

have become with this policy of goodness carried out ruthlessly. Scarcely had he come to power than he undertook to establish a more rational policy. Alas, he believed in what he was doing. His aim was not to be adored like Catherine or to build an armed nation like Frederick—he had the soul of a *philosophe*. He wanted an ordered government. He wanted to translate into fact the lessons of the thinkers whom he loved. And what happened?

To be sure, the Austrian monarchy was not without resources. It drew substantial income from the old lands where it had originated—from the valleys of the Alpine regions and the Dalmatian shores. These valleys comprised as many governments with distinct administrations where authority was exercised through Estates, councils or extensive privileges. All these regions, however, underwent almost the same vicissitudes and by reason of this fact had comparable institutions and traditions. Geography rather than history separated them.

Everything remained feudal there until 1748. A land register of the French type, the result of compiling surveys of unequal value, gave some idea of the status of landed property. That which was noble or ecclesiastic and held by privilege ceased to be exempt from taxes.

In addition, Maria Theresa recognized that if the different Estates regularly paid her almost all they owed, it was because many of them had secret coffers, veritable private treasuries, in which they accumulated funds in the good years. This system led to embezzlement. So in 1762 it was possible for the empress, without modifying the size of the sums she demanded, to turn to her own profit a situation that was not without its dangers, because it gave eventual particularism a powerful weapon.

First, embezzlement was rooted out, especially by transforming the authority of the Estates into liability. The Estates now were no longer charged with anything but the levying of imposed sums and had to pay advances to Vienna, which, from this period on, sent its orders directly to municipal and seigneurial officials and received the receipts directly. The Estates remained responsible for the return of these taxes and had to make up any shortages. Likewise, the nobles were responsible for their vassals. This liability on the part of Estates and seigneurs was based on their right to sell lands which did not pay or to seize the revenues if they were entailed property. Thus, even as she preserved that which was fundamental in the old division of authority, Maria Theresa was able to assure herself of revenue and to control and disarm an old remnant of particularism. At the same time that she increased the authority of the manorial lord, she provoked the overthrow of the feudal system.

Taxes on urban trades, fixed on the basis of income, were also added to the old impositions on the soil, and Maria Theresa progressively piled new charges on top of these. In 1763 a poll tax, bearing on families divided into twenty-four classes, was established throughout the Empire in the name of "tax liquidation." Every family was supposed to consist of five children and was taxed additionally for each extra child. For these reasons it can easily be seen that here was an extremely primitive economy, where, as in Russia, a man served as a measure as well as an instrument of value. More modern in character, a tax on revenue from capital over a certain level offered more difficulties in its collection.

Responsible seigneurs and municipal officials did not mean that a period of thoroughly modern economy had been reached. On the contrary, responsibility led to the renewal of the authority of the magnates over the people, a tightening of the feudal system. In any case, it served Maria Theresa, who had need of regular resources. The magnates saw in it an advantage tinged with patriotism which made them both pass over the new charges they would have to bear and renounce old particularist traditions the more easily.

To these resources drawn from the old familial Estates were added the contributions from the lands incorporated by annexation. Bohemia, victim of the first success of the Hapsburgs in the Thirty Years' War, was treated like a vanquished state. Since the seventeenth century the nobles had paid taxes like all others. Besides additional taxes created in the eighteenth century, Bohemia had to pay a double contribution, one fixed at 12 million *livres*, the other variable. The first was levied on lands, and a land register, which had been in preparation for almost a century, divided lands according to their productivity. Here, too, arable land was classified according to the quantity of seed sown or the ruggedness of the terrain. Woods and meadows paid over 20 per cent of their yield. Added to this tax on land was a levy on town houses, which were also divided into classes on the basis of the income they produced.

But this tax, which produced little revenue even in Prague, must have been negligible elsewhere.

These assessments, as noted, formed only the regular contribution. To the latter a special tax was added annually, one which bore on a different resource each time, the rotation being established over a period of years according to the nature of economic crises and proportional to their severity. It was calculated on the difference between the resources and the needs of the Treasury.

A Council at Prague watched over the assessment and collection of these taxes. This supreme tribunal condemned those who falsified their declarations or failed to keep the land survey up to date. It delegated commissions to gather the funds to be collected and sent to Vienna accompanied by invoices. Here again, municipal and seigneurial officials were invested with great authority and it can easily be seen that the degree of subjection of Bohemia was of great help to the Emperor in organizing a regular administration there, one which became a model that was extended to the older states.

More difficult was the collection of revenue from the middle class. At Pressburg sat a royal Chamber which exploited the dues from royal estates, customs duties and a salt tax, while a Chamber of Mines sat at Chemnitz. There is only uncertain information about the resources which the Treasury drew from Hungary.

All the same, the traditional revenues must have seemed rather small in comparison with the great expenses incurred by the monarchy in waging its Hungarian wars, for customs duties on the Hungarian borders increased abnormally, as if the Emperor wanted to recover all that was due him. Was this perhaps a means of pressuring the nobles to accept a program of tax reform in this kingdom?

To be sure, the independent character of Hungary's feudal lords, proud of their privileges, did have its other side, and the powerful aid which Maria Theresa was able to draw from this kingdom at the beginning of her wars is well-known. Here again, as in Russia, the backward state of the peasantry was no negligible force. The *pandurs*, or "thieves," whom the Baron von der Trenck[7] was able to dislodge from

7 An Austrian military commander who tried to raise an irregular army to fight the Turks, a venture that was not successful. [Editor's note.]

a fortress in Slavonia in 1741 so as to enroll them into the army and whose numbers were added to by outlaws drawn from everywhere, are one example. But in the last analysis, such a system offered only uncertain guarantees in a Europe which was growing more modern.

Thus in Austria, Bohemia, and Hungary, we see their ruler seeking new resources, in as much as the bulk of taxes which have been mentioned above were absorbed by the Chambers for War to meet the needs of an army and the defense of a vulnerable territory.

These new resources could be expected to come from trade. A tax on the salt traffic was easily established in a country with a small merchant marine. To it were added taxes on beverages and a monopoly over mines which wars facilitated. One fifth of mine production was surrendered to the crown, which bought the rest at low prices and stored it in warehouses on the Prussian model. Lastly, tobacco was not made a monopoly but was heavily taxed. Resorting to the farm system was often necessary. A third of the tax farmers' profits had to be turned over to the Treasury, in addition to, obviously, the cost of the contract award.

No mention has been made here of either the resources of the Austrian Netherlands or those of the Italian possessions, which could not have been of great help to the monarchy. Let us note only that, in Italy, Charles VI had wisely resumed control over an administration which the Spanish, breaking with the tradition of the Sforzas, had gravely neglected. Numerous feudal dues, the farming out of economic rights, the salt tax, and so on, were added to a *taille* to which, here again, Charles VI devoted great efforts, notably by undertaking a great thousand-year land register in which he returned to the old, solid tradition of monthly payments. Through it the direct authority of the court of Vienna developed slowly, at the expense of the Tribunal of Assessments, which was dependent on the Assembly of the State, composed of deputies from the towns and syndics from the Italian provinces.

Maria Theresa supported this policy of encroachment by prudently maintaining the poll tax at a low level. She at least assured its collection according to her instructions. It cost her nothing to promise that the rates would be perpetual and irrevocable!

No mention will be made here of the system of taxes peculiar to the Netherlands. It is known that it was based on the prosperity of trade. Berlin estimated a revenue from there which seems lower than must have been the case. In any event, it is difficult for us to know what this income represented in new money in the hands of the Emperor.

All in all, we observe great variety and uncertainty in the over-all exactions that the Emperor effected in his territories. To be sure, it was deplorable that the resources of this government were still so feudal in character. But following a tradition of the seventeenth century, Charles VI and Maria Theresa had progressively modernized the system of tax collection. Here again, the keystone of the system that would permit the establishment of innovations atop the old arrangements which were linked to the soil was the institution of a monetary device.

In 1703 Leopold gave 4 millions from his revenues to a bank established and guaranteed by the municipality of Vienna. He would very much have liked to order that all bills of exchange be paid through the intermediary of this bank. He would also have wanted his share of the credit of the bank to be met with the help of fictitious revenues. But the city of Vienna intervened — it had no intention of running so many risks!

The Emperor, however, needed credit from Vienna. Slowly the greater part of the real revenues of the crown went to the bank to guarantee the sums it had advanced. In 1765 the bank had become primarily a state organization, regulating the circulation of money. Maria Theresa created a *Ministerial Banco-hof Deputation*, which controlled the whole enterprise in her name.

This bank received deposits for which it remitted notes that were good as money, yet redeemable and bearing interest at 5 per cent. Many of these deposits were made through compulsion, since the law ordered, for example, that endowments for hospitals and churches be paid into it. Moreover, the king borrowed from it, and notes were issued on his guarantee. The government also issued notes on the credit of the Estates, but they were generally sustained by the credit of the Bank of Vienna.

Thus a considerable circulation of paper money developed throughout the Empire. Soon the interest on the notes could be reduced; soon the crown was able to indulge in inflation through paper money whenever it was in difficulty, without harming its credit. This, thanks to the prudence of Haugwitz,[8] who always knew how to link loans with an improvement in financial organization and an increase in the transfer of imperial revenues to the profit of the bank.

Thus, at the advent of Joseph II, important resources could be mobilized to benefit the crown, and the currency was no longer at the mercy of exhausted mines or imports from abroad. The Emperor controlled important assets. This is what destroyed him because he wanted to substitute, for the prudence of his mother, a sudden wave of reforms—the standardization of law codes, courts, and administration from the North Sea to the Adriatic.

Confusion quickly resulted. All the officials of the crown, the syndics and the high municipal officials were overwhelmed by the new procedures that were hard to substitute for the old, which had developed only slowly. The various manorial lords had accepted the reforms of the empire gradually only because their vanity was continually soothed and their moral authority reinforced, although the latter became increasingly fictitious as they were deprived of their material authority and control over their own finances. But to proclaim such principles abruptly was to show the king's hand. Not having seen the skillfulness of Maria Theresa and Charles VI and by rushing matters, Joseph II broke the fragile instrument of his authority.

What did the "liberation" of the serfs signify when it was materially impossible for the Emperor to give this fine word any true meaning? But once spoken, it shook the whole structure. Without changing the real status of any individual, it provoked occasional famines, frequent violent seigneurial reactions, and difficulties in collecting revenue everywhere.

In fact, the religious and philosophic content of the declarations and measures of Joseph II would lead Belgium to revolt. But the prince really failed because he wanted to be too ruthless a *philosophe*. The sadness of his last years is well-known: then he had to go back on all his decisions, leaving the Empire weakened, almost amputated, and compromised beyond any hope of resuming reform for a long time to come.

IV

The reader who has struggled through the minute detail of all these internal affairs of the cabinets of Europe will perhaps have a general idea of the power of the State at the end of the eighteenth century.

Everywhere rulers wanted to imitate Louis XIV—to strengthen the State by putting all economic resources at its service, resources that were largely destined for war, the old instrument of Western prestige. In order to succeed they, like the French monarchy of the seventeenth century, needed to place themselves in the forefront of progress in material life and control it through their reforms, while still benefiting from the old adulation of the people for its king.

In Russia where this affection was enormous because of the naïveté of the population, Catherine could permit only superficial reforms which succeeded as a result of the religious and moral credit of the monarchy. In Prussia Frederick the Great could count only on the friends he made for himself and paid for in money and military glory. So he was led to assume far more effective control over the economic apparatus by basing it on the military apparatus. In Russia Catherine was able to proclaim great philosophic principles that her entourage scarcely understood and which caused no stir among the people. In Prussia Frederick was more prudent and he was wise if brutal in escorting Voltaire to the border.

In Austria the situation was far more delicate. There the population was of the Catholic faith and the culture of that faith. It was enough for Joseph II not to be strictly orthodox to be suspect. Most important, his subjects were too devout not to be disturbed by philosophic proclamations that threw everything into disorder. Lastly, the varied economic systems which he governed did not lend themselves to uniformity. Moreover, everywhere they were advanced enough to invite a little respect for and a defense of the institutions which had hitherto preserved them. In the Netherlands particularly, reformism was a menace to everyone. To be sure, any reform in Austria was not impossible, since Charles VI and Maria Theresa had succeeded in promoting a

---

[8] Prince Friedrich Wilhelm von Gaugwitz (1700–1765) served as Marie Theresa's chancellor; he was instrumental in instituting a series of internal reforms aimed at improving the financial condition of the imperial government. [Editor's note.]

The Early Modern Era

new life everywhere, by instituting modern money and reshaping the old institutional framework. But such reform had to be carried out in successive stages from one area of the Empire to another, playing with the security of the Empire in one place, with that of religion in another, and with material interests elsewhere. This calculated tactfulness did not lend itself to public proclamations.

Thus it was that of the two countries where the basis of civilization was already too refined and too rich to permit a public display of principle, Austria was in the more delicate situation, and its ruler the more obviously limited and prudent. How bitter it was for the good Emperor to see how his rival Catherine, with so much impunity, gave verbal proof of a philosophy (which he perhaps had good reason to consider inoperative) whose effects were not known and had echoes only in the West. Nothing but a path of cautious reform was open to Joseph II; he could only hate this Frederick the Great who knew how to follow it better — and at the expense of imperial power.

Such were the various vicissitudes of the enlightened despotism in fashion everywhere, but particularly reputed in the larger States: vicissitudes which everywhere saw seated more or less solidly on their thrones, princes concerned with logical action and a firmly based material strength in which money served to create money and to strengthen the army.

All did indeed follow the example of the Sun King. All were worthy pupils, and the majority were able, in the bargain, to offer themselves the luxury of appearing to be inspired by the *philosophes* who were in fashion in France.

France, alas, had no resources other than this very fashion. In the seventeenth century it had offered the striking example of what royal power might be. In the eighteenth century it presented only the gloss with which the other princes tinged their aspirations to power.

We must not be deceived: no reform in Europe was due to the ideas of the *philosophes*. Indeed, Frederick the Great mocked Montesquieu, Voltaire, Rousseau and the Physiocrats when he wanted arsenals, outfitted storehouses of grain, or distributed cattle and seed. Catherine only flirted with the *philosophes*, and the good Joseph was almost led to complete ruin for having taken their talk for gospel truth.

Nothing in the real and solid institutions of Europe owed anything whatsoever to the France of the eighteenth century; they owed almost everything to the France of the seventeenth.

And the rest came from England. There has been no discussion here of the details of the machines of all kinds which equipped workshops and factories — they were frequently German but more often English. Most important, and a capital innovation for these countries without mines of precious metals and with difficult or restricted access to the Atlantic, they thought of England and its monetary system. Everywhere state banks were established, prospered, and rendered precisely that kind of service to the sovereign which the Bank of England had rendered to its government. But all these potentates had a great advantage over the rulers of England. Except in Austria (and here again to a far lesser degree than in England) they had no wide and powerful political opinion to fear, one capable of casting on their money that discredit that it had no other way of expressing to the ruler. Russians believed in the bank note because they adored their tsar, while the English had chosen their king as a measure of their confidence in their money. As a result the Enlightened Despots, more fortunate still than Louis XIV, could create a monetary instrument before the conditions which would have naturally given birth to it in their countries were realized. They thus outpaced public opinion and might use against it the financial credit which it had let itself lose.

The bank note was the product of psychological forces. It was believed in because it had been believed in. It would be believed in tomorrow although it served a policy that was detested, because yesterday it had been believed in on the word of a crown that was respected.

Thus, in the form of money, the despots accumulated a reserve of confidence of a kind from which they were to profit and which would serve them effectively in the difficult years ahead.

How much luckier than Louis XIV! At the height of his reign the latter could have created a bank and bank notes, and the adoration of his subjects would have allowed the move. The same would undoubtedly have been the case even with Henry IV, who thought of a bank of issue, but, too unsophisticated, he did not recognize what a treasure he was disdaining. The imprudent Regent, nimble as he was, spoiled everything through his blindness.[9]

Thus while the despots throughout the Continent were accumulating treasure through the naive simplicity of their peoples, the King of France gave his people full, public proof that a bank might be the worst instrument of royal arbitrariness. He antagonized the public opinion which he should have called upon to support his designs.

Thus, as monarchies were being consolidated elsewhere, the one in France was cutting itself off from its economic roots like an oak about to come crashing down. If France now no longer provided the world with realistic models but rather with a veneer of ideas, it was because the political body of the old monarchy was already decaying within and dying from a loss of vigor.

But was this thought always to remain a veneer? Were there not other prosperous institutions in France alongside this disappearing monarchial body which were ready to support a State with a different balance? Could the other princes of Europe always mock this thought, and were there no fertile fields in their own midst which were sown by or despite them and which were preparing to bear fruit? If Continental Europe remained at a stage where its political thought drew more from the example of Louis XIV than from the French court of the eighteenth century, was this not precisely a reason to think that the time would come when French thought of the eighteenth century would soon serve for something other than preambles to proclamations?

Such was one drama of the European mind near the end of the eighteenth century, and reform was an integral part of the objective values of French philosophic thought. If French philosophy had been merely a declaration, it would, in fact, have been only the gilt which Frederick, Catherine and Maria Theresa applied to their real attitudes, just as stylish furniture was covered with *vernis Martin*. The good Joseph was the victim of the ideas of the *philosophes* for having seen their solid virtues.

But perhaps this philosophy was fatal to Joseph only because it was applied too soon. Perhaps it held a destructive power which Frederick, Catherine and Maria Theresa had to be quick in deriding because they would have little time left to do so.

But there was a second drama in the West. All the powers studied here resembled each other in many ways, the greatest being their imitation of Louis XIV. From England they borrowed only techniques, not methods of government. They inverted these techniques, so to speak, by placing them to a use far different from the one that had given them birth across the Channel. In England public opinion was responsible for creating the Bank of England and consolidating its bank notes. In Eastern Europe the bank note duped public opinion to the profit of a bank which was nothing more than an extension of the royal treasury.

Thus a split was perhaps being prepared between the continental West and the maritime West. It was the old quarrel between land and sea.

[9] Philip, Duke of Orléans, Regent of France (1715–1732) during Louis XV's minority, permitted the Scotsman John Law to set up a Royal Bank, which became disastrously involved with Law's Mississippi Company ("Mississippi Bubble") and had to suspend payments in 1720. [Editor's note.]

HANS ROSENBERG

BUREAUCRATIZED AUTOCRACY

The evolutionary aspects of Enlightened Despotism are broadly sketched by Professor Hans Rosenberg of the University of California at Berkeley in the "Preface" to his book, *Bureaucracy, Aristocracy, and Autocracy*. Professor Rosenberg, outlining the development of "centralizing authoritarianism," pays particular attention to the role of the bureaucrats (whom he calls "new bureaucrats" to distinguish them from the feudal office holders) in the formation of the modern state. These new bureaucrats, Rosenberg finds, are far more important in the development of Enlightened Absolutism and Despotism than the rulers, or despots, themselves.

The whittling away of the powers of the assemblies of estates ushered in a new era in the history of the ownership, control, and management of the means of political domination. The emergence of centralizing authoritarianism found conspicuous expression in the partial or total eclipse, as organs of government, of the Spanish *cortes*, the French *etats*, the south Italian *parliamenti*, the German and Austrian *Stände*, and the Russian *zemskii sobor*. Their decline was both the cause and the effect of the establishment of a princely monopoly over the central power in the state.

Through this momentous usurpation of preponderant influence, backed up by superior military force, the *Ständestaat* gave way to an absolute state in the sense that the legal authority of the prince was released from the restraints which natural law, rivaling jurisdictions, old-standing customs, and the special liberties of the ruling groups had imposed upon him. In real life, unchecked authority did not mean unlimited power, and the claim to omnipotence was scarcely more than wishful thinking. But despite its pretentious legal façade, at the prime of its development the absolute monarchy was an exacting fiscal and military police state. In accord with the revised ideas of Roman imperial absolutism, the exclusive right to make policy and law and to direct enforcement at will was concentrated in a single individual. The newly proclaimed "sovereignty" of the state was embodied in the person of the monarch.

In politics and governmental administration the abandonment of the proprietary conception of rulership was extremely slow. The differentiation between kingship as a public trust and a personal status advanced faster in theory than in practice. Wherever princely despotism did become the legitimate government, the identification of the dynastic interest with *raison d'etat* and *salus publica* was the official mainspring of political integration. In consequence, obedience to the monarch and his appointed designees supplanted, in principle, voluntary coöperation by the old co-owners of public jurisdictions. Even the hitherto independent few — the hopes

and desires of the many hardly mattered — were now expected to bow their heads and to take orders.

The rise of centralized domination under the leadership of autocrats, whether kings, princes, prime ministers, or political cardinals, wrought profound changes in the functions of the central government; in the methods of political and administrative management; in the recruitment and behavior of men in authority; and in the conception of the rights and duties of officeholding.

Absolutism also altered the nature of political power. The new state rulers were not content to add to their "patrimony" the traditional jurisdictions of the estates and to absorb most of their functions. They also built a new bureaucratic empire. They raised sizable permanent armies, imposed ever larger taxes, multiplied fiscal exactions. They extended and intensified the regulative and administrative intervention of the dynastic government into the sphere of private rights and local home rule. And they made a place for the Crown as a strong commercial competitor and monopolist in production and distribution.

Thus, the makers of the absolute monarchy did not merely learn to handle old institutions in a new way. They also invented novel and more effective instruments of compulsion. By constructing a large-scale apparatus of finance, administration, and military might operated by a class of appointed career executives accountable to them, they became the founders of a thoroughly bureaucratized state with many strikingly "modern" features. The great political entrepreneurs had the wit to realize that "a bureaucratized autocracy is a perfected autocracy."

An aggressive, methodical, and often oppressive machine of hierarchical state management by dictation and subordination came to prevail over the less elaborate, more slovenly, and infinitely more personal medieval contrivances. Dynastic absolutism itself was only a passing historic phenomenon. But it gave birth to an administrative system which survived to enter the common heritage of contemporary civilization.

The growth of the power of the central authority meant the growth of the power of the executive bureaucracy. Everywhere throughout the formative stage, new, removable bureaucrats and not the "old" patrimonial officials and notables were in the lead. The *nouveaux arrivés* challenged the diehard notion that the privileged should continue to derive the right to govern by inheritance or purchase without special training and without devoting their energies to it exclusively. The power of the monarch to nominate officers at his discretion, unconfirmed by the estates and in violation of ancient usage, and to regulate the functions and status of the incumbents as he saw fit, deeply affected both the practice and theory of government.

The crown's arrogated power to appoint and to remove at will made possible the resurgence and rapid expansion of autocratic personnel administration. The rise of absolutism furnished an important basis for gaining authority, income, wealth, external dignity, social honors, and for the extraction of deference from the lower orders. It raised a dependent parvenu elite of commissioned government managers to a position of functional superiority in the polity.

Henceforth, centrally directed executive government was far more ramified than in medieval times. Impersonal relations were to prevail over personal ties, since administrative *étatisme* was growing into a big business. Its operators originated as "dynastic servants." But unlike the professional officials in the feudal states, they were, a few relics of the past notwithstanding, clearly separated from the princely household.

The new bureaucrats were not modern civil servants, but their forerunners. They were dynastic rather than public servants. They served the welfare of the government of the autocratic prince, not that of the governed. The well-being of the subjects was not an end in itself but a means to bolster the position of the government. Nowhere in Europe did the conversion of dynastic bureaucrats into public agents present itself as a serious issue before the end of the eighteenth century. Only thereafter did allegiance to the king-employer as a person or to the crown as the institutional embodiment of authority or to the aristocratic few begin to merge into loyalty to the abstract ideas of the State or of popular sovereignty.

Government bureaucracy and civil service are not synonymous terms or identical concepts. The modern civil service is a special type of responsible bureaucracy. It deserves its name only if it equates the public interest with the general welfare. In reality, during the nineteenth century the evolving civil service elites of the European world showed a strong propensity toward attaching themselves to the interests and ideals of limited groups rather than to "the people and egalitarian conceptions of civic right and political liberty. The tardy adjustment demonstrated how great was the vitality of the ancient aristocratic societies.

The New Monarchy, as it is sometimes called, modified but did not destroy the confused mass of jurisdictions which had been transmitted from the past. It merely made a start in disengaging public prerogatives from the law of private property, from vested family interests, and from the grip of the possessors of legal, social, and political privilege. The new bureaucrats epitomized this trend which in medieval times had been noticeable only in the cities.

France, the most populous political unit of Europe in the sixteenth and seventeenth centuries, was then the chief model of the absolute monarchy. Here law and political theory drew a sharp distinction between the numerous patrimonial officials, the strongly entrenched *officiers*, and the rising small body of absolutist bureaucrats, the *commissaires*. All the modernized states of Europe, in their own peculiar and fleeting ways, developed striking analogies to this dual personnel pattern which reflected two antagonistic principles of officeholding and the coëxistence of two distinct managerial hierarchies.

The *officiers*, as defined and protected by French law, gave concrete expression to the close association of public authority with rights of private ownership, which the feudal state had passed on to its successors. The *officiers* were holders of administrative and judicial jobs whose appointment had legally to be approved by the crown. Actually, in the course of the fourteenth and fifteenth centuries, when the French *Ständestaat* was built, the purchase of offices was common enough to reduce royal confirmation to a formality. Through this practice the buyer gained a personal proprietary title to a particular *charge* or *fonction*.

The Early Modern Era

Sale of offices on a large scale was peculiar to France. There it grew rapidly during the dislocating price revolution of the sixteenth and early seventeenth centuries. Fiscal expediency accounted for this further growth which was to prove a blight to the public and disastrous to the long-term interests of the "sovereign" monarch striving for supreme mastery. The financial straits of the crown coincided with a strong craving for public distinction. This demand came not from the increasingly impoverished class of noble landed *rentiers*, but from socially ambitious families who had made fortunes in trade, in finance, or in the legal profession. As in the immediately preceding centuries, officeholding was one of the chief means by which men from the middle ranks of society entered the old upper class. All over Europe, the expansion of acquisitive business enterprise gave a fresh impetus to social mobility and to the amalgamation of private and public activity.

The *Paulette* of 1604, named after the secretary of state Paulet, provided a firm legal foundation for the perpetuation of venal authority and the sanctity of commercialized government administration in France. The office was made transferable at the will of the incumbent who in return for this right was obligated to pay an annual fee to the crown. In theory and practice, the office was recognized as a regularly established public function as well as an object of private ownership. It was distinct from an "ordinary" capital investment, since it was a springboard of legal privilege, a secure base of personal power, and often also a means of acquiring prestige titles and noble status. The income derived from it was not so much in wages and allowances as in fees and perquisites. The *officier* owned his post and appendant rights almost like a piece of real estate which he had either bought with hard cash or inherited or acquired as a dowry. He was the "old" bureaucrat and hence a semi-autonomous, virtually irremovable and largely unaccountable functionary with strong regional and local attachments.

The *commissaire* appeared in the sixteenth century as an irregular and more carefully selected representative of the king. He differed fundamentally from the *officier*, with regard to both legal status and political function. The *commissaire* was the new bureaucrat, the official champion of monarchical centralization, and a salaried subordinate, although his emoluments were seldom confined to a fixed stipend. He was a "permanent probationer," subservient to the wishes of his ruler. Entrusted with a revocable *commission*, he was subject to specific instructions regulating his functions and duties, to disciplinary controls, to sudden transfer or dismissal. He was the creature but also the maker and chief direct beneficiary of the absolute form of government.

The concept of the *commissaire* was distinct from that of the *officier*. Historic reality, however, was less precise and more perplexing. Actually the two categories shaded into each other, and sometimes the lines of demarcation became hopelessly blurred. Everywhere a more or less substantial percentage of the rising *commissaires* was originally recruited from the ranks of the old official hierarchy. They were then, literally speaking, "commissioned officers."

From the outset, the power elite of "commissars" was built up, like their age-old competitors, on gradations of rank and permeated with hierarchical conceptions. Their initial political status was that of a mere transmission belt. They were commissioned by the monarch to ensure his sovereignty by curbing or destroying the powers of the traditional leadership groups in general and by working out a *modus vivendi* with the corporate organizations of the *officiers* in particular. They had to make a place for themselves in a neatly stratified and predominantly noncompetitive society, founded on status, unequal rights, class privileges, and the persistent aristocratic conviction "that the inequalities which distinguish one body of men from another are of essential and permanent importance. In such a social order, the commissars, loosely scraped together from heterogeneous strata, could not relax until they, too, had arrived.

The long and bitter struggle of these interlopers for dominance in the management of public administration, for political leadership, and for recognition as a superior status group was concentrated on two fronts. They could not attain their ends without putting into their place the old political and executive elites and without effecting their own emancipation from monarchical autocracy.

Nowhere in Europe under the absolutist Old Regime were the new administrative bureaucracy and the time-honored bodies of aristocratic rulership implacable enemies. The upper brackets of the commissar class found their social identity in close interaction with those very forces who as independent *seigneurs* or as semi-independent *officiers* had heretofore owned the means of government and administration. The commissars gained an assured social position and extended their power by infiltration and limited amalgamation, chiefly through holding interlocking positions. Thus they developed into a social elite which was not merely a self-perpetuating official aristocracy but also a highly prominent segment of the nobility and of the plutocracy. Thus they fortified themselves as a political hierarchy. As a group, they grew almost independent of effective royal control in the exercise of delegated administrative and judicial tasks. But in addition, and whether or not they came from the new or the old bureaucracies, the top executives, and sometimes even strategically placed subaltern officials, eventually managed to capture the lion's share in the central power of political decision.

This whole process was accompanied by the regrouping of all the competing governing elites. The principal political result was the subtle conversion of bureaucratized monarchical autocracy into government by an oligarchical bureaucracy, self-willed, yet representative of the refashioned privileged classes. Everywhere, earlier or later, dynastic absolutism was superseded by bureaucratic absolutism before the absolute state itself was seriously challenged by modern liberalism.

The transition to the more advanced stage in the evolution of the Old Regime began to be quite conspicuous in France in the late days of Louis XIV, in Russia under the successors of Peter I, and in the monarchy of the Austrian Habsburgs during the reign of Maria Theresa. In Prussia this development did not become clearly discernable before the latter part of the eighteenth century. The main reason for this delay was not so much the fact that the Hohenzollerns were relative latecomers in practicing political integration by coercion, but rather the accident that here princely leadership was nominal only from 1688 to 1713. At the helm of the Prussian absolute state, prior to the French Revolution, stood three men who for long periods ruled autocratically in person: the Elector Frederick William, later called the Great Elector (1640–1688), King Frederick William I (1713–1740), and Frederick II, better known as Frederick the Great (1740–1786).

In substance, but on a grander scale and with the aid of perfected methods, the commissars played a social and political role which closely resembled that of their far distant professional forebears. The bureaucratic managers of the reformed feudal monarchies had supplied the initial kernel of the growing body of patrimonial officials. And the elite of this old hierarchy had succeeded in trimming the discretionary powers of the prince, but had been forced to share the spoils of victory with the large landowners and the urban patricians.

So enormous was the influence of the historic heritage that the absolute dynastic state turned out to be merely another phase in the history of the inveterate struggle for the abridgment of royal prerogatives. As for the social forces in the state, the "modern Old Regimes" were indeed not more than a variation of the aristocratic monarchy, a monarchy dominated by aristocratic power groups of bureaucrats and notables. Related by direct descent to the *Ständestaaten* and the feudal polities, the absolute monarchies retained certain traits of their predecessors. At the same time, however, they were far more centralized and bureaucratized, more active and more strictly utilitarian, more machine-like, more authoritarian, and more efficient in the use of material resources and in the direction and coördination of human energy. . . .

5

JEAN-JACQUES ROUSSEAU—
DEMOCRAT OR TOTALITARIAN?

Jean-Jacques Rousseau was born in Geneva, Switzerland, on June 28, 1712. His mother having died when he was but a few days old, Rousseau was brought up by his father, a watchmaker. When he was fifteen he left Geneva and spent the next dozen years wandering across Switzerland, Savoy, northern Italy, and southern

France, earning his living as a lackey, an engraver, tutor, and music copyist. In 1742 he settled in Paris where, in addition to copying and composing music, he cultivated the friendship of several noted French writers, among them the renowned *philosophe* Denis Diderot. Diderot, taking an interest in Rousseau's career, asked him in the late 1740's to write several articles on music for the great French edition of the *Encyclopédie*. From that time Rousseau devoted his life increasingly to literary pursuits.

In 1749 Rousseau submitted an essay to the Dijon Academy which won a first prize and was published in the following year under the title *A Discourse on the Arts and Sciences*. Delighted with this initial success, Rousseau composed, again for the academy at Dijon, a second essay which, though it did not win first prize, became famous as a *Discourse on the Origin of Inequality among Men* (1755). Both *Discourses* created something of a sensation among the Enlightened circles of Europe for branding Society itself as the great corrupter of mankind, thus at once attacking the ideas of progress and original sin.

In 1756 Rousseau left Paris, retreating to a cottage near the forest of Montmorency where he wrote his most famous works: *Julie, or the New Heloise* (1761); *Émile, or on Education* (1762); and *The Social Contract* (1762). The latter work by enunciating a "democratic thesis" of government so incensed the French authorities that Rousseau fled to Switzerland and thence, in 1766, to the "home of exiles," England. Returning secretly to France in 1767, Rousseau lived in obscurity until his death in July, 1778.

After his death, Rousseau's reputation fluctuated with the temper of the times. During the French Revolution, for example, the Jacobin clubs proclaimed Rousseau the architect of popular democracy. At the same time, the Romantic poet, Lord Byron, pictured him as

The apostle of affliction, he who threw
Enchantment over passion, and from woe
Wrung overwhelming eloquence.

Byron's reaction to Rousseau was typical of the Romantics: a mixture of awe and amusement. Later nineteenth-century critics, less tolerant of Rousseau's idiosyncrasies, called him an "emotional enthusiast," a "super-tramp," and "a self-torturing sophist." It was only in the early twentieth century that a balanced judgment of the man and his writings appeared in the works of Gustave Lanson. Lanson, a professor of literature at the Sorbonne, discovered in Rousseau's works a thread of continuity based on the statement from *Émile* that "Nature has created man happy and good, but society depraves him and makes him miserable." Lanson and later critics like E. H. Wright, Charles W. Hendel, Ernst Cassirer, and Sir Ernest Barker helped to dignify the accounts of Rousseau the man and to underscore the serious intent and continuity of his writings. Yet, in view of all this learned commentary, Rousseau remains an enigma: a passionate defender of the individual in society who in his famous work on the *Social Contract* (1762) was willing to see individual rights sacrificed to the corporate state; a sensitive man who could write a great treatise on education, *Émile*, yet abandon his own children to an orphanage; a hedonist who later reverted to a Calvinistic asceticism; a *philosophe* who was intrigued by the gay life of the Parisian salons yet fled Paris for a hermit's cottage near the woods of Montmorency. Rousseau's life was filled with contradictions and false starts; or, perhaps better put, it was a long pilgrimage in search of the grail of perfection.

ERNEST HUNTER WRIGHT

CREATOR OF THE DEMOCRATIC IDEAL

The consistency rather than the inconsistency in Rousseau's thought is what strikes Ernest Hunter Wright, formerly professor of literature at Columbia University. Wright contends in his book, *The Meaning of Rousseau* (1928), that the great Swiss thinker was well aware of the dangers of democracy and that he filled his great work on the *Social Contract* with "precautions against error," safeguards for the public-minded citizen to heed lest he stray either toward despotism or anarchy. Wright believes that Rousseau's ideal state was just that, something the citizen should strive for, a quest for what ought to be. Wright thus counters the legend created by Edmund Burke, John Morley, and the French critic Taine that Rousseau was a wild-eyed reformer, a sophist, and a word-monger, unaware of the consequences of the ideas he released on an unsuspecting world.

That the state described was far to seek in Rousseau's day is very evident. The governments in power were proceeding mainly on a very different principle, and that is why the *Inequality* was written to deplore them. That the state is still beyond us is but too apparent. Even that it will remain somewhat beyond us for all time might go unsaid but for the fact that many of the critics seem to start and end with the idea that Rousseau thought it could be instituted at a human nod. It is frankly an ideal, though it has already had a large effect in practice, and the only question left for us is whether the ideal is a good one. What has been objected to it?

That it is abusable is evident enough. Of course a demagogue may counterfeit a public spirit for his personal ends, and so may any group. Of course a busybody may forget the common cause to meddle in his neighbour's private business. Of course it takes a certain wisdom to be citizen enough to know that

obedience to the law is liberty, and a certain prudence to act consonantly. The ideal has been grievously abused, whether by men who understood its meaning or by others who were ignorant of it. Rousseau foresaw a thousand ways of injuring law and liberty in the betrayal of his principle, and was decidedly uncomfortable about what he well knew to be the desperate science. So apprehensive was he as to say outright that few peoples were intelligent and public-spirited enough to compass liberty, and that for the rest some other polity were better; so apprehensive that he filled a good half of his book [*Social Contract*] with precautions against error; and indeed so apprehensive that in spite of an occasional hope of adapting the ideal to some people like the Poles or Corsicans, his more usual mood was one of a despair perhaps too deep lest it could never be approximated in human society, and lest the most arbitrary despotism, the most "perfect Hobbism," should prove the only possible alternative. For he

From Ernest Hunter Wright, *The Meaning of Rousseau*, (1928), pp. 101–112. Reprinted by permission of the author.

was sure the sovereign must be absolute if the state would live; and if the sovereign could not be the people, it would have to be a master. He never doubted the ideal, but he often wondered how far it could go in practice. Yet he thought best to state it once for all, and let it work as it could. Whatever its worth, it may be no more abusable than any other social principle. And a principle is not invalidated by abuses merely, else the golden rule would be the most discredited of maxims.

It is hard to say whether the *Contract* has been oftener indicted for an individualism that will run to anarchy or for an absolutism that will bring the final tyranny. The people rule, and may do as they please; the people is supreme, and its pleasure will be despotism; so run the unsisterly opinions. On the whole, the first is older and more popular, the second later and more learned; but the two have come from every decade and from every kind of critic, and have even found a common home in season with a single critic. Vaughan can see them both implicit in the marvellous diatribes of Burke which are probably the main source of the Anglo-Saxon creed about our book. In 1790 Burke is aghast at the men who are disbanding France into her original *moleculae,* or murdering a nation to give every man his own sweet will. But six years later he is in a rage because individuality is left out of their scheme and the state is all in all for them; because they are surrendering the last morsel of their liberty for a sop to Leviathan. Of course Burke is speaking of two sets of revolutionists, with the Terror and much else between them, and apart from the intemperate eloquence of age he may be mainly right about them both; but he cannot well be right in implying or openly declaring that they are both doing the will of Rousseau. Yet in some sort of amity the two opinions have come down the century to us, now in diatribe and now in eulogy, and are still assuring us on the one hand that our treatise is a charter for individual licence and on the other that it "leaves no jot of liberty" to any individual, but is "one of the most potent implements of tyranny that maniac ever forged."

Though famous in their sponsors, the opinions cannot both be right unless our treatise is a tissue of such incoherence as to merit no attention. But without answering that it is also assailed by Burke and others for a logic which they call too unrelenting, we may simply ask if there is anything of signal incoherence in the summary as given of it. In the light of such a summary both opinions seem to be untenable. The

book is meant for neither individualist nor absolutist. In the struggle between state and individual which has been the torment of political philosophy from Aristotle down, it offers a proposal for a peace. Whatever the proposal may be worth, we have already stated it so fully that we may now be brief upon it. The individual must have liberty for progress, but the state that fosters progress must have power to do its work. The liberty must be secure, for a precarious liberty is none at all, but the power must be supreme, for contingent power is the lack of it. So the two must remain full and unconflicting. And our author would so render them in law that cannot of its nature lack supremacy but cannot of its nature limit liberty. The reasoning that leads him to such law may be assailed in other ways — as a sheer abstraction, as ideal or "metaphysical" perhaps; but not as individualist or absolutist.

For it is such reasoning that arouses what has nearly always been the main objection to the book, especially in lands that speak the tongue of Burke. The whole thing is airy logic — logic soaring in a void above the reach of fact or care of consequence. The age of sophisters has come indeed, with Rousseau as the worst and loudest of them, and "the glory of Europe is extinguished forever" with a libertine logician fiddling on the thin strings of intellectual figment in the ruins. Morley[1] carries on the charge more temperately than most of its continuators, and in periods so masterly that we may borrow all our illustrations from him. Over and over he tells us that many of the problems in our treatise are such pure dialectic as "never had any other than an abstract and phantasmatic existence," and that "the slightest attempt to confront them with actual fact would have shown them to be not merely valueless, but meaningless." A "symmetrical" humour made Rousseau's "vision too narrow" for his complex subject, and led only to his "geometrical method" of handling the kind of "desperate absurdity" that makes "fanatics." Many of his pages are mere "logical deductions from verbal definitions" that lead only to questions which "were never worth asking" and to answers which "nobody will take the trouble to deny" because they are "nonsense." For though he is "firmly possessed with the infallibility of his own dreams," he is merely "basing his political institutions on a figment," as if he "had never really settled the ends for which government exists"; so he can give us "not the least help toward the solution of any

[1] John Morley in his book, *Rousseau.* [Editor's note.]

problem of actual government." Never mind if he is nothing but a sentimentalist still, who offers mere "emotion for the discovery of law," for all his logic is the fig-leaf of his sentiment. And never mind if Morley, after reassuring us in closing that he is innocent of all "attempt to palliate either the shallowness or the practical mischievousness" of the book, gives us a last surprise by showing how it fired thousands of "generous breasts" all over Europe to a "virile and patriotic energy" so great as to create a new social world which reminds Morley of the new world of science after Newton. Such a surprise is very common for the reader of the criticism of Rousseau. But Rousseau, of all men, must not have the credit; he did but "involuntarily and unconsciously contribute to the growth of those new and progressive ideas, in which for his own part he lacked all faith" — even though he was "firmly possessed with the infallibility" of them.

All this from a famous liberal known for moderation, all this from a single chapter of the best book in the language on our subject. We would not be unfair to its author, nor could he have so understood us; for the opinions we have quoted from his early masterpiece deepened steadily within him during the half-century of service that ensued upon their utterance. If we were looking for excitement we could fill a hundred pages with quotations from as many authors whose intemperance would leave the present excerpts rather pale. But these should be enough to serve the purpose.

There is no denying that there is a truth behind them. Every reader of the *Social Contract* must have felt it. There is more abstraction in the book than practical experience, and at cardinal points. "It is as if the edifice were built of wood instead of human beings, so precisely are the pieces fitted into place by rule and line." Slip this into Burke or Morley, and the words will fit to all perfection; but it is not Burke or Morley now protesting — it is no other than Rousseau in person. Such is Emile's first objection to the *Social Contract* as abridged for his instruction. And his tutor has an answer ready. "True," he says, "but we must remember that the right is not dependent upon human passion, and that our first duty was to settle the true principle of social right. Now that we have found it, we may look and see what men have made of it, *et vous verrez de belles choses!*" So Rousseau knew at least what he was doing when he built his doctrine mainly out of logic. If his admission lay obscure in some far corner of his work, a critic might be

more excusable for missing it and for implying that Rousseau never thought of it and never dreamed of any other key to social theory than that of formal logic; but time and again the admission is explicit, and by implication it is omnipresent. It is clear, for instance, in his reference to Montesquieu, so famous for another way in social theory. "The illustrious Montesquieu" is the only man who could have found the true principle of social right, "but he took care to avoid the principles of politics and gave all his attention to the laws of actual governments; and the two matters are as different as may be. But whoever would pass judgement on an actual government must study both of them; he must know what ought to be if he would judge what is."

Rousseau's quest is mainly for what ought to be, and Montesquieu's for what has been and is. The one would find the right first and apply it as may be expedient, and the other looks for the expedient in the faith that nothing else is right. It is no disrespect to either to say this. It is fortunate enough that neither tried to be the other; as fortunate, in a minor way, as that a Plato did not try to be an Aristotle, or, in a more comparable instance, as that Edmund Burke would seldom follow abstract reason very far on any of the principles which it was his sovereign principle to flout. But we do not escape principles by flouting them, we only assert others; and if Burke had ever deigned to justify his sovereign principle in final reason, he might have had his troubles. Rousseau had his own in following Montesquieu in the details of practical experience; partly because he found so little room for rivalry, mainly because he was not made for sifting masses of detail but rather for carving out a principle. So he is weakest in the latter portion of his book, where observation and experience count for most; he is weakest in "examples," here as in *Émile*. He is stronger in the earlier portion, where he must rely on reason pure and simple. In that reliance he will find a single right society, as did Plato long before him on the same ground — on the ground that there can be one kind of justice only. On the ground of observation and experience, Montesquieu will hold a single right society to be pure fiction.

These are the two ways for the political philosopher. He may gather all the facts of variable experience in the hope that he may then deduce a principle from them, even though it prove that any principle is inconceivable. Such is on the whole the way of Montesquieu or Burke. Or he may first look for a principle in reason, in the hope that he may mould the facts in some proportion to its image. Such is on the whole the way of Plato or Rousseau. On the whole, of course; it would be tedious to show that we must use some combination of the two, since the purest reason must have facts to go on, and since we cannot even gather facts without some reason for so doing. We must "study both." We are all using both the methods all the time, and they often yield about the same results in practice, as they did indeed for Montesquieu and Rousseau; for in practical conclusions about government the two men are pretty much at one. There is little ground for any man who may prefer one method to revile his neighbour for employing the other; and when the results are similar, the men will be left fighting over nothing but their badges. There would probably have been no better magistrate for Rousseau's commonwealth than Burke, for all his eloquent derision of its author.

Now Rousseau does not so much choose between the two ways as endorse them both but try to show that one of them must take precedence. Though he was one of the earliest men of genius to offer ample praise to the great Montesquieu, he still thought that the study of what ought to be must come first, else the study of what is, however thorough, could not know its purpose. He was sure the endless gathering of facts was useless in the absence of a principle to judge them by. And he was sure the principle must come from reason, for he saw no hope of its emerging by some spontaneity from the facts alone; as well hope that the golden rule will rise out of a list of all our deeds as that the golden age will be discoverable in the facts of our history. That is why he wove the Social Contract mainly out of logic. In our Darwinian day the other method has the upper hand, in social science as in all else; in the still Cartesian day of Rousseau, his own way was in far higher favour. The century was out for universals, in spite of Montesquieu, and Rousseau was of it. For whatever be the common notion, he probably owes more in general method to Descartes than to any other predecessor, and the Social Contract may well be the best example of Cartesian reasoning since Descartes himself.

But reasoning it is, of full intention; and that is what has caused most of the criticism. For the main target of the scorn of Burke and Morley is simply the use of reason as such in a realm where they believe it to be unemployable and pernicious. Nor is their belief at all unusual. Many a man considers that our safest policy is to feel our way from point to point as best we can, rather than to map out a complete itinerary at the start and try to cling to it. But there need be no derision for the other men who think that we must know where we are going if we are to find the way. And such men may say that cavilling at reason as such in any realm is a little too much like cavilling at the Republic, a favourite adolescent pastime, because it is not "practical," or even at Euclid because there are no straight lines in nature, or at any abstract thought at all because there is nothing but brute fact before our eyes. The mind's eye has another vision, which alone may better the brute fact around us. Undoubtedly the vision may be wrong, and dangerous. Undoubtedly it may be misinterpreted, and made more dangerous. We have said that reason is a perilous weapon in our hands. We are always busy sweeping its past wrecks away, and we should always bear in mind that the reason we employ in so doing is about as dangerous for us as for our predecessors. But we may cavil at them for their errors in it, not for the attempt to use it.

We may say all this and still be proud of an ancestral policy now known as "muddling through." We may still admire the results of a millennium of it in the land of Burke and Morley; and when Mr. Chamberlain assures the Commons that the policies of that land have never rested upon logic and under heaven never will, we may fling up a proud cap for the intuitive experience, for the genius of compromise . . . for whatever it is that the policies do rest on. But it will be better not to claim that there is a philosophy of muddling; or rather, to admit at once that there must be some species of philosophy if ever we shall muddle through. It will be no shame to us if we conclude that we must have some end in mind, or get nowhere; and the moment we inquire the end, we are off into political philosophy, where we shall need all of the reason we can muster, and where we cannot gracefully assail our predecessors for the use of it. In all admiration we may risk the thought that Edmund Burke was the sublimest "muddler through" our race has borne; and possibly the only thing that ill became his noble mind was the rage he vented upon some of the men who may have helped to form it.

The popular persuasion that the Social Contract is some species of abomination in decadence might remain unnoticed if it had not been encouraged in the masses by distinguished critics who presumably had read the book before they scandalized the public with a tale of its uncleanliness. A "horrible" book, says Jules Lemaître,[2] an "odious" book; it "makes one shudder." For "never . . . has a writer done more harm to man." In whole or in part the thing is not only "mediocre," "obscure," "chaotic," "full of contradictions," "extraordinary for incoherence," "swarming with fallacies," "absolutely unusable," "inept," "absurd," "superstitious," "tyrannical," "paradoxical," "nonsensical," and many other things repugnant to mere reason; but it is morally "dangerous," "pernicious," "murderous," "maniacal." Many other interesting appellatives may be found in the twenty-four pages from which these have come, and the remainder of the book. It is a melancholy thing to know that in the flower of his fame Lemaître tacitly agreed to say these things, when he engaged to write the lectures in his volume for delivery to a select audience of monarchists, *before he had read Rousseau through;* but it is a little pleasant to learn, if the story be true, that even these effusions were too feeble for his hearers, since one of the ladies present made complaint: *Monsieur, vous n'avez pas été assez injuste!* Is there any other author, old or new, whose critics are in such a state that the story could be true or that there could be a point in inventing it? But though the phrases are of genius, they are beneath further notice, and a sentence will suffice. Close your Lemaître, and open your *Contract:* do you see abomination, or the constitution of every free state in the modern world?

For it is time to say that all the argument we have been hearing about sovereignty and freedom, all the demonstration of the unison of law and liberty, is only an elaborate vindication of the faith in "government of the people, by the people, and for the people." If it does not give a final proof that this is the one polity of reason, it has so far held its own at least in that no other polity has been proposed that most of us consider better. With whatever errors in detail, it has frankly remained unrefuted in the face of all the major criticisms here reviewed as well as of some minor ones not mentioned. It is not peculiarly abusable, it is neither individualist nor absolutist, it is not irrationally rational, it is not "decadent." As a theory we have pretty well accepted it, and seemingly because we have to come to it when we face the problem of the state in reason.

But how well does it work in practice? And is it possible that the theory of reason will not fit a human race of waifs and strays so well as something

rather more irrational? Possibly no living man is wise enough to answer that inquiry, though there are exceeding few whose minds are not made up upon it. Democracy is either something like divine right for them or it is sheer nonsense; there are very few indeed who really think of it as of a thing on trial. But the *Social Contract,* with its high abstractions all brought down into the terms of practice, is on trial to-day if ever human idea was. If we are to ask how it is working, we may well begin by asking how the other policies open to us would seem to work. There would seem to be but four of them; no more at least appear to have been offered, and perhaps no more are thinkable. Instead of giving sovereignty to the people, we may do the following things with it:

1. Take it from the people and annihilate it. Give up any kind of state except the "state of nature." This is the proposal of the anarchist; but we need not ask if it would be desirable, because it is impossible.

2. Leave it with the people, but restrict it. This is done whenever the people agree to rule within a certain limit and to claim no power beyond it, as in any bill of rights. Their agreement may be very wise in practice, and may long endure; but the very act of making it will prove them sovereign over this and all agreements they may make; and it is impossible to keep them from revising or annulling the agreement if they think it wiser so to do. So we do not put a limit on the sovereign in this manner, but provide a way of working only. It is not a real alternative.

3. Leave it with the people, but divide it so among them that it rests in no one place. This is the familiar way of checks and balances in different branches of a government. There is little to be said against it, and our author recommends it as another way of working. But it does not touch the sovereignty. Back of the divided powers is the power that apportions and maintains them, and that power is the only sovereign. So this too is not a real alternative.

4. Take it from the people and confer it on an individual or group. This is what most states have done, and what a number are still doing; and it is a real alternative. To be sure, a united people may depose a monarch or a group at any time, and so resume the sovereignty, for there can be no way to take this power from them. In this sense they are the sovereign by necessity. But there is a great difference between appointing an agent to administer the law

---

[2] A French biographer of Rousseau. [Editor's note.]

The Early Modern Era

that they have made and submitting to a master in agreement to obey the law that he proclaims. And therein is the true alternative.

So the four have really come to one. The first remains impossible, and the second and the third unreal; the fourth alone is of concern. The only question is whether it is better for the people to create their own law or to choose a master to proclaim it for them. One of these two things we all shall do. Which do we think will work best? Most of the men in Rousseau's time believed it best to give the power away; most of us to-day think otherwise. And we offer argument from theory and history alike. For we are no less theoretical if we are at times none too articulate, but only the more sweeping in assumption; and when we are most articulate, we are likely to be found repeating that "Obedience to the law that we have made is liberty" and that "To renounce our liberty is to renounce the state of man—is rights and even his duties." And in history we feel that the lessons upon monarchy and aristocracy are not alluring, even by the side of the poor lessons often given by democracy; so we have come to think there may be a better chance for a free people to seek and find their good than for a master to give up his own in their behalf. Doubtless a century is not so long nor we so wise that we can call this proof, but we incline to faith in it. We believe the theory works.

We ought to say with our author that it will not work for every people. It requires a certain wisdom and a certain public spirit. It will fail whenever people are too ignorant to understand it or too selfish to keep faith with it. It will fail for savages or for decadents; they are better with another polity at their own cost. But in the temperate zone of culture interlying we believe it works. We have no illusion of its working anywhere to all perfection. And we know it works exactly in proportion to the public spirit we provide

for it. That will hold, of course, in any state; but we believe there is a better chance for public spirit to develop in a state which is in truth the public thing. We may leave aside scholastic jargon and say simply that the general will is nothing but the total sum of public spirit; and that it is no airy figment, but the sole foundation for a fit society. The one means to the right society is the right men, and no device of theory will avail without them.

But if the citizens must make the state, the state in turn must make true citizens. Public spirit can grow only in the exercise of it. This need leave us in no quandary as to which must come first, for the state and citizen will grow together, and will further each the other to the ends of interest to them both. Above all, the state will have the education of the individual, and a proper education is the sovereign way of making a true citizen. That is why our author gave another book to education, with a summary of the *Social Contract* for a final lesson in it. And so the *Contract* and *Emile* come into unision. The one would form a natural man to take his part in the natural society delineated in the other.

For the society would seem to be the one that will fulfill our nature. If we err in thinking it will work, we must some day try the other kind again—we must find a master, and see whether he will do better by us, after all. Reason seems to tell us to go on with our present experiment, and history to second the advice with the evidence at her disposal. But she has not finished with her testimony and deposed the whole truth. We are still so near our start toward the ideal which has here been set before us that the brief experiment so far is inconclusive. And indeed our history will always be continuing, and beginning all anew before our eyes; so it may never have a final answer for us. If we ask of history only, we may wait till it is over to discover what was right. We may have to find the answer, after all, in reason.

KINGSLEY MARTIN

SPOKESMAN FOR SMALL COMMUNITY FEDERALISM

Several important questions concerning the interpretation of Rousseau are posed by Kingsley Martin, the former editor of *New Statesman and Nation,* in his work *French Liberal Thought in the Eighteenth Century* (originally published in 1929, revised in 1954). The *Social Contract,* Martin states, like the Bible and *Das Kapital,* can be "variously interpreted by enthusiasts, endlessly commented on by scholars, and triumphantly quoted by rival schools. . . ." Martin himself believes that the "truest interpretation of the *Social Contract* is some form of federalism," and that Rousseau believed that federalism could best be attained in small communities. Rousseau's teachings have thus been adopted at various times by the Girondins, utopian socialists, communists, and syndicalists.

This last aspect of Rousseau — the cautious reformer, the respectful disciple of Montesquieu, the revolutionary who even hesitated to abolish serfdom — has been usually forgotten, but other parts of his teaching have had long, complicated and surprising histories. No one can be as fairly quoted in support of opposite theories as Rousseau. His doctrines were capable of extension and elaboration in directions which would have astonished him. His influence was probably increased by the fact that some passages in his works were mystical and obscure: *The Social Contract* could be treated like the Bible and *Das Kapital* — it could be variously interpreted by enthusiasts, endlessly commented on by scholars, and triumphantly quoted by rival schools, each certain of possessing the true milk of the master's teaching.

To some, Rousseau is an extreme individualist, hating all forms of social coercion, and denying the right of State or Church to impose its will upon any individual. The ideal of both the early *Discours* was a simple life, in which property would be held in common, and each man would be able to live as he pleased, earning his own living by his labour under the coercion of hunger only, untroubled by governments and heedless of conventions. Rousseau's own life and expressed inclinations supported this interpretation of his main teaching, and the apostles of the simple life, as well as the philosophic anarchists and early Utopian communists, found inspiration in his work. Godwin's *Political Justice*[1] is a logical continuation of *The Origin of Inequality. The Social Contract* was equally useful to the exponents of an opposite theory of government. For them the State, the result of the general wills of all the individuals who compose it, is everything, and the individual whose actual will is recalcitrant counts for nothing. He has ceased to have rights of any sort against the State, he must be content with his opportunity to contribute to the general will. So far from being an exponent of natural rights, Rousseau is fairly quoted by authoritarians as a precursor of an extreme collectivism, in which neither private property nor religious liberty is free from the interference of government. Rousseau's division between the actual and real wills of individuals, the assumption that moral purposes can be fully developed only in the ideal State, led to nineteenth-century Idealism. Kant could base an individualist theory upon it, but the followers of Hegel easily used it to support a transcendental theory of the State, which, as the embodiment of the highest and best in the community, became valuable in itself and was alone able to give value to individual life. The confusion between the

---

[1] William Godwin (1756–1836) was an English social theorist; his *Political Justice* attacked private property. [Editor's note.]

From Kingsley Martin, *French Liberal Thought in the Eighteenth Century* (London: Turnstile Press, 1954), pp. 214–219. Reprinted by permission of J. M. Dent and Sons Ltd., and of Harper and Row, Inc. (Torch book edition.)

ideal democracy—in which the general will should give effect to the highest aspirations of individuals—and the actual dominance of class government in Prussia was the more easily made because the division between the ideal and the actual is never very clear in *The Social Contract* itself. The application of Rousseau to the more democratic conditions of England made by the Oxford idealists was more logical, but it resulted in a denial of individual rights as complete as that in the German followers of Hegel.

The truest interpretation of *The Social Contract* is some form of federalism: the Commune of 1870 is so far the nearest approach to a practical realization of Rousseau's theory. He had expressly said that the ideal freedom at which he aimed was attainable only in a small community, and had added that no freedom was possible in a large State unless it were divided into districts and given a federal constitution. The Girondists were attracted by this theory; nineteenth-century communists based a revolutionary philosophy upon it; syndicalists gave a new twist to its development by applying it to industrial groups instead of geographical areas. Exponents of mediaeval federalism have found support in Rousseau's refusal to admit the validity of representation and have developed for their own purposes his argument that a social group other than the State may embody the will of its constituent members in relation only to the purpose for which the particular association has been formed. Those who accept the corporation theory of the State are therefore indebted to Rousseau, as well as their bitterest opponents, the idealist protagonists of unified sovereignty.

In the Revolution itself much of Rousseau's theory was inevitably misunderstood or neglected. For Rousseau had solved the problem of reconciling liberty and authority by postulating a State so small that the practical difficulties of reconciliation scarcely arose. He had himself seen that his argument applied only to the small community. He knew what economists have often forgotten—that, while the consideration of a simple case may sometimes elucidate the nature of a complex problem, it cannot provide a solution for it. The economic problems of a million persons are not those of Robinson Crusoe multiplied by a million, nor can the political problems of a modern community of men be solved by a statement of conditions which would be ideal for a small community of gods. If you simplify both your people and your conditions the result may be logical, suggestive, and even inspiring, but it

cannot serve the purposes of the legislator and administrator. So much Rousseau had himself implicitly admitted when asked to apply himself to the art of government. When his followers, steeped in his phrases, tried to transform them into constitutions the only mechanism to their hand was that of representation. They could not stop to consider Rousseau's view, that the human will could not be represented and that representation really involved a different form of government. They did not consider the problem of how the "general will" could be made effective in a modern State: there is no hint in their writings or speeches of the need for organized parties or of an independent civil service.

Robespierre could not wait for a democratic meeting before taking action. He assumed, as naturally as Louis XIV. had assumed, that his own will represented the general will of the community. Rousseau's federalism, embodied in the Girondist proposal to give power to the communes of France, appeared political madness when foreign enemies were at the door. When the need for autocracy had passed away the only possible interpretation of *The Social Contract* seemed to be representative government and majority rule. Rousseau had supplied the populace with the cry of popular sovereignty, and in the French Revolution this could only mean the right to vote. Orators who quoted Rousseau were never tired of reminding their audiences that the people themselves were now sovereign, every common man exercising his share of the divine right of the French monarch. For the moment there seemed no difficulty. In the enthusiasm engendered by the struggle against the aristocrats and the Austrians, both the patriotism and the democratic virtue which Rousseau had acclaimed as the true basis of a political society seemed to be realized throughout France. Sebastian Mercier, a fervent disciple of Rousseau, expressed his astonishment, in 1791, that Rousseau could have imagined that democracy was only applicable to a State the size of Geneva, while the Abbé Sièyes popularized and gave effect to *The Social Contract* by his pamphlet *Qu'est-ce que le Tiers État?* He saw none of Rousseau's difficulties, had no objection to representation, no view that the only valid legislation is of a purely general character which affects everyone equally; he was content to expound the doctrine of popular sovereignty in a form which people could understand. "What is the Third Estate?" the first page of his pamphlet asks, and the reply is: "Everything." "What has it so far been in the political order?" "Nothing." "What is its demand?" "To be something." In the event, as the result of revolutionary movements in many countries, the Third Estate of Europe became something, and the arguments which led to a middle-class franchise were available for a later generation which urged that a property qualification was inconsistent with democratic theory.

Rousseau's disciples were easily reconciled to the exclusion of the working class from its theoretical share in government. They were also persuaded by utilitarian arguments to tolerate representation. The elected representative would maintain his constituents' liberty because his interest would lie in obeying the will of his masters. Those who respected British practice more than democratic theory were content that the representative should retain some independence and owe his constituents, in Burke's phrase, "not his industry only, but his judgment." Sterner democrats, who feared that representatives would develop "sinister" or "particular" interests (here Bentham and Rousseau meant the same thing), were anxious to make them delegates liable to frequent re-election. Jeffersonian democracy, directly inspired by Rousseau, had little influence on the Federal Constitution; it was more successful in the case of some State constitutions which ensure administrative inefficiency by providing for the annual or biennial elections of their legislatures and officers. Further instalments of direct democracy have been added in many parts of the world, and Rousseau's influence is to be traced wherever civil servants and judges are directly elected and liable to recall, and where referenda and plebiscites may override the authority of parliaments.

These were later victories of the democratic principle. At the Revolution itself the task of interpreting democratic doctrine was in the hands of men of property. The peasantry and the urban middle class, which controlled the Revolution except when the Parisian mob was out of hand, had long been burdened by an arbitrary executive which did not respect any rights of property, person or thought. They desired political power commensurate with their economic power; the practical method of obtaining it was the one which the great landowners of Eng-

land had discovered in the seventeenth century. A Parliament elected by themselves should make the laws and see that they were enforced by a responsible executive. Thus European States in the nineteenth century were commonly governed by parliaments which represented the energetic and wealthy middle class: this class claimed to be "the people"; its sovereignty was the sovereignty of the people and middleclass government was therefore democracy.

To mention the schools of thought that paid homage to Rousseau and to explain the developments of political practice which have been influenced by him is enough to show the varied possibilities of his teaching. But in truth Rousseau was a genius whose real influence cannot be traced with precision because it pervaded all the thought that followed him. Rousseau was the originator of a religious movement of which the Catholic revival was only one of the beneficiaries. He paved the way for men as various as Bernardin de Saint-Pierre, Chateaubriand, Victor Hugo and Lamennais.[2] Everything anti-rational, whether it was religious, romantic or merely sentimental, profited by his teaching. Men will always be sharply divided about Rousseau; for he released imagination as well as sentimentalism; he increased men's desire for justice as well as confusing their minds, and he gave the poor hope even though the rich could make use of his arguments. In one direction at least Rousseau's influence was a steady one: he discredited force as a basis for the State, convinced men that authority was legitimate only when founded on rational consent and that no arguments from passing expediency could justify a government in disregarding the claims of individual freedom or in failing to promote social equality.

[2]Bernardin de Saint-Pierre (1737-1814) was a friend and disciple of Rousseau; he wrote extensively on nature and religion. François René de Chateaubriand (1768-1848) was the leading literary figure in France in the first half of the nineteenth century and a prime exemplar of literary Romanticism; his *Génie du christianisme* exerted an especially powerful influence in reestablishing the respectability of religion after the assault made on it by the men of the Enlightment. Victor Hugo (1802–1885) was another prolific and influential representative of Romanticism. Hugues Félicité Robert de Lamennais (1782–1854) was a priest who wrote extensively in defense of Catholicism and in favor of freedom of the church from state domination. [Editors' note.]

ERNEST BARKER

ADVERSARY OF PARLIAMENTARY DEMOCRACY

Sir Ernest Barker, a renowned English political scientist, underscores in his edition of the *Social Contract* what he calls Rousseau's "cardinal difficulty," his use of the word "democracy," by which he means "the unguided democracy of a primary assembly. . . ." It is the application of the Rousseau idea of democracy to actual circumstances that causes the difficulty. In this transmutation of an ideal into reality, Rousseau, Barker claims, discards the parliamentary form of government for what may be called "in the last resort . . . a totalitarian [form of government]."

We touch at this point on a cardinal difficulty in Rousseau's thought. He wants to use his two-edged sword in defence of *primary* democracy, with no representatives, without any parties, and within the confines of the small State which primary democracy demands. He rejects representative government, or *parliamentary* democracy. But he only does so to find in the issue that he has rejected democracy itself. The unguided democracy of a primary assembly without any parties is a *souverain fainéant*. A "mayor of the palace" must be provided; and we are left in the issue with Pepin of Heristal acting as "legislator" for the *souverain*.

Rousseau belonged by origin to the city-state of Geneva, to whose "magnificent, most honoured, and sovereign seigneurs" he dedicated his *Discours sur l'Égalité*. The free institutions and the civic life of Geneva affected his thought. We may almost say that they Hellenized his views into a belief in primary democracy, making him at once the votary of the contemporary Swiss canton and the apostle of the ancient civic republics of Athens and Sparta. We may also say, in another phrase, that they hypostatized his abstract idea of a sovereign general will, and turned it into a mundane matter of government by a primary assembly. There is much to be said in favour of the idea of the general will, taken in and by itself. The problem is the translation of the idea; its application in actual life; the discovery of the organ through which it acts. It is here that Rousseau sails into troubled waters; and it is here that we have to study the tacks and shifts of his thought.

We must begin our study with his version of the contract. He is like Hobbes in that he postulates the entire surrender of himself by each individual in the moment of the contract: he is unlike in that he regards each individual as surrendering himself to no man, but "alienating himself with all his rights to the whole community" (I, c. 6).[1] All, in the sense of all the individuals surrendering, form the *état;* all, in the sense of the community to which surrender is made, form the *souverain*; and all are thus, at one and the same time, a passive body of subjects and an active body of sovereigns. Here Rousseau enunciates his famous paradox, "Each, giving himself to all, gives himself to nobody": in other words, each gives himself to himself, and each is still his own master. The paradox conceals a paralogism. I surrender all myself—and I surrender it all to 999 others as well as myself: I only receive a fraction of the sovereignty of the community; and ultimately I must reflect that if I am the thousandth part of a tyrant, I am also the whole of a slave. Leviathan is still Leviathan, even when he is corporate.

There is a further difference, however, between the Leviathan of Hobbes and the Leviathan of Rousseau, over and above the difference that the one Leviathan is a sole person and the other a community of persons. The Leviathan of Hobbes is at once a legislative and an executive, uniting all the powers. The community which forms Rousseau's Leviathan is purely a legislative, confining itself to the generali-

[1] References enclosed in parentheses are to Barker's edition of *Social Contract*. [Editor's note.]

From Sir Ernest Barker, ed., *Social Contract* (The World's Classics) (London, New York, and Toronto: Oxford University Press, 1947, 1948, 1952), pp. xlv–liv. Reprinted by permission.

ties of legislation. For particular acts of authority the community institutes a *gouvernement,* an intermediary body for the execution of the laws which it makes, standing between itself as *souver in* and itself in its capacity of *état* (III, c. i). This government, however, is only a temporary and limited commission: while the sovereign community exists of itself, and its sovereignty is inalienable and indivisible, the government exists by grace of the sovereign, and its power can be resumed or divided at will by the sovereign. There is thus no contract of government for Rousseau; he will only recognize the one contract of society: "there is only one contract in the State, that of association, and it excludes all others" (III, c. 16).

But though the community may thus alienate executive power to a commission (temporarily, and subject to the resumption or division of such power as it may will), it never alienates legislative power to representatives. That would be to alienate sovereignty, which is impossible. Here Rousseau differs fundamentally from Locke, who, if he had envisaged the possibility of the community acting itself as legislative, had also assumed that it would normally act through its representatives. Rousseau dismisses with a cavalier gesture any idea of parliamentary democracy: representation is derived from the iniquitous and absurd system of feudal government; representatives in counsel are like mercenaries in war; the English people thinks it is free, and deceives itself greatly—it is only free during a general election (III, c. 15). Banishing parliamentary democracy, he accordingly preaches the doctrine of a primary legislative, sovereign over an executive which serves as its *commissaire.*

There is an old lesson of politics—the principle of balance (John Stuart Mill could even call it the principle of antagonism)—which teaches us that, in actual life, States need a strong executive as well as a strong legislative. There is also another lesson of politics—perhaps more recent, but certainly no less important—which teaches us that a strong executive and a strong legislative must not simply confront one another, on a system of division of powers, but must also co-operate with one another, in a system of reciprocity and mutual confidence. Rousseau paid little heed to the first of these lessons; and we can hardly blame him (after all he was writing in 1762, and a developed cabinet system of reciprocity between the executive and the legislative power still lay in the future) for not thinking of the second. He

was hardly concerned with practical necessities: he was hot in pursuit of the logical symmetry of an ideal scheme of popular sovereignty. We may therefore limit our criticism to an inquiry into its logic. Was it, after all, symmetrical; and was it a consistent scheme?

On his scheme the generality was to be the sovereign body, in the capacity of a legislative; and the reason was that the generality, and only the generality, could be trusted to will a general will, and to rise superior to particular and sectional interests. Was this a well-founded trust? Hardly; for when his journey begins the traveller finds that he has to traverse ranges—and they are somewhat mountainous ranges—of logical difficulty. In the first place he has to distinguish a real general will from a mere will of all—the will of a true collectivity from a mere aggregate of wills. How is this to be done? Rousseau answers, "By the presence or absence of party-lines in voting" (II, c. 3). If party is present, and a great clique carries the day, the general good will be sacrificed; if there are no parties, and each individual votes individually, the individual selfishnesses in voting will cancel one another, and the general good will be the residuum. In an age which still interpreted party as faction (the age, for example, of Bolingbroke[2] and the theory of the superiority of *la patrie* to *le parti*) this was perhaps a natural view; and yet it is hardly logical to argue that individualism in voting is the royal road which leads to collectivism in decision. Party, after all, is a necessary means of precipitating in a set form a programme of the general good, and of realizing that programme in the strength of concerted action; and Burke was wiser than Rousseau when he argued at the end of his pamphlet on *The Present Discontents* (published eight years after the *Contrat Social*) that party was "a body of men united for promoting . . . the *national* interest upon some particular principle." The true freedom of the citizen consists in the citizen's choice; and where is the citizen's choice unless there are alternative programmes, presented by different parties, between which choice can be made? It is not the absence, but the presence, of party—if party is only organized as a body of opinion about the national interest and the general good, and not

[2] Viscount Bolingbroke (Henry St. John) (1678–1751) was a Tory leader in England during the reign of Queen Anne; he played an important role in the conduct of foreign affairs during this era. He was also an influential writer on political philosophy, voicing in his writings many of the ideas of the Enlightenment concerning the natural order of society and the need for rational conduct. [Editor's note.]

The Early Modern Era

corrupted into a sum of personal interests—which is the true criterion of the existence of a general will.

In the second place—and here we reach another range of logical difficulty—the question arises whether the whole people, if it be set to legislate for itself, can ever discover for itself the general good which, ex *hypothesi*, it really wishes to enact. To distil the requirements of the general good in an actual measure of legislation is something which requires both an intellectual effort of sustained reflection (or, better, sustained discussion) and a moral effort of abstinence from private and sinister interests: it will not come of itself, through the automatic cancellation of private interests by one another. Rousseau himself is aware of the necessity of distillation; but he will not trust representatives to do this necessary work. He accordingly introduces a wise legislator—antique in idea, but contemporary history has shown us that he may be terribly modern in practice—as a *deus ex machina* to tell the people what they ought to will. "Of itself, the people always wishes the good; of itself, it does not always see it" (II, c. 6). Here emerges the "leader" and "guide". . . . Here too, as we have already noticed, the sword of Rousseau turns round in his hand, and shows its other edge.

In effect, and in the last resort, Rousseau is a totalitarian. We need not exaggerate the importance of the "legislator" to arrive at this result. Omit the legislator altogether: the result is still there. Imagine Rousseau a perfect democrat: his perfect democracy is still a multiple autocrat. He leaves no safeguard against the omnipotence of the *souverain*. It is significant that the *Contrat Social* ends with the suggestion of religious persecution. The man who has publicly acknowledged the articles of the civil faith, which it belongs to the sovereign to determine, and who has then acted as if he did not believe in those articles—*qu'il soit puni de mort*. Rousseau was so far from believing in *les droits de l'homme* that he went to the other extreme. He was so convinced that it was enough for the individual to enjoy political rights (as a fraction of the collectivity) that he forgot the necessity of his enjoying the rights of "civil and religious liberty." The English Whigs and their philosopher Locke, with all their faults, were wiser in their generation.

There is still a third range of logical difficulty, less terrible than the second, but still sufficiently formidable. How can the great state of modern times reconcile its size to a primary legislative? Rousseau himself realized that his theory suited only the small community, such as Greece had known and Switzerland still knew; and he would have reconciled it to the greater size of the modern state either by advocating a movable metropolis, if a state had many towns, or by suggesting some system of federalism. The suggestion of federalism remained merely a suggestion: the advocacy of a movable metropolis may remind us of an early phase in the history of Trade Unionism (described in the first chapter, entitled "Primitive Democracy," of the Webbs[3] book on *Industrial Democracy*), when trade union branches in different towns were made in rotation the "governing branch" of the whole of that union for a fixed period. The phase soon passed; and the later development of Trade Unionism admirably shows (though sometimes with lapses back to "the primitive") the impracticability of Rousseauism, and the need of representative institutions in any large society which seeks to follow the arduous path of true self-government.

Here we may leave the *Contrat Social*. . . .

You can find your own dogmas in Rousseau, whether you belong to the Left (and especially to the left of the left) or whether you belong to the Right (and especially to the right of the Right). The only dogmas which it is difficult to find are those of the Centre—the Centre to which the English Whigs, whom a later generation called Liberals, have really always belonged, though they have always professed to belong to the Left. There is no comfort for the Centre in all the shot fabric of Rousseau's book. That is why it is natural, and even permissible, to prefer the hodden grey of Locke's cloth to the brilliant but parti-coloured silk of Rousseau. . . . Yet what a magic has style—above all when the language is French. It makes the tour of the world, and it carries with it everywhere the ideas which it has adorned. It is curious to reflect what would have happened to Rousseau's ideas if they had been given, about 1760, to an English writer in Cambridge, or a German writer in the University of Halle, and he had been told to express them to the best of his ability. Would the English writer have set the Cam on fire—let alone the Thames? Or the German the Saale—let alone the Rhine? . . .

[3] Sidney and Beatrice Webb, British writers and leaders of the Fabian Society whose books helped to popularize Socialism in England and to promote the cause of the Labour Party. [Editor's note.]

J. L. TALMON

PRECURSOR OF TOTALITARIANISM

If Sir Ernest Barker suggests that Rousseau's thought borders on the authoritarian, Professor J. L. Talmon of the Hebrew University of Jerusalem in his work on *The Rise of Totalitarian Democracy* pushes Rousseau over the line toward authoritarianism by asserting that Rousseau is one of the chief representatives of totalitarian Messianism in the eighteenth century, and as such must be held in part responsible for the rise of the totalitarian ideologies of the nineteenth and twentieth centuries.

THE PSYCHOLOGICAL BACKGROUND

Rousseau often uses the words nature and the natural order in the same sense as his contemporaries to indicate the logical structure of the universe. He also uses nature, however, to describe the elemental as opposed to the effort and achievement of the spirit in overcoming and subduing the elemental. The historical state of nature before organized society was the reign of the elemental. The inauguration of the social state marked the triumph of the spirit.

It must be repeated that to the materialists the natural order is, so to speak, a ready-made machine to be discovered and set to work. To Rousseau, on the other hand, it is the State, when it has fulfilled its purpose. It is a categorical imperative. The materialists reached the problem of the individual versus the social order only late in their argument. Even then, supremely confident of the possibility of mutual adjustment, they failed to recognize the existence of the problem of coercion. To Rousseau the problem exists from the beginning. It is indeed the fundamental problem to him.

A motherless vagabond starved of warmth and affection, having his dream of intimacy constantly frustrated by human callousness, real or imaginary, Rousseau could never decide what he wanted, to release human nature or to moralize it by breaking it; to be alone or a part of human company. He could never make up his mind whether man was made better or worse, happier or more miserable, by

people. Rousseau was one of the most ill-adjusted and egocentric natures who have left a record of their predicament. He was a bundle of contradictions, a recluse and anarchist, yearning to return to nature, given to reverie, in revolt against all social conventions, sentimental and lacrimose, abjectly self-conscious and at odds with his environment, on the one hand; and the admirer of Sparta and Rome, the preacher of discipline and the submergence of the individual in the collective entity, on the other. The secret of this dual personality was that the disciplinarian was the envious dream of the tormented paranoiac. The *Social Contract* was the sublimation of the *Discourse on the Origins of Inequality*. Rousseau speaks of his own predicament, when describing in *Émile* and elsewhere the unhappiness of man, who, after he left the state of nature, fell prey to the conflict between impulse and the duties of civilized society; always "wavering between his inclinations and his duties," neither quite man nor quite citizen, "no good to himself, nor to others," because never in accord with himself. The only salvation from this agony, if a return to the untroubled state of nature was impossible, was either a complete self-abandonment to the elemental impulses or to "denature (*dénaturer*) man" altogether. It was in the latter case necessary to substitute a relative for an absolute existence, social consciousness for self-consciousness. Man must be made to regard himself not as a "unité numérique, l'entier absolu, qui n'a de rapport qu'à lui-même", but as a "unité fonctionnaire qui tient au dénominateur et dont la valeur est dans son rapport avec l'entier, qui

From J. L. Talmon, *The Rise of Totalitarian Democracy,* (London, 1952) pp. 38–44, 45–49. Reprinted by permission of Martin Secker and Warburg Ltd.

The Early Modern Era

est le corps social."[1] A fixed rigid and universal pattern of feeling and behaviour was to be imposed in order to create man of one piece, without contradictions, without centrifugal and anti-social urges. The task was to create citizens who would will only what the general will does, and thus be free, instead of every man being an entity in himself, torn by egotistic tensions and thus enslaved. Rousseau, the teacher of romantic spontaneity of feeling, was obsessed with the idea of man's cupidity as the root cause of moral degeneration and social evil. Hence his apotheosis of Spartan ascetic virtue and his condemnation of civilization in so far as civilization is the expression of the urge to conquer, the desire to shine and the release of human vitality, without reference to morality. He had that intense awareness of the reality of human rivalry peculiar to people who have experienced it in their souls. Either out of a sense of guilt or out of weariness, they long to be delivered from the need for external recognition and the challenge of rivalry.

Three other representatives of the totalitarian Messianic temperament to be analysed in these pages show a similar paranoiac streak. They are Robespierre, Saint-Just and Babeuf. In recent times we have had examples of the strange combination of psychological ill-adjustment and totalitarian ideology. In some cases, salvation from the impossibility of finding a balanced relationship with fellow-men is sought in the lonely superiority of dictatorial leadership. The leader identifies himself with the absolute doctrine and the refusal of others to submit comes to be regarded not as a normal difference of opinion, but as a crime. It is characteristic of the paranoiac leader that when thwarted he is quickly thrown off his precarious balance and falls victim to an orgy of self-pity, persecution mania and the suicidal urge. Leadership is the salvation of the few, but to many even mere membership of a totalitarian movement and submission to the exclusive doctrine may offer a release from ill-adjusted egotism. Periods of great stress, of mass psychosis, and intense struggle call forth marginal qualities which otherwise may have remained dormant, and bring to the top men of a peculiar neurotic mentality.

THE GENERAL WILL AND THE INDIVIDUAL

It was of vital importance to Rousseau to save the ideal of liberty, while insisting on discipline. He was very proud and had a keen sense of the heroic.

Rousseau's thinking is thus dominated by a highly fruitful but dangerous ambiguity. On the one hand, the individual is said to obey nothing but his own will; on the other, he is urged to conform to some objective criterion. The contradiction is resolved by the claim that this external criterion is his better, higher, or real self, man's inner voice, as Rousseau calls it. Hence, even if constrained to obey the external standard, man cannot complain of being coerced, for in fact he is merely being made to obey his own true self. He is thus still free; indeed freer than before. For freedom is the triumph of the spirit over natural, elemental instinct. It is the acceptance of moral obligation and the disciplining of irrational and selfish urges by reason and duty. The acceptance of the obligations laid down in the Social Contract marks the birth of man's personality and his initiation into freedom. Every exercise of the general will constitutes a reaffirmation of man's freedom.

The problem of the general will may be considered from two points of view, that of individual ethics and that of political legitimacy. Diderot in his articles in the Encyclopaedia on the *Législateur* and *Droit naturel* was a forerunner of Rousseau in so far as personal ethics are concerned. He conceived the problem in the same way as Rousseau: as the dilemma of reconciling freedom with an external absolute standard. It seemed to Diderot inadmissible that the individual as he is should be the final judge of what is just and unjust, right and wrong. The particular will of the individual is always suspect. The general will is the sole judge. One must always address oneself for judgment to the general good and the general will. One who disagrees with the general will renounces his humanity and classifies himself as "dénaturé." The general will is to enlighten man "to what extent he should be man, citizen, subject, father or child," "et quand il lui convient de vivre ou de mourir."[2] The general will shall fix the nature and limits of all our duties. Like Rousseau, Diderot is anxious to make the reservation in regard to man's natural and most sacred right to all that is not contested by the "species as a whole." He nevertheless hastens, again like Rousseau, to add that the general will shall guide us on the nature of our ideas and desires. Whatever we think and desire will be good, great and sublime, if it is in keeping

[1] Not as "a numerical unity, an absolute whole, who has only to have rapport with himself," but as "a functional unity who is held to a denominator and whose value is in his relationship with the entirety that is the social body." [Editor's note.]

[2] "and when it is fitting for him to live or die." [Editor's note.]

with the general interest. Conformity to it alone qualifies us for membership of our species: "ne la perdez donc jamais de vue, sans quoi vous verrez les notions de la bonté, de la justice, de l'humanité, de la vertu, chanceler dans votre entendement."[3] Diderot gives two definitions of the general will. He declares it first to be contained in the principles of the written law of all civilized nations, in the social actions of the savage peoples, in the conventions of the enemies of mankind among themselves and even in the instinctive indignation of injured animals. He then calls the general will "dans chaque individu un acte pur de l'entendement qui raisonne dans le silence des passions sur ce que l'homme peut exiger de son semblable et sur ce que son semblable est en droit d'exiger de lui."[4] This is also Rousseau's definition of the general will in the first version of the *Social Contract*.

Ultimately the general will is to Rousseau something like a mathematical truth or a Platonic idea. It has an objective existence of its own, whether perceived or not. It has nevertheless to be discovered by the human mind. But having discovered it, the human mind simply cannot honestly refuse to accept it. In this way the general will is at the same time outside us and within us. Man is not invited to express his personal preferences. He is not asked for his approval. He is asked whether the given proposal is or is not in conformity with the general will. "If my particular opinion had carried the day, I should have achieved the opposite of what was my will; and it is in that case that I should not have been free." For freedom is the capacity of ridding oneself of considerations, interests, preferences and prejudices, whether personal or collective, which obscure the objectively true and good, which, if I am true to my true nature, I am bound to will. What applies to the individual applies equally to the people. Man and people have to be brought to choose freedom, and if necessary to be forced to be free.

The general will becomes ultimately a question of enlightenment and morality. Although it should be the achievement of the general will to create harmony and unanimity, the whole aim of political life is really to educate and prepare men to will the

[3] "Never let that escape from your view without which you would see the ideas of benevolence, of justice, of humanity, of virtue falter in your understanding." [Editor's note.]

[4] "In each individual a pure act of the understanding which argues in the silence of the passions concerning that which man can demand of his fellow-man and over that which his fellow-man has a right to demand of him." [Editor's note.]

general will without any sense of constraint. Human egotism must be rooted out, and human nature changed. "Each individual, who is by himself a complete and solitary whole, would have to be transformed into part of a greater whole from which he receives his life and being." Individualism will have to give place to collectivism, egoism to virtue, which is the conformity of the personal to the general will. The Legislator "must, in a word, take away from man his resources and gives him instead new ones alien to him, and incapable of being made use of without the help of other men. The more completely these natural resources are annihilated, the greater and the more lasting are those which he acquires, and the more stable and perfect the new institutions, so that if each citizen is nothing and can do nothing without the rest, and the resources acquired by the whole are equal or superior to the aggregate of the resources of all individuals, it may be said that legislation is at the highest possible point of perfection." As in the case of the materialists, it is not the self-expression of the individual, the deployment of his particular faculties and the realization of his own and unique mode of existence, that is the final aim, but the loss of the individual in the collective entity by taking on its colour and principle of existence. The aim is to train men to "bear with docility the yoke of public happiness," in fact to create a new type of man, a purely political creature, without any particular private or social loyalties, any partial interests, as Rousseau would call them.

THE GENERAL WILL, POPULAR SOVEREIGNTY, AND DICTATORSHIP

Rousseau's sovereign is the externalized general will, and, as has been said before, stands for essentially the same as the natural harmonious order. In marrying this concept with the principle of popular sovereignty, and popular self-expression, Rousseau gave rise to totalitarian democracy. The mere introduction of this latter element, coupled with the fire of Rousseau's style, lifted the eighteenth-century postulate from the plane of intellectual speculation into that of a great collective experience. It marked the birth of the modern secular religion, not merely as a system of ideas, but as a passionate faith. Rousseau's synthesis is in itself the formulation of the paradox of freedom in totalitarian democracy in terms which reveal the dilemma in the most striking form, namely, in those of will. There is such a thing as an objective general will, whether willed or not willed by anybody. To become a reality it must be willed by the people. If the people does not will it, it must be made to will it, for the general will is latent in the people's will.

Democratic ideas and rationalist premises are Rousseau's means of resolving the dilemma. According to him the general will would be discerned only if the whole people, and not a part of it or a representative body, was to make the effort. The second condition is that individual men as purely political atoms, and not groups, parties or interests, should be called upon to will. Both conditions are based upon the premise that there is such a thing as a common substance of citizenship, of which all partake, once everyone is able to divest himself of his partial interests and group loyalties. In the same way men as rational beings may arrive at the same conclusions, once they rid themselves of their particular passions and interests and cease to depend on "imaginary" standards which obscure their judgment. Only when all are acting together as an assembled people, does man's nature as citizen come into active existence. It would not, if only a part of the nation were assembled to will the general will. They would express a partial will. Moreover, even the fact that all have willed something does not yet make it the expression of the general will, if the right disposition on the part of those who will it was not there. A will does not become general because it is willed by all, only when it is willed in conformity to the objective will.

Exercise of sovereignty is not conceived here as the interplay of interests, the balancing of views, all equally deserving a hearing, the weighing of various interests. It connotes the endorsement of a truth, self-identification on the part of those who exercise sovereignty with some general interest which is presumed to be the fountain of all identical individual interests. Political parties are not considered as vehicles of the various currents of opinion, but representatives of partial interests, at variance with the general interest, which is regarded as almost tangible. It is of great importance to realize that what is to-day considered as an essential concomitant of democracy, namely, diversity of views and interests, was far from being regarded as essential by the eighteenth-century fathers of democracy. Their original postulates were unity and unanimity. The affirmation of the principle of diversity came later, when the totalitarian implications of the principle of homogeneity had been demonstrated in Jacobin dictatorship.

This expectation of unanimity was only natural in an age which, starting with the idea of the natural order, declared war on all privileges and inequalities. The very eighteenth-century concept of the nation as opposed to estates implied a homogeneous entity. Naïve and inexperienced in the working of democracy, the theorists on the eve of the Revolution were unable to regard the strains and stresses, the conflicts and struggles of a parliamentary democratic régime as ordinary things, which need not frighten anybody with the spectre of immediate ruin and confusion. Even so moderate and level-headed a thinker as Holbach[5] was appalled by the "terrible" cleavages in English society. He considered England the most miserable country of all, ostensibly free, but in fact more unhappy than any of the Oriental despot-ridden kingdoms. Had not England been brought to the verge of ruin by the struggle of factions and contradictory interests? Was not her system a hotch-potch of irrational habits, obsolete customs, incongruous laws, with no system, and no guiding principle? The physiocrat Letronne declared that "the situation of France is infinitely better than that of England; for here reforms, changing the whole state of the country, can be accomplished in a moment, whereas in England such reforms can always be blocked by the party system." . . . .

Rousseau puts the people in place of the Physiocratic enlightened despot. He too considers partial interests the greatest enemy of social harmony. Just as in the case of the rationalist utilitarians the individual becomes here the vehicle of uniformity. It could be said without any exaggeration that this attitude points towards the idea of a classless society. It is conditioned by a vague expectation that somewhere at the end of the road and after an ever more intensive elimination of differences and inequalities there will be unanimity. Not that this unanimity need be enforced of itself. The more extreme the forms of popular sovereignty, the more democratic the procedure, the surer one may be of unanimity. Thus Morelly[6] thought that real democracy was a régime

[5] Baron d'Holbach (1723–1789) was a French philosopher of German birth who contributed scientific materials to Diderot's *Encyclopédie* and who wrote philosophical tracts attacking religion and advancing a materialistic philosophy. [Editor's note.]

[6] Morelly was an eighteenth-century French political philosopher about whom almost nothing is known; in his writings he described the idealistic communistic society in which the will of the people would rule supreme. [Editor's note.]

where the citizens would unanimously vote to obey nothing but nature. The leader of the British Jacobins, Horne Tooke, standing trial in 1794, defined his aim as a régime with annual parliaments, based on universal suffrage, with the exclusion of parties, and voting unanimously.

Like the Physiocrats Rousseau rejects any attempt to divide sovereignty. He brands it as the trick of a juggler playing with the severed limbs of an organism. For if there is only one will, sovereignty cannot be divided. Only that in place of the Physiocratic absolute monarch Rousseau puts the people. It is the people as a whole that should exercise the sovereign power, and not a representative body. An elected assembly is calculated to develop a vested interest like any other corporation. A people buys itself a master once it hands over sovereignty to a parliamentary representative body.

Now at the very foundation of the principle of direct and indivisible democracy, and the expectation of unanimity, there is the implication of dictatorship, as the history of many a referendum has shown. If a constant appeal to the people as a whole, not just to a small representative body, is kept up, and at the same time unanimity is postulated, there is no es-. cape from dictatorship. This was implied in Rousseau's emphasis on the all-important point that the leaders must put only questions of a general nature to the people, and, moreover, must know how to put the right question. The question must have so obvious an answer that a different sort of answer would appear plain treason or perversion. If unanimity is what is desired, it must be engineered through intimidation, election tricks, or the organization of the spontaneous popular expression through the activists busying themselves with petitions, public demonstrations, and a violent campaign of denunciation. This was what the Jacobins and the organizers of people's petitions, revolutionary *journées*, and other forms of direct expression of the people's will read into Rousseau.

Rousseau demonstrates clearly the close relation between popular sovereignty taken to the extreme, and totalitarianism. The paradox calls for analysis. It is commonly held that dictatorship comes into existence and is maintained by the indifference of the people and the lack of democratic vigilance. There is nothing that Rousseau insists on more than the active and ceaseless participation of the people and of every citizen in the affairs of the State.

The State is near ruin, says Rousseau, when the citizen is too indifferent to attend a public meeting. Saturated with antiquity, Rousseau intuitively experiences the thrill of the people assembled to legislate and shape the common weal. The Republic is in a continuous state of being born. In the pre-democratic age Rousseau could not realize that the originally deliberate creation of men could become transformed into a Leviathan, which might crush its own makers. He was unaware that total and highly emotional absorption in the collective political endeavour is calculated to kill all privacy, that the excitement of the assembled crowd may exercise a most tyrannical pressure, and that the extension of the scope of politics to all spheres of human interest and endeavour, without leaving any room for the process of casual and empirical activity, was the shortest way to totalitarianism. Liberty is safer in countries where politics are not considered all-important and where there are numerous levels of non-political private and collective activity, although not so much direct popular democracy, than in countries where politics take everything in their stride, and the people sit in permanent assembly.

In the latter the truth really is that, although all seem to be engaged in shaping the national will, and are doing it with a sense of elation and fulfilment, they are in fact accepting and endorsing something which is presented to them as a sole truth, while believing that it is their free choice. This is actually implied in Rousseau's image of the people willing the general will. The collective sense of elation is subject to emotional weariness. It soon gives way to apathetic and mechanical behaviour.

Rousseau is most reluctant to recognize the will of the majority, or even the will of all, as the general will. Neither does he give any indication by what signs the general will could be recognized. It being willed by the people does not make the thing willed the expression of the general will. The blind multitude does not know what it wants, and what is its real interest. "Left to themselves, the People always desire the good, but, left to themselves, they do not always know where that good lies. The general will is always right, but the judgment guiding it is not always well informed. It must be made to see things as they are, sometimes as they ought to appear to them."

The Early Modern Era

THE GENERAL WILL AS PURPOSE

The general will assumes thus the character of a purpose and as such lends itself to definition in terms of social-political ideology, a pre-ordained goal, towards which we are irresistibly driven; a solely true aim, which we will, or are bound to will, although we may not will it yet, because of our backwardness, prejudices, selfishness or ignorance.

In this case the idea of a people becomes naturally restricted to those who identify themselves with the general will and the general interest. Those outside are not really of the nation. They are aliens. This conception of the nation (or people) was soon to become a powerful political argument. Thus Sieyès claimed that the Third Estate alone constituted the nation. The Jacobins restricted the term still further, to the *san-culottes*. To Babeuf the proletariat alone was the nation, and to Buonarroti only those who had been formally admitted to the National Community.[7]

The very idea of an assumed preordained will, which has not yet become the actual will of the nation; the view that the nation is still therefore in its infancy, a "young nation," in the nomenclature of the *Social Contract*, gives those who claim to know and to represent the real and ultimate will of the nation—the party of the vanguard—a blank cheque to act on behalf of the people, without reference to the people's actual will. And this, as we hope later on to show it has, may express itself in two forms or rather two stages: one—the act of revolution; and the other—the effort at enthroning the general will. Those who feel themselves to be the real people rise

[7] Abbé Sieyès (1748–1836) was an important statesman in France just before and during the Revolution. François Babeuf (1760–1797) was an agitator with strong socialistic leanings; ultimately he was executed for plotting the overthrow of the Directory. P. M. Buonarroti (1761–1873) was likewise leader of the more radical elements during the period of the Revolution; he was exiled for his involvement in agitation against the Directory. [Editor's note.]

against the system and the men in power, who are not of the people. Moreover, the very act of their insurrection, e.g. the establishment of a Revolutionary (or Insurrectionary) Committee, abolishes *ipso facto* not only the parliamentary representative body, which is in any case, according to Rousseau, a standing attempt on the sovereignty of the people, but indeed all existing laws and institutions. For "the moment the people is legitimately assembled as a sovereign body, the jurisdiction of the government wholly lapses, the executive power is suspended, and the person of the meanest citizen is as sacred and inviolable as that of the first magistrate; for in the presence of the person represented, representatives no longer exist." The real people, or rather their leadership, once triumphant in their insurrection, become Rousseau's Legislator, who surveys clearly the whole panorama, without being swayed by partial interests and passions, and shapes the "young nation" with the help of laws derived from his superior wisdom. He prepares it to will the general will. First comes the elimination of men and influences not of the people and not identified with the general will embodied in the newly established Social Contract of the Revolution; then the re-education of the young nation to will the general will. The task of the Legislator is to create a new type of man, with a new mentality, new values, a new type of sensitiveness, free from old instincts, prejudices and bad habits. It is not enough to change the machinery of government, or even reshuffle the classes. You have to change human nature, or, in the terminology of the eighteenth century, to make man virtuous.

Rousseau represents the most articulate form of the *esprit révolutionnaire* in each of its facets. In the *Discourse on Inequality* he expresses the burning sense of a society that has gone astray. In the *Social Contract* he postulates an exclusively legitimate social system as a challenge to human greatness.

JOHN W. CHAPMAN

PRECURSOR OF "MODERN" LIBERALISM

According to John W. Chapman, in his book *Rousseau—Totalitarian or Liberal?*, Rousseau's doctrines are the forerunners of modern liberalism, not modern totalitarianism. Both Rousseau and the modern liberals, says Chapman, "think of man as ambivalent" in his aspirations for a better world; both agree that the problems of community and the "common life" are of the utmost importance to modern man and that the solution to these problems entails a difficult pilgrimage from ignorance to enlightenment. Chapman's position represents the antithesis to Barkers' and Talmon's.

It is true that Rousseau wrote before technical progress enabled democratic government to be carried on over much larger areas than in the past. The deliberative state, as we know it, is possible only on the basis of the scope and rapidity of modern means of communication. Nevertheless, Rousseau's capacity for political invention was clearly limited. It broke down completely, as we have seen, in his effort to solve the problem of how to keep government responsive to the general will. The best he could do was to recommend the device of the periodical assembly, hallowed in his eyes by Roman practice; and to insure its effectiveness, he was led to advocate the totalitarian idea of a civil religion. Here Rousseau's faith in the liberated reason of men faltered, and he sought to achieve liberal ends by authoritarian means.

In analytical terms, Rousseau's theory of human nature and dynamics may be regarded as a synthesis of the views of Hobbes and Locke, in which the principle of transformation partially replaces the principle of association as an explanation of man's relation to his social environment. Because of this principle of transformation in his view of man, Rousseau's political theory differs markedly from the classical liberal democratic pattern of thought. Human dynamics do include associative processes. On this point, Rousseau and the classical liberals are in agreement. But exclusive reliance on these processes involves for Rousseau, as it does not for the classical liberals, violation of man's moral potentialities. It means achievement of the appearance, at the expense of the substance, of moral ideals, utilitarian behavior without moral freedom. Rousseau's patriotic citizen is not James Mill's economic man, but both are creatures of association, lacking insight and individuality.

Rousseau's differences from classical liberalism relate him to modern liberalism. The modern liberal shares with Rousseau a conception of man's social dependence that goes beyond anything found in classical liberal doctrine. The reason is that both think of man as a creature with potentialities that may develop only in an appropriate social medium. There is "nature" within him; he has a "self-realizing principle" that his society may either thwart or fulfil. Social and political institutions must take account of man's autonomous tendencies.

In addition, both the modern liberal and Rousseau think of man as ambivalent, although for Rousseau ambivalence approaches contradictoriness when the strain of psychological hedonism is uppermost in his thinking. He conceives of human ambivalence as a conflict between productive and egoistic tendencies. The former are rooted in man's reason and conscience, while the latter appear as bias in favor of his personal good, which impairs his capacity for moral deliberation and action. A modern liberal such as Lindsay[1] thinks of man as a being who rec-

[1] Alexander Dunlop Lindsay (1879–1952) was a late master of Balliol College, Oxford, who wrote extensively on the nature of the modern democratic state. [Editor's note.]

From John W. Chapman, *Rousseau—Totalitarian or Liberal?* (New York: Columbia University Press, 1956), pp. 140–144.

ognizes the existence of obligations to his fellows, but whose moral and intellectual limitations prevent him from fully meeting these obligations without the aid of elaborate institutional supports. But no difference in principle of a substantial kind is involved here. Both Lindsay and Rousseau think of the state as essentially the institutional expression of man's moral purpose, which purpose includes recognition of an obligation to neutralize his selfish tendencies and their effects. For them, the state is the means by which man releases his moral potential and seeks to realize goodness and justice; it is not merely a device by which men are enabled to control one another. Neither pictures man as the egoistic yet plastic creature of the utilitarians. Both see man's need for liberty in his capacity for moral growth, in his "perfectibility," as Rousseau would say. These ideas about man and the state which relate Rousseau to modern liberalism also differentiate them both from classical liberalism.

Rousseau and modern liberals also agree in principle on how to achieve social harmony. The general will may be expressed only through deliberation of the people. Above all others, this idea connects Rousseau's thought to the theory of the deliberative state. It is true that Rousseau's formulation of it is a vast oversimplification of the political process. "If, when the people, being furnished with adequate information, held its deliberations, the citizens had no communication one with another, the grand total of small differences would always give the general will, and the decision would always be good." On the basis of this formula for expression of the general will, Rousseau, by assuming that the people are sufficiently informed, all but assumes away the political problem as the modern liberal sees it. Social processes are apt to be blind precisely because people are not sufficiently informed as to the implications of their ideas and actions. Part of the purpose of discussion is to enhance their awareness of these. Much of the administrative machinery of government is devoted to their analysis. But this qualification does not vitiate the point that on the principle of discussion as the way to transcend the biases of individuals, Rousseau and modern liberals stand together.

The difference between them is on the source of these biases. Rousseau is thinking primarily in terms of the necessity for overcoming distortions in individuals' judgments on the requirements of justice and the general welfare. It is the intrinsic fallibility of man's judgment based on his propensity to rationalize and his tendency to seek his personal good without regard for that of others that concern Rousseau, and for which he sees a remedy in the joint effort of group deliberation. The modern liberal, however, is thinking primarily of discussion as a means for discovering and eliminating destructive consequences of partially blind social and economic processes. For the modern liberal, it is not only the limitations of man's moral nature, but also the nature of his society, that make discussion the imperative of the democratic process. But both the theory of the general will and the theory of the deliberative state seek to enhance the role of reason in human life. Unlike Bosanquet[2] and the philosophers of the Enlightenment, neither Rousseau nor modern liberals assume the existence of a movement toward social harmony immanent in historical and economic processes. For them, in Lindsay's words, a truly political society is a "purposive society."

Finally, we observe that both Rousseau and the modern liberals repudiate the atomism of classical liberal democratic theory. But for neither does man's social dependence involve sacrifice of his individuality. Modern liberalism is concerned with the problem of community and the promotion of what Lindsay calls a "common life." This conception requires not depreciation but rather maximization of individuality. As Carleton Kemp Allen puts it:

The notion that the man who values, guards, and cultivates his own individuality is setting himself in opposition to the interest of society is a profound misunderstanding. It is the essence of democracy that the public interest cannot flourish without the cultivation of the individual's interest in himself. The Together-Will must be the aggregation of real and vigorous individual wills; otherwise it becomes that devouring monster, mass emotion, goaded by unconscionable and overweening individual will.

This view of the relation between community and individuality is of the essence of Rousseau's theory of the general will. He is concerned for man's moral autonomy as well as his political freedom, for his capacity to make his own appraisals of values and to be independent. These are the prerequisites to his

[2] Bernard Bosanquet (1848–1923) was an English philosopher strongly influenced by Hegel; his writings on the state stressed the importance of a communal spirit emerging from individual cooperation. [Editor's note.]

attaining an appropriate relation to society and to the expression of the general will. Here is no atomistic theory of man's relation to society. Rather it is a theory which, while giving full weight to man's dependence on his society, sees in him capacities for autonomy and responsibility and demands that he exercise them.

Despite his deviations from this ideal—and notably so in his proposals for intensification of social sentiment—individual autonomy is the key to Rousseau's moral and political theory. Human dynamics are such that without independence men remain slaves of their socially accentuated egoistic tendencies. Their moral potentialities lie dormant, and society drifts toward prideful materialism. This drift may be defeated either by their achievement of moral freedom or by their indoctrination with patriotism combined with devotion to justice and the general welfare. Only the first involves no violation of man's nature as Rousseau discerns it, of man's capacity for moral creativity. The latter destroys this capacity.

William Ernest Hocking once said the liberal spirit "is human nature's revolt against its perpetual tendency to egoism." This is the spirit which moves in Rousseau's work.

JOAN McDONALD

THE CONSERVATIVE

Contrary to Chapman's findings, Mrs. McDonald, writing in a book recently published by the University of London, believes that Rousseau is essentially a conservative, "imbued with classical philosophy, free from the idea of progress and looking to the past rather than to the future." With Mrs. McDonald's interpretation the student has come full circle of Rousseau's critics.

How far can it be argued that Rousseau's theory of the general will is totalitarian? The charges made against Rousseau are twofold. Firstly, he insisted that the general will could not be expressed by representatives. It is argued that an attempt to apply this theory would lead to direct democracy, and that such a system would in turn lead inevitably to dictatorship. Secondly, it is argued that by insisting that the general will was the expression of man's higher self, Rousseau opened the way to a new form of dictatorship. Men could now be forced along a course dictated to them by their rulers in defiance of their expressed will, because their rulers could claim to be acting in accordance with their real will. If, moreover, it is accepted that for the general will to be expressed it is necessary to reach unanimity on all political issues, then in practice the state must be to a high degree coercive, and must be active in educating the citizen to will correctly. The individual must be subjected to constant pressure throughout his life, must be absorbed in communal activities and submitted to emotional and highly organized demonstrations of unity which allow him no opportunity to think for himself. Since what Rousseau called the "private and personal loyalties" are the greatest enemies to social unanimity there must be a progressive elimination of all individual differences and inequalities. Hence it is argued that from Rousseau's theory of the general will stem dictatorship, collectivism and ultimately communism.

The function of the legislator in the *Social Contract* has been compared with that of the modern revolutionary dictator, and the "general will" has been identified with "the party line." During a revolution, it is argued, those who rise against the established laws and institutions claim that they express the real will of the nation. In fact, however, it is not the people who become the legislators, but their leaders. These men act on behalf of the nation, and they use

From Joan McDonald, *Rousseau and the French Revolution, 1762–1791* (London, 1965), pp. 27–40. Reprinted by permission of The Athlone Press.

The Early Modern Era

their power to prepare for the people what they, as their leaders, believe is best for them. This involves the elimination of those individuals who do not conform and the re-education of what is left by all those forms of pressure and mass stimulation familiar to the student of modern totalitarian societies.

This linking of Rousseau's theory with nineteenth- and twentieth-century developments is open to criticism. Tyrannies are a form of government well known to historians of every era. They have their genesis in the reaction of societies to circumstances, and as far as modern tyrannies are concerned, it seems reasonable to assume that they would have taken much the same form had Rousseau never expounded his theory of the general will.

If we are to understand Rousseau's concept of the general will it is essential that we should consider his ideas not in relation to events which he could not possibly have foreseen, but against the background of his own times and the evils which he was attacking. When we speak of Rousseau's theories "involving" or "implying" this or that inevitable consequence, we must bear in mind that they did not necessarily "involve" or "imply" anything of the sort to Rousseau. The modern reader of the *Social Contract* might be conscious of the dangers of placing power in the hands of the people, and may regard popular sovereignty as synonymous with some form of popular tyranny. At the time when Rousseau was writing the experience of totalitarian democracy had yet to come, and therefore what Rousseau and his contemporaries understood by the phrase "sovereignty of the people" could obviously not be what the twentieth-century student of politics understands by it. On the other hand the social and political evils which Rousseau attacked were real to the eighteenth-century mind. Inequality, privilege and despotism were a part of the experience of Rousseau and his contemporaries. It was necessary to stress equality of rights and equality under the law because these things were lacking in eighteenth-century society. The questions which Rousseau asked himself were: How can liberty and equality be guaranteed? By what means is it possible to maintain the rule of law? He perceived that so long as the power of making the law was to be vested in one individual, the people would continue to be subject to an arbitrary will. He perceived that so long as minorities could claim privileges and exemptions it would be impossible to establish a just society. In his theory of sovereignty he was groping after a new concept of society in which liberty, equality and the rule of law would be guaranteed by the equal right of every citizen to participate in making the laws. It must be remembered that in the eighteenth century the people were the still untried receptacle for power, and the eighteenth century held, on the whole, an optimistic view of human nature. Rousseau himself believed that men's innate potentialities could be developed in a just society in such a way that the people would rise to the role of responsible citizenship. He did not believe that any one man, once aware of his political rights, would deliberately and consciously act in such a way as to destroy his own liberty. These assumptions show the wide gap which separates eighteenth-century conceptions from those based on subsequent experience.

When Rousseau wrote that the general will could not be represented and could only be expressed by the entire people, he did not intend to invest in the people all those powers which he was taking away from the despot. Rousseau, it has been pointed out, was the greatest of Montesquieu's disciples, and as such an exponent of the separation of powers. The form of government which he thought the best was an elective aristocracy, in which the powers of legislation would be vested in the people and the judicial and administrative functions in the magistrates. Sovereignty was indivisible and inalienable, but the work of government ought, he believed, to be delegated. Admittedly this distinction between legislation and government was easier to draw in Rousseau's day than it is in ours. The executive was expected to govern within the framework of certain fundamental laws which it could not change. This was the view expressed in the Remonstrances of the Parlements, and it was the view which Rousseau also took.

Moreover, Rousseau made it clear that only in certain circumstances could his theories be applied with any degree of success. For the general will to find expression it was necessary that the society should be very small and closely knit by the bonds of custom and common interest. In such a society the occasions when the people were called upon to act in their sovereign capacity would in fact be very few. Firstly, the actual size of the state and secondly, the strength of custom would reduce the need for great activity on the part of the legislative power. Indeed Rousseau did not believe it to be either necessary or advisable that the sovereign should be perpetually in action. In the *Discours sur l'Économie Politique* he stated that the sovereign should not be assembled at every unforeseen event.

It is clear that the same factors which made unnecessary the continual activity of the sovereign would also limit the role of the magistrates. Ideally, Rousseau believed that habit should replace authority in the regulation of men's lives. The magistrates were called upon to deal with the details of government within the framework of well-known laws. Thus there is no question, in Rousseau's small society, of the individual becoming the victim of perpetual political pressure exercised by leaders who wish to give the appearance of legality to their arbitrary actions. If we are to understand Rousseau's theory of popular sovereignty we must consider the idea in a context very different from that familiar to our own century.

Again, Rousseau never advocated that the individual should be stripped of his property and deprived of all personal ties and loyalties to stand in defenceless isolation in the face of an omnipotent state. We must distinguish between what he wrote of the large monarchical state and what he wrote of the small society in which he visualized the possible realization of his theories. He clearly argued that in great states intermediate bodies should be as many and as varied as possible, because they provided the bulwarks of tradition against the corrosive tide of despotism. He did not, however, regard the great monarchical state as the political organization best designed for man's happiness. His aim was to consider the conditions in which there would be no need for those estates and corporations whose jealously guarded privileges divided French society and utterly perverted the justice and equality of the laws. In a small republic they would be superfluous because the people would be bound closely together by the strong ties of common interest, tradition and kinship, and every citizen would feel himself to be a part of the society to which he belonged.

As for the system of property in itself, the subject is one to which Rousseau made frequent reference, and there does not appear to have been any confusion in his mind on this issue. He frequently attacked inequalities of wealth, but such attacks were not unusual in eighteenth-century philosophy and should not be regarded as attacks on the institution of property as such. Rousseau with characteristic intensity went so far as to say that the first man who

enclosed a piece of land and said, "This is mine," was the originator of all the subsequent ills which befell societies. Even here, however, he was not attacking the institution of property. His view of property was similar to that held by Locke; he believed that property was that with which a man had mixed his labour. In a man's property, he wrote in *Émile*, there is a part of himself, and he can claim it against all the world. But whereas Locke regarded it as perfectly in keeping with the natural order for a man to commute his right to property in return for a wage, Rousseau held that the concentration of property in the hands of a few destroyed men's natural independence—it caused some individuals to be dependent on the wills of others, which Rousseau regarded as contrary to nature. It is in this sense that he attacked property in the *Second Discourse*. Rousseau held that each man had a natural right to the amount of property necessary to satisfy his own essential needs, and that no one had a right to more. He regarded it as the duty of the state to maintain this principle, in order that the equality and independence which men enjoyed in the natural state should be perpetuated in the civil state, and in order that society should be protected from the moral evils and political dangers attendant upon great extremes of wealth on the one hand and poverty on the other. Only in one sense could Rousseau be regarded as favouring a class-less society; that is, in so far as his ideal society was "middle-class."

A modern student of Rousseau, trying to judge whether or not his theories were totalitarian would probably regard as even more significant his attitude to minorities; but here also it would be misleading to judge Rousseau's thought outside the context of his own times. The idea of institutionalizing dissentient opinion by means of political parties was quite alien to the theory and practice of eighteenth-century politics. Political theorists presupposed both the possibility and the advisability of unanimity in society. The British political divisions were regarded, by continental observers, as an aberration, peculiar to these islands. Moreover, the British ruling classes themselves did not conceive of sovereignty in terms of the interplay of interests and the balancing of views all equally deserving of a hearing.

En effet, s'il n'y avait point de convention antérieure, où serait, à moins que l'élection ne fût unanime, l'obligation pour le petit nombre de se soumettre au choix du grand? et d'où cent qui veulent un maître ont-ils le droit de voter pour dix qui n'en veulent point? La loi de la pluralité des

The Early Modern Era

suffrages est elle-même un établissement de convention, et suppose, au moins une fois, l'unanimité.[1]

Rousseau accepted the logical conclusions of his principles. If there came to exist within a society a group of citizens whose interests were fundamentally opposed to those of the rest, then in his view there was no longer one society. There were two societies and two general wills. This identity of interest may be regarded as idealistic, and Rousseau recognized that in practice it would be impossible to achieve except in a very small, conservative state. A large state, he believed, must inevitably by tyrannical toward some section of its people:

Les mêmes lois ne peuvent convenir à tant de provinces diverses qui ont des moeurs différentes, qui vivent sous de climats opposes, et qui ne peuvent souffrir la même forme de gouvernement.[2]

As the boundaries of the state were enlarged, so the relation between customs and laws became weaker and the coercive power of the state had to be proportionately increased. Only when the state was restricted to the limits of a group whose interests and customs were homogeneous was it possible to formulate the general will and to promulgate laws which would not violate the conscience of any minority or individual.

Assuming these conditions Rousseau held that any individual who did not will the general will could justifiably be forced nevertheless to conform to it. He drew the well-known conclusion:

Ce qui ne signifie autre chose sinon qu'on le forcera d'être libre.[3]

This was certainly dangerously epigrammatic, but even the most liberal governments insist that all the members of the state must conform to certain minimum standards of behaviour, without which the existence of society would not be possible at all.

Moreover, since some ethical standards accepted by a society are higher than those which would otherwise be accepted by many individuals who are members of it, the coercive power of the state is commonly regarded as justifiably used to ensure conformity to these standards. The crucial point is reached, of course, when, in a conflict between the state and the individual, there is doubt whether the ethical standards upheld by the state are in fact higher than those maintained by the individual. This situation, however, is precisely the one which Rousseau tried to avoid. At least we can say that when Rousseau put forward his theory of the general will he was not providing a pretext by which people should be forced to conform to a system of ideas imposed upon them. The general will is not, in fact, an anticipation of the "party line." Rousseau, writing in the middle of the eighteenth century, could not possibly have envisaged the techniques which have been devised and utilized by the modern state to mould mass opinion. The very idea that human beings can be "conditioned" to accept a body of beliefs and to act in a way convenient to their rulers is alien to Rousseau's thought. This idea is modern. Elements of it may be found in the works of some eighteenth-century writers, but it is diametrically opposed to Rousseau's views about the educative role of society. Education for Rousseau was essentially a process of self-realization.

Rousseau regarded the general will as the means whereby the individual's consciousness of justice might be given expression in the laws. His intention was not to sacrifice the individual to the collective entity, but to consider how society could best be adapted to the essential nature of man. Like his contemporaries and immediate predecessors, Rousseau began his search for social justice by considering human beings outside society. He considered, that is, the essential nature of man before he considered the kind of society in which men can live happily. Like Pufendorf,[4] Rousseau held that all men had implanted in them by nature "un principe intérieur pour se gouverner eux-mêmes." Thus they were in this respect independent of one another, each following his own inner voice. It was in this sense that he regarded men as equal, for it was against nature for one man to be subordinated to the will of another. Rousseau sought to ensure that in society the right of the individual to control his own destiny

[1] "In effect, if there had not been a prior convention, then where—if the elections were not unanimous—would be the obligation of the minority to submit to the choice of the majority? And from where would the hundred who wished for a master have the right to vote for the ten who did not wish one? The law of majority voting is itself an establishment of convention, and supposes, at least on one occasion unanimity." [Editor's note.]

[2] "The same laws cannot be entirely suitable to diverse provinces which have different customs, which live under opposite climates, and which cannot accept the same form of government." [Editor's note.]

[3] "This means nothing less than that he will be forced to be free."—[Editor's note.]

[4] Samuel Pufendorf (1623–1694) was a German jurist who laid down in his writings the basic principles of international law. [Editor's note.]

would be preserved. He believed that the only way to achieve this was for all men to be equal under the laws which all had equally participated in making. Thus the Rousseauist theory of the general will is based on the principle that each man has a right to control his own life.

It was, however, not enough in Rousseau's view that all should participate in making the laws. For the general will to be expressed it was necessary that the decisions which the people reached should be just. This does not mean that they should be forced to accept and to will according to an external standard incompatible with the individual conscience. On the contrary, it was only when the individual conscience became the criterion of judgement that Rousseau believed the general will could be expressed. Indeed, he specifically stated that for the general will to be expressed each individual should "think only his own thoughts." He expressed this idea even more clearly in the *Discours sur l'Économie Politique* where he asserted that for the general will to be expressed it was necessary for each citizen to "act according to the rules of his own judgement and not to behave inconsistently with himself."

Rousseau did not detect any menace to individual liberty in the assumption that to every political issue that arose there was only one answer conformable with justice, and that the whole people could be expected to accept that answer. He held the view that was common to his age, that men were possessed of a single, unitary will. The conflicts which arose in men's minds were not, he believed, natural to them. They were the products of corrupt conventions which exacted conformity to social standards incompatible with the individual sense of justice. It was on this sense of justice that the general will was based. Where men's minds had not been corrupted by evil institutions there was no obstacle, in Rousseau's view, to the expression of the general will, and no reason why the citizens should not reach agreement on all matters of fundamental importance.

This view may be considered as unduly optimistic, but at least it is not the case that Rousseau thought in terms of adapting men to society. On the contrary, his aim was to preserve and to give a new moral context to man's natural liberty. Two inseparable conditions were necessary for legislation: every individual must have participated in making the laws, and the laws themselves had to be the expression of the individual sense of justice.

How was it possible to ensure that in the course of his transposition from the natural to the social state, man's will was not corrupted? This is a crucial point in Rousseau's political thought. It was in the course of this change that the innate potentialities of the individual were realized. In the *Second Discourse* he argued that it was only as a result of living together in communities that men began to appreciate the idea of justice, and to realize that new standards of behaviour were demanded of them which were not necessary so long as they were solitary creatures. Unfortunately, by the time this realization came, it was often too late. Some individuals had already seen how they could take advantage of the new conditions to further their own selfish ends. Thus when the state took form it was based on injustice and perpetuated the inequality and privilege which had already arisen.

In the *Social Contract* Rousseau described how a society, at the very outset of its existence, could establish conventions by which the process of corruption described in the *Second Discourse* could be avoided. It was in this context that he visualized the work of the great legislator, a man who could see further than his fellow citizens and who would establish just conventions at the very foundations of society. Thus the individual's innate potentialities would be developed in relation to a virtuous concept of citizenship. Instead of being corrupted by contact with his fellow men he would realize, in society, his full moral stature. It is therefore in relation to this great crossroads in the history of mankind, the assumption of social responsibility, that Rousseau's description of the legislator should be considered.

Essentially, Rousseau was a conservative, imbued with classical philosophy, free from the idea of progress and looking to the past rather than to the future. He regarded the legislator as the great man who achieved his superhuman task in the dawn of history. Thereafter the longevity of a society depended on the degree to which its people remained faithful to their ancient traditions of virtue. Any departure from custom was a falling away from the primitive standards of virtue and a step downward in the inevitable process of decay and disruption to which all societies were subject. Thus, unlike nineteenth- and twentieth-century philosophers, Rous-

The Early Modern Era

seau looked back to his superman, not forward. His concept of the legislator may reasonably be supposed to have originated in his study of ancient history, and particularly of Plutarch, rather than in any intuitive glimpse of the modern dictator. The great legislators he quoted were Lycurgus, Solon and Moses. He did not envisage the great leader as Professor Toynbee describes him, as the man who "breaks the crust of custom" and thus releases forces which carry society a stage further in the process of its development. On the contrary, Rousseau regarded the task of the great man as setting society firmly in the mould of custom. He quoted Montesquieu: "At the birth of societies rulers of republics establish institutions and afterwards the institutions mould the rulers."

Rousseau admittedly considered the possibility of an old state being regenerated by a violent revolution, but he thought that the cases when this happened were extremely rare and the intention dangerous. It was precisely at such times that usurpers were likely to establish themselves, so that the people, far from gaining their liberty, bound themselves more tightly than before.

Les usurpateurs amènent ou choisissent toujours ces temps de troubles pour faire passer, à la faveur de l'effroi public, des lois destructives que le peuple n'adopterait jamais de sang-froid. Le choix du moment de l'institution est un des caractères les sûrs par lesquels on peut distinguer l'oeuvre du Legislateur d'avec celle du tyran.[5]

In order to understand Rousseau's intentions it is necessary to consider his theory of the general will within the self-contained logic of his political theory, and to place this against the background of his own century. It must be recognized that the ideal principles of the *Social Contract* were developed in relation to an ideal society. Rousseau did not believe that the general will could find expression except in a very small state in which the citizens were closely bound by common interests and traditions, and by a high regard for the virtuous customs of their ancestors. To neglect what Rousseau wrote about small states and then to criticize his theories in relation to the modern Leviathan must inevitably lead to distortion. Rousseau obviously knew nothing of modern forms of dictatorship, but he did attack

[5] Usurpers always bring about or choose times of trouble to pass, by means of public terror, destructive laws which the people would never adopt in cooler moments. The choice of the moment for the institution of laws is one of the surest characteristics by which one can distinguish the work of the Legislator from that of a tyrant. [Editor's note.]

those forms of dictatorship with which he was familiar. Whereas the Physiocrats favoured "legal" or "enlightened" despotism, Rousseau, on the contrary, stated that legal despotism was a contradiction in terms, and held that the individual was the best judge of his own interests.

Rousseau's aim was to discuss the conditions in which men could preserve their natural liberty, equality and independence. His success or failure must be judged in relation to the kind of society which he believed would provide those conditions, and not in relation to some other society which he could not have foreseen and which he certainly would have condemned if he had. It is indeed possible to argue that Rousseau's theory contained some elements which would be unacceptable to later liberal thought. For example, the state which he visualized was essentially static. It was assumed that once the contract had been established no further social development was desirable. The state would have to be limited in members to those whose economic interests were easily reconciled, and would have to exclude economic interests which were divergent. Any discussion of differences arising in the same society with a view to compromise would appear to be ruled out by Rousseau's theory. The demand that the individual should think only his own thoughts seems to suggest that discussion was not regarded as a means whereby unanimity could properly be reached. The very assumption that for any society there was only one course of action which could be regarded as just, and that every individual in that society must accept that course as just, owning himself mistaken if he had originally thought otherwise, makes Rousseau's theory of the general will seem oppressive.

However, such considerations only throw into higher relief the great divergences between Rousseau's political thought and the character of modern totalitarian democracy. The repressive qualities of Rousseau's small state are more akin to those of Calvinist Geneva or Plato's ideal state, than to the great totalitarian state of the twentieth century. The citizen who shuts himself up to think his own thoughts whenever a decision must be made in the state has more affinities with the Puritan, closeted alone with his Bible, than with the party member struggling to bring his thoughts into line with an externally imposed philosophy.

Thus we must guard against the tendency to see the

Social Contract as the first step in a process of revolution by which, over the past two hundred years, traditional governments have been overthrown and the sovereignty of the people established; and equally against seeing the French Revolution as the first practical expression of the process which Rousseau initiated. But we must now turn to the specific problem of the relation between the thought of Rousseau and the practice of the Revolution.

1234567890